ILL

DATE DUE

50827858			
MAR 3 1 2009			
GAYLORD			PRINTED IN U.S.A.

Mountaineering In The Sierra Nevada

Clarence King

Publishing Statement:

This important reprint was made from an old and scarce book.

Therefore, it may have defects such as missing pages, erroneous pagination, blurred pages, missing text, poor pictures, markings, marginalia and other issues beyond our control.

Because this is such an important and rare work, we believe it is best to reproduce this book regardless of its original condition.

Thank you for your understanding and enjoy this unique book!

MOUNTAINEERING IN THE SIERRA NEVADA.

I.

THE RANGE.

THE western margin of this continent is built of a succession of mountain chains folded in broad corrugations, like waves of stone upon whose seaward base beat the mild small breakers of the Pacific.

By far the grandest of all these ranges is the Sierra Nevada, a long and massive uplift lying between the arid deserts of the Great Basin and the Californian exuberance of grain-field and orchard; its eastern slope, a defiant wall of rock plunging abruptly down to the plain; the western, a long, grand sweep, well watered and overgrown with cool, stately forests; its crest a line of sharp, snowy peaks springing into the sky and catching the *alpenglow* long after the sun has set for all the rest of America.

The Sierras have a structure and a physical character which are individual and unique. To Professor Whitney and his corps of the Geological Survey of California is due the honor of first gaining a scientific knowledge of the form, plan, and physical conditions of the Sierras. How many thousands of miles, how many toilsome climbs, we made, and what measure of patience came to be expended, cannot be told; but the general harvest is gathered in, and already a volume of great interest (the forerunner of others) has been published.

1   A

The ancient history of the Sierras goes back to a period when the Atlantic and Pacific were one ocean, in whose depths great accumulations of sand and powdered stone were gathering and being spread out in level strata.

It is not easy to assign the age in which these submarine strata were begun, nor exactly the boundaries of the embryo continents from whose shores the primeval breakers ground away sand and gravel enough to form such incredibly thick deposits.

It appears most likely that the Sierra region was sub-merged from the earliest Palæozoic, or perhaps even the Azoic, age. Slowly the deep ocean valley filled up, until, in the late Triassic period, the uppermost tables were in water shallow enough to drift the sands and clays into wave and ripple ridges. With what immeasurable patience, what infinite deliberation, has nature amassed the materials for these mountains! Age succeeded age; form after form of animal and plant life perished in the unfolding of the great plan of development, while the suspended sands of that primeval sea sunk slowly down and were stretched in level plains upon the floor of stone.

Early in the Jurassic period an impressive and far-reaching movement of the earth's crust took place, during which the bed of the ocean rose in crumpled waves towering high in the air and forming the mountain framework of the Western United States. This system of upheavals reached as far east as Middle Wyoming and stretched from Mexico probably into Alaska. Its numerous ridges and chains, having a general northwest trend, were crowded together in one broad zone whose western and most lofty member is the Sierra Nevada. During all of the Cretaceous period, and a part of the Tertiary, the Pacific beat upon its seaward foot-hills, tearing to pieces the rocks, crumbling and grinding the shores, and, drifting the powdered stone and pebbles beneath its waves, scattered them again in layers. This submarine table-land fringed the whole base of the range and extended westward an unknown distance under the sea. To this perpetual sea-wearing of the Sierra Nevada base was added the detritus made by the cutting out of cañons, which in great volumes continually poured into the Pacific, and was arranged upon its bottom by currents.

In the late Tertiary period a chapter of very remarkable events occurred. For a second time the evenly laid beds of the sea-bottom were crumpled by the shrinking of the earth. The ocean flowed back into deeper and narrower limits, and, fronting the Sierra Nevada, appeared the present system of Coast Ranges. The intermediate depression, or sea-trough as I like to call it, is the valley of California, and is therefore a more recent continental feature than the Sierra Nevada. At once then from the folded rocks of the Coast Ranges, from the Sierra summits and the inland plateaus, and from numberless vents caused by the fierce dynamical action, there poured out a general deluge of melted rock. From the bottom of the sea sprung up those fountains of lava whose cooled material forms many of the islands of the Pacific, and, all along the coast of America, like a system of answering beacons, blazed up volcanic chimneys. The rent mountains glowed with outpourings of molten stone. Sheets of lava poured down the slopes of the Sierra, covering an immense proportion of its surface, only the high granite and metamorphic peaks reaching above the deluge. Rivers and lakes floated up in a cloud of steam and were gone forever. The misty sky of these volcanic days glowed with innumerable lurid reflections, and, at intervals along the crest of the range, great cones arose, blackening the sky with their plumes of mineral smoke. At length, having exhausted themselves, the volcanoes burned lower and lower, and, at last, by far the greater number went out altogether. With a tendency to extremes which " development" geologists would hesitate to admit, nature passed under the dominion of ice and snow.

The vast amount of ocean water which had been vaporized floated over the land, condensed upon hill-tops, chilled the lavas, and finally buried beneath an icy covering all the higher parts of the mountain system. According to well-known laws, the overburdened summits unloaded themselves by a system of glaciers. The whole Sierra crest was one pile of snow, from whose base crawled out the ice-rivers, wearing their bodies into the rock, sculpturing as they went the forms of valleys, and brightening the surface of their tracks by the friction of stones and sand which were bedded, armor-like, in their nether surface. Having made their way down the slope of the Sierra, they met a lowland temperature of sufficient warmth to arrest and waste them. At last, from causes which are too intricate to be discussed at present, they shrank slowly back into the higher summit fastnesses, and there gradually perished, leaving only a crest of snow. The ice melted, and upon the whole plateau, little by little, a thin layer of soil accumulated, and, replacing the snow, there sprang up a forest of pines, whose shadows fall pleasantly to-day over rocks which were once torrents of lava and across the burnished pathways of ice. Rivers, pure and sparkling, thread the bottom of these gigantic glacier valleys. The volcanoes are extinct, and the whole theatre of this impressive geological drama is now the most glorious and beautiful region of America.

As the characters of the *Zauberflöte* passed safely through the trial of fire and the desperate ordeal of water, so, through the terror of volcanic fires and the chilling empire of ice, has the great Sierra come into the present age of tranquil grandeur.

Five distinct periods divide the history of the range. First, the slow gathering of marine sediment within the early ocean, during which incalculable ages were consumed.

Second, in the early Jurassic period this level sea-floor came suddenly to be lifted into the air and crumpled in folds, through whose yawning fissures and ruptured axes outpoured wide zones of granite. Third, the volcanic age of fire and steam. Fourth, the glacial period, when the Sierras were one broad field of snow, with huge dragons of ice crawling down its slopes, and wearing their armor into the rocks. Fifth, the present condition, which the following chapters will describe, albeit in a desultory and inadequate manner.

From latitude 35° to latitude 39° 30' the Sierra lifts a continuous chain, the profile culminating in several groups of peaks separated by deep depressed curves or sharp notches, the summits varying from eight to fifteen thousand feet; seven to twelve thousand being the common range of passes. Near its southern extremity, in San Bernardino County, the range is cleft to the base with magnificent gateways opening through into the desert. From Walker's Pass for two hundred miles northward the sky line is more uniformly elevated; the passes averaging nine thousand feet high, the actual summit a chain of peaks from thirteen to fifteen thousand feet. This serrated snow and granite outline of the Sierra Nevada, projected against the cold clear blue, is the blade of white teeth which suggested its Spanish name.

Northward still the range gradually sinks; high peaks covered with perpetual snow are rarer and rarer. Its summit rolls on in broken forest-covered ridges, now and

then overlooked by a solitary pile of metamorphic or irruptive rock. At length, in Northern California, where
it breaks down in a compressed medley of ridges, and
open, level expanses of plain, the axis is maintained by a
line of extinct volcanoes standing above the lowland in
isolated positions.   The most lofty of these, Mount Shasta,
is a cone of lava fourteen thousand four hundred and
forty feet high, its broad base girdled with noble forests,
which give way at eight thousand feet to a cap of glaciers
and snow.

Beyond this to the northward the extension of the
range is quite difficult to definitely assign, for, geologically
speaking, the Sierra Nevada system occupies a broad area
in Oregon, consisting of several prominent mountain
groups, while in a physical sense the chain ceases with
Shasta ; the Cascades, which are the apparent topographical continuation, being a tertiary structure formed chiefly
of lavas which have been outpoured long subsequent to
the main upheaval of the Sierra.

It is not easy to point out the actual southern limit
either, because where the mountain mass descends into
the Colorado desert it comes in contact with a number of
lesser groups of hills, which ramify in many directions,
all losing themselves beneath the tertiary and quartenary
beds of the desert.

For four hundred miles the Sierras are a definite ridge,
broad and high, and having the form of a sea-wave.   Buttresses of sombre-hued rock, jutting at intervals from a
steep wall, form the abrupt eastern slopes ; irregular forests, in scattered growth, huddle together near the snow.
The lower declivities are barren spurs, sinking into the
sterile flats of the Great Basin.

Long ridges of comparatively gentle outline characterize
the western side, but this sloping table is scored from

summit to base by a system of parallel transverse cañons,
distant from one another often less than twenty-five miles.
They are ordinarily two or three thousand feet deep, falling at times in sheer, smooth-fronted cliffs, again in sweeping curves like the hull of a ship, again in rugged V-shaped
gorges, or with irregular, hilly flanks opening at last
through gateways of low, rounded foot-hills out upon the
horizontal plain of the San Joaquin and Sacramento.

Every cañon carries a river, derived from constant melting of the perpetual snow, which threads its way down
the mountain, — a feeble type of those vast ice-streams
and torrents that formerly discharged the summit accumulation of ice and snow while carving the cañons out
from solid rock. Nowhere on the continent of America is
there more positive evidence of the cutting power of rapid
streams than in these very cañons. Although much is
due to this cause, the most impressive passages of the
Sierra valleys are actual ruptures of the rock; either the
engulfment of masses of great size, as Professor Whitney
supposes in explanation of the peculiar form of the Yosemite, or a splitting asunder in yawning cracks. From
the summits down half the distance to the plains, the
cañons are also carved out in broad, round curves by glacial action. The summit gorges themselves are altogether
the result of frost and ice. Here, even yet, may be studied
the mode of blocking out mountain peaks; the cracks
riven by unequal contraction and expansion of the rock;
the slow leverage of ice, the storm, the avalanche.

The western descent, facing a moisture-laden, aerial
current from the Pacific, condenses on its higher portions a great amount of water, which has piled upon the
summits in the form of snow, and is absorbed upon the
upper plateau by an exuberant growth of forest. This
prevalent wind, which during most undisturbed periods

blows continuously from the ocean, strikes first upon the western slope of the Coast Range, and there discharges, both as fog and rain, a very great sum of moisture; but, being ever reinforced, it blows over their crest, and, hurrying eastward, strikes the Sierras at about four thousand feet above sea-level. Below this line the foot-hills are oppressed by an habitual dryness, which produces a rusty olive tone throughout nearly all the large conspicuous vegetation, scorches the red soil, and, during the long summer, overlays the whole region with a cloud of dust.

Dull and monotonous in color, there are, however, certain elements of picturesqueness in this lower zone. Its oak-clad hills wander out into the great plain like coast promontories, enclosing yellow, or in spring-time green, bays of prairie. The hill forms are rounded, or stretch in long longitudinal ridges, broken across by the river cañons. Above this zone of red earth, softly modelled undulations, and dull, grayish groves, with a chain of mining towns, dotted ranches and vineyards, rise the swelling middle heights of the Sierras, a broad billowy plateau cut by sharp sudden cañons, and sweeping up, with its dark, superb growth of coniferous forest to the feet of the summit peaks.

For a breadth of forty miles, all along the chain, is spread this continuous belt of pines. From Walker's Pass to Sitka one may ride through an unbroken forest, and will find its character and aspect vary constantly in strict accordance with the laws of altitude and moisture, each of the several species of coniferous trees taking its position with an almost mathematical precision. Where low gaps in the Coast Range give free access to the western wind, there the forest sweeps downward and encamps upon the foot-hills, and, continuing northward, it advances toward the coast, securing for itself over this whole distance about the same physical conditions; so that a tree which finds itself at home on the shore of Puget's Sound, in the latitude of Middle California has climbed the Sierras to a height of six thousand feet, finding there its normal requirements of damp, cool air. As if to economize the whole surface of the Sierra, the forest is mainly made up of twelve species of coniferæ, each having its own definitely circumscribed limits of temperature, and yet being able successively to occupy the whole middle Sierra up to the foot of the perpetual snow. The average range in altitude of each species is about twenty-five hundred feet, so that you pass imperceptibly from the zone of one species into that of the next. Frequently three or four are commingled, their varied habit, characteristic foliage, and richly colored trunks uniting to make the most stately of forests.

In the centre of the coniferous belt is assembled the most remarkable family of trees. Those which approach the perpetual snow are imperfect, gnarled, storm-bent; full of character and suggestion, but lacking the symmetry, the rich, living green, and the great size of their lower neighbors. In the other extreme of the pine-belt, growing side by side with foot-hill oaks, is an equally imperfect species, which, although attaining a very great size, still has the air of an abnormal tree. The conditions of drought on the one hand, and rigorous storms on the other, injure and blast alike, while the more verdant centre, furnishing the finest conditions, produces a forest whose profusion and grandeur fill the traveller with the liveliest admiration.

Toward the south the growth of the forest is more open and grove-like, the individual trees becoming proportionally larger and reaching their highest development. Northward its density increases, to the injury of indi-

1 *

vidual pines, until the branches finally interlock, and at last on the shores of British Columbia the trunks are so densely assembled that a dead tree is held in its upright position by the arms of its fellows.

At the one extremity are magnificent purple shafts ornamented with an exquisitely delicate drapery of pale golden and dark blue green; at the other the slender spars stand crowded together like the fringe of masts girdling a prosperous port. The one is a great continuous grove, on whose sunny openings are innumerable brilliant parterres ; the other is a dismal thicket, a sort of gigantic canebrake, void of beauty, dark, impenetrable, save by the avenues of streams, where one may float for days between sombre walls of forest. From one to the other of these extremes is an imperceptible transition ; only in the passage of hundreds of miles does the forest seem to thicken northward, or the majesty of the single trees appear to be impaired by their struggle for room.

Near the centre is the perfection of forest. At the south are the finest specimen trees, at the north the densest accumulations of timber. In riding throughout this whole region and watching the same species from the glorious ideal life of the south gradually dwarfed toward the north, until it becomes a mere wand ; or in climbing from the scattered drought-scourged pines of the foot-hills up through the zone of finest vegetation to those summit crags, where, struggling against the power of tempest and frost, only a few of the bravest trees succeed in clinging to the rocks and to life, — one sees with novel effect the inexorable sway which climatic conditions hold over the kingdom of trees.

Looking down from the summit, the forest is a closely woven vesture, which has fallen over the body of the range, clinging closely to its form, sinking into the deep cañons, covering the hill-tops with even velvety folds, and only lost here and there where a bold mass of rock gives it no foothold, or where around the margin of the mountain lakes bits of alpine meadow lie open to the sun.

Along its upper limit the forest zone grows thin and irregular ; black shafts of alpine pines and firs clustering on sheltered slopes, or climbing in disordered processions up broken and rocky faces. Higher, the last gnarled forms are passed, and beyond stretches the rank of silent, white peaks, a region of rock and ice lifted above the limit of life.

In the north, domes and cones of volcanic formation are the summit, but for about three hundred miles in the south it is a succession of sharp granite aiguilles and crags. Prevalent among the granitic forms are singularly perfect conoidal domes, whose symmetrical figures, were it not for their immense size, would impress one as having an artificial finish.

The alpine gorges are usually wide and open, leading into amphitheatres, whose walls are either rock or drifts of never-melting snow. The sculpture of the summit is very evidently glacial. Beside the ordinary phenomena of polished rocks and moraines, the larger general forms are clearly the work of frost and ice ; and although this ice-period is only feebly represented to-day, yet the frequent avalanches of winter and freshly scored mountain flanks are constant suggestions of the past.

Strikingly contrasted are the two countries bordering the Sierra on either side. Along the western base is the plain of California, an elliptical basin four hundred and fifty miles long by sixty-five broad; level, fertile, well watered, half tropically warmed ; checkered with farms of grain, ranches of cattle, orchard, and vineyard, and

homes of commonplace opulence, towns of bustling thrift.
Rivers flow over it, bordered by lines of oaks which seem
characterless or gone to sleep, when compared with the
vitality, the spring, and attitude of the same species higher
up on the foot-hills.   It is a region of great industrial
future, within a narrow range, but quite without charms
for the student of science.   It has a certain impressive
breadth when seen from some overlooking eminence, or
when in early spring its brilliant carpet of flowers lies as
a foreground over which the dark pine-land and white
crest of the Sierra loom indistinctly.

From the Mexican frontier up into Oregon, a strip of
actual desert lies under the east slope of the great chain,
and stretches eastward sometimes as far as five hundred
miles, varied by successions of bare white ground, effer-
vescing under the hot sun with alkaline salts, plains
covered by the low ashy-hued sage-plant, high, barren,
rocky ranges, which are folds of metamorphic rocks, and
piled-up lavas of bright red or yellow colors ; all overarched by a sky which is at one time of a hot metallic
brilliancy, and again the tenderest of evanescent purple
or pearl.

Utterly opposed are the two aspects of the Sierras from
these east and west approaches.   I remember how stern
and strong the chain looked to me when I first saw it
from the Colorado desert.

It was in early May, 1866.   My companion, Mr. James
T. Gardner, and I got into the saddle on the bank of the
Colorado River, and headed westward over the road from
La Paz to San Bernardino.   My mount was a tough, mag-
nanimous sort of mule, who at all times did his very best ;
that of my friend, an animal still hardier, but altogether
wanting in moral attributes.   He developed a singular
antipathy for my mule, and utterly refused to march within

a quarter of a mile of me; so that over a wearying route
of three hundred miles we were obliged to travel just beyond the reach of a shout. Hour after hour, plodding
along at a dog-trot, we pursued our solitary way without
the spice of companionship, and altogether deprived of
the melodramatic satisfaction of loneliness.

Far ahead of us a white line traced across the barren
plain marked our road. It seemed to lead to nowhere,
except onward over more and more arid reaches of desert.
Rolling hills of crude color and low gloomy contour rose
above the general level. Here and there the eye was arrested by a towering crag, or an elevated, rocky mountain
group, whose naked sides sank down into the desert, unrelieved by the shade of a solitary tree. The whole aspect
of nature was dull in color, and gloomy with an all-per-
vading silence of death. Although the summer had not
fairly opened, a torrid sun beat down with cruel severity,
blinding the eye with its brilliance, and inducing a painful, slow fever. The very plants, scorched to a crisp, were
ready, at the first blast of a sirocco, to be whirled away
and ground to dust. Certain bare zones lay swept clean
of the last dry stems across our path, marking the track
of whirlwinds. Water was only found at intervals of
sixty or seventy miles, and, when reached, was more of
an aggravation than a pleasure,— bitter, turbid, and
scarce; we rode for it all day, and berated it all night,
only to leave it at sunrise with a secret fear that we
might fare worse next time.

About noon on the third day of our march, having
reached the borders of the Chabazon Valley, we emerged
from a rough, rocky gateway in the mountains, and I
paused while my companion made up his quarter of a
mile, that we might hold council and determine our
course, for the water question was becoming serious;

springs which looked cool and seductive on our maps proving to be dried up and obsolete upon the ground.

A fresh mule and a lively man get along, to be sure, well enough ; but after all it is at best with perfunctory tolerance on both sides, a sort of diplomatic interchange of argument, the man suggesting with bridle, or mildly admonishing with spurs ; but when the high contracting parties get tired, the *entente cordiale* goes to pieces, and actual hostilities open, in which I never knew a man to come out the better.

I had noticed a shambling uncertainty during the last half-hour's trot, and those invariable indicators, " John's " long, furry ears, either lopped diagonally down on one side, or lay back with ill omen upon his neck.

Gardner reached me in a few minutes, and we dismounted to rest the tired mules, and to scan the landscape before us. We were on the margin of a great basin whose gently shelving rim sank from our feet to a perfectly level plain, which stretched southward as far as the eye could reach, bounded by a dim, level horizon, like the sea, but walled in to the west, at a distance of about forty miles, by the high frowning wall of the Sierras. This plain was a level floor, as white as marble, and into it the rocky spurs from our own mountain range descended, like promontories into the sea. Wide, deeply indented white bays wound in and out among the foot-hills, and, traced upon the barren slopes of this rocky coast, was marked, at a considerable elevation above the plain, the shore-line of an ancient sea, — a white stain defining its former margin as clearly as if the water had but just receded. On the dim, distant base of the Sierras the same primeval beach could be seen. This water-mark, the level white valley, and the utter absence upon its surface of any vegetation, gave a strange and weird aspect to the country,

as if a vast tide had but just ebbed, and the brilliant
scorching sun had hurriedly dried up its last traces of
moisture.

In the indistinct glare of the southern horizon, it needed
but slight aid from the imagination to see a lifting and
tumbling of billows, as if the old tide were coming; but
they were only shudderings of heat. As we sat there
surveying this unusual scene, the white expanse became
suddenly transformed into a placid blue sea, along whose
rippling shores were the white blocks of roofs, groups of
spire-crowned villages, and cool stretches of green grove.
A soft, vapory atmosphere hung over this sea; shadows,
purple and blue, floated slowly across it, producing the
most enchanting effect of light and color. The dreamy
richness of the tropics, the serene sapphire sky of the
desert, and the cool, purple distance of mountains, were
grouped as by miracle. It was as if Nature were about
to repay us an hundred-fold for the lie she had given the
topographers and their maps.

In a moment the illusion vanished. It was gone,
leaving the white desert unrelieved by a shadow; a blaze
of white light falling full on the plain; the sun-struck air
reeling in whirlwind columns, white with the dust of the
desert, up, up, and vanishing into the sky. Waves of
heat rolled like billows across the valley, the old shores
became indistinct, the whole lowland unreal. Shades of
misty blue crossed over it and disappeared. Lakes with
ragged shores gleamed out, reflecting the sky, and in a
moment disappeared.

The bewildering effect of this natural magic, and perhaps the feverish thirst, produced the impression of a
dream, which might have taken fatal possession of us,
but for the importunate braying of Gardner's mule, whose
piteous discords (for he made three noises at once) ban-

ished all hallucination, and brought us gently back from the mysterious spectacle to the practical question of water. We had but one canteen of that precious elixir left; the elixir in this case being composed of one part pure water, one part sand, one part alum, one part saleratus, with liberal traces of Colorado mud, representing a very disgusting taste, and very great range of geological formations.

To search for the mountain springs laid down upon our maps was probably to find them dry, and afforded us little more inducement than to chase the mirages. The only well-known water was at an oasis somewhere on the margin of the Chabazon, and should, if the information was correct, have been in sight from our resting-place.

We eagerly scanned the distance, but were unable, among the phantom lakes and the ever-changing illusions of the desert, to fix upon any probable point. Indian trails led out in all directions, and our only clew to the right path was far in the northwest, where, looming against the sky, stood two conspicuous mountain piles lifted above the general wall of the Sierra, their bases rooted in the desert, and their precipitous fronts rising boldly on each side of an open gateway. The two summits, high above the magical stratum of desert air, were sharply defined and singularly distinct in all the details of rock-form and snow-field. From their position we knew them to be walls of the San Gorgonio Pass, and through this gateway lay our road.

After brief deliberation we chose what seemed to be the most beaten road leading in that direction, and I mounted my mule and started, leaving my friend patiently seated in his saddle waiting for the *afflatus* of his mule to take effect. Thus we rode down into the desert, and hour after hour travelled silently on, straining our eyes forward to a spot of green which we hoped might mark our oasis.

So incredulous had I become, that I prided myself upon having penetrated the flimsy disguise of an unusually deceptive mirage, and philosophized, to a considerable extent, upon the superiority of my reason over the instinct of the mule, whose quickened pace and nervous manner showed him to be, as I thought, a dupe.

Whenever there comes to be a clearly defined mental issue between man and mule, the stubbornness of the latter is the expression of an adamantine moral resolve, founded in eternal right. The man is invariably wrong. Thus on this occasion, as at a thousand other times, I was obliged to own up worsted, and I drummed for a while with Spanish spurs upon the ribs of my conqueror; that being my habitual mode of covering my retreat.

It *was* the oasis, and not the mirage. John lifted up his voice, now many days hushed, and gave out spasmodic gusts of baritone, which were as dry and harsh as if he had drunk mirages only.

The heart of Gardner's mule relented. Of his own accord he galloped up to my side, and, for the first time together, we rode forward to the margin of the oasis. Under the palms we hastily threw off our saddles and allowed the parched brutes to drink their fill. We lay down in the grass, drank, bathed our faces, and played in the water like children. We picketed our mules knee-deep in the freshest of grass, and, unpacking our saddle-bags, sent up a smoke to heaven, and achieved that most precious solace of the desert traveller, a pot of tea.

By and by we plunged into the pool, which was perhaps thirty feet long, and deep enough to give us a pleasant swim. The water being almost blood-warm, we

B

absorbed it in every pore, dilated like sponges, and came out refreshed.

It is well worth having one's juices broiled out by a desert sun just to experience the renewal of life from a mild parboil. That About's "Man with the Broken Ear," under this same aqueous renovation, was ready to fall in love with his granddaughter, no longer appears to me odd. Our oasis spread out its disk of delicate green, sharply defined upon the enamel-like desert which stretched away for leagues, simple, unbroken, pathetic. Near the eastern edge of this garden, whose whole surface covered hardly more than an acre, rose two palms, interlocking their cool, dark foliage over the pool of pure water. A low, deserted cabin with wide, overhanging flat roof, which had long ago been thatched with palm-leaves, stood close by the trees.

With its isolation, its strange warm fountain, its charming vegetation varied with grasses, trailing water-plants, bright parterres in which were minute flowers of turquoise blue, pale gold, mauve, and rose, and its two graceful palms, this oasis evoked a strange sentiment. I have never felt such a sense of absolute and remote seclusion ; the hot, trackless plain and distant groups of mountain shut it away from all the world. Its humid and fragrant air hung over us in delicious contrast with the oven-breath through which we had ridden. Weary little birds alighted, panting, and drank and drank again, without showing the least fear of us. Wild doves fluttering down bathed in the pool and fed about among our mules.

After straining over one hundred and fifty miles of silent desert, hearing no sound but the shoes of our mules grating upon hot sand, after the white glare, and that fever-thirst which comes from drinking alkali-water, it was a deep pleasure to lie under the palms and look up at their slow-moving green fans, and hear in those shaded recesses the mild, sweet twittering of our traveller-friends, the birds, who stayed, like ourselves, overcome with the languor of perfect repose.

Declining rapidly toward the west, the sun warned us to renew our journey. Several hours' rest and frequent deep draughts of water, added to the feast of succulent grass, filled out and rejuvenated our saddle-animals. John was far less an anatomical specimen than when I unsaddled him, and Gardner's mule came up to be bridled with so mollified a demeanor that it occurred to us as just possible he might forget his trick of lagging behind; but with the old tenacity of purpose he planted his forefeet, and waited till I was well out on the desert.

As I rode, I watched the western prospect. Completely bounding the basin in that direction, rose the gigantic wall of the Sierra, its serrated line sharply profiled against the evening sky. This dark barrier became more and more shadowed, so that the old shore line and the lowland, where mountain and plain joined, were lost. The desert melted in the distance into the shadowed masses of the Sierra, which, looming higher and higher, seemed to rise as the sun went down. Scattered snow-fields shone along its crest ; each peak and notch, every column of rock and detail of outline, were black and sharp.

On either side of the San Gorgonio stood its two guardian peaks, San Bernardino and San Jacinto, capped with rosy snow, and the pass itself, warm with western light, opened hopefully before us. For a moment the sun rested upon the Sierra crest, and then, slowly sinking, suffered eclipse by its ragged black profile. Through the slow hours of darkening twilight a strange ashy gloom overspread the desert. The forms of the distant mountain chains behind us, and the old shore line upon the Sierra base, stared at us with a strange weird distinctness.   At last all was gray and vague, except the black silhouette of the Sierras cut upon a band of golden heaven.

We at length reached their foot and, turning northward, rode parallel with the base toward the San Gorgonio.   In the moonless night huge rocky buttresses of the range loomed before us, their feet plunging into the pale desert floor.   High upon their fronts, perhaps five hundred feet above us, was dimly traceable the white line of ancient shore.   Over drifted hills of sand and hard alkaline clay we rode along the bottom of that primitive sea.   Between the spurs, deep mountain alcoves, stretching back into the heart of the range, opened grand and shadowy; far at their head, over crests of ridge and peak, loomed the planet Jupiter.   A long, wearisome ride of forty hours brought us to the open San Gorgonio Pass.   Already scattered beds of flowers tinted the austere face of the desert; tufts of pale grass grew about the stones, and tall stems of yucca bore up their magnificent bunches of bluish flowers.   Upon all the heights overhanging the road gnarled struggling cedars grasp the rock, and stretch themselves with frantic effort to catch a breath of the fresh Pacific vapor.   It is instructive to observe the difference between those which lean out into the vitalizing wind of the pass, and the fated few whose position exposes them to the dry air of the desert.   Vigor, soundness, nerve to stand on the edge of sheer walls, flexibility, sap, fulness of green foliage, are in the one; a shroud of dull olive-leaves scantily cover the thin, straggling, bayonet-like boughs of the others: they are rigid, shrunken, split to the heart, pitiful.   We were glad to forget them as we turned a last buttress and ascended the gentle acclivity of the pass.

Before us opened a broad gateway six or seven miles

from wall to wall, in which a mere swell of green land
rises to divide the desert and Pacific slopes. Flanking
the pass along its northern side stands Mount San Bernardino, its granite framework crowded up above the beds
of more recent rock about its base, bearing aloft tattered
fragments of pine forest, the summit piercing through a
marbling of perpetual snow up to the height of ten thousand feet. Fronting it on the opposite wall rises its com-
peer, San Jacinto, a dark crag of lava, whose flanks are
cracked, riven, and waterworn into innumerable ravines,
each catching a share of the drainage from the snow-cap,
and glistening with a hundred small waterfalls.

Numerous brooks unite to form two rivers, one running
down the green slope among ranches and gardens into the
blooming valley of San Bernardino, the other pouring
eastward, shrinking as it flows out upon the hot sands,
till, in a few miles, the unslakable desert has drunk it
dry.

There are but few points in America where such extremes of physical condition meet. What contrasts, what
opposed sentiments, the two views awakened! Spread
out below us lay the desert, stark and glaring, its rigid
hill-chains lying in disordered grouping, in attitudes of the
dead. The bare hills are cut out with sharp gorges, and
over their stone skeletons scanty earth clings in folds,
like shrunken flesh ; they are emaciated corses of once
noble ranges now lifeless, outstretched as in a long sleep.
Ghastly colors define them from the ashen plain in which
their feet are buried. Far in the south were a procession
of whirlwind columns slowly moving across the desert in
spectral dimness. A white light beat down, dispelling
the last trace of shadow, and above hung the burnished
shield of hard, pitiless sky.

Sinking to the *west* from our feet the gentle golden-

green *glacis* sloped away, flanked by rolling hills covered
with a fresh vernal carpet of grass, and relieved by scattered groves of dark oak-trees.   Upon the distant valley
were checkered fields of grass and grain just tinged with
the first ripening yellow.   The bounding Coast Ranges
lay in the cool shadow of a bank of mist which drifted in
from the Pacific, covering their heights.   Flocks of bright
clouds floated across the sky, whose blue was palpitating
with light, and seemed to rise with infinite perspective.
Tranquillity, abundance, the slow, beautiful unfolding of
plant life, dark shadowed spots to rest our tired eyes
upon, the shade of giant oaks to lie down under, while
listening to brooks, contralto larks, and the soft distant
lowing of cattle.

I have given the outlines of aspect along our ride across
the Chabazon, omitting many amusing incidents and some
genre pictures of rare interest among the Kaweah Indians,
as I wished simply to illustrate the relations of the Sierra
with the country bordering its east base, — the barrier
looming above a desert.

In Nevada and California, farther north, this wall rises
more grandly, but its face rests upon a modified form of
desert plains of less extent than the Colorado, and usually
covered with sage-plants and other brushy *compositæ* of
equally pitiful appearance.   Large lakes of complicated
saline waters are dotted under the Sierra shadow, the
ancient terraces built upon foot-hill and outlying volcanic
ranges indicating their former expansion into inland seas ;
and farther north still, where plains extend east of Mount
Shasta, level sheets of lava form the country, and open
black, rocky channels, for the numerous branches of the
Sacramento and Klamath.

Approaching the Sierras anywhere from the west, you
will perceive a totally different topographical and climatic

condition. From the Coast Range peaks especially one obtains an extended and impressive prospect. I had fallen behind the party one May evening of our march across Pacheco's Pass, partly because some wind-bent oaks trailing almost horizontally over the wild-oat surface of the hills, and marking, as a living record, the prevalent west wind, had arrested me and called out compass and note-book; and because there had fallen to my lot an incorrigibly deliberate mustang to whom I had abandoned myself to be carried along at his own pace, comforted withal that I should get in too late to have any hand in the cooking of supper. We reached the crest, the mustang coming to a conspicuous and unwarrantable halt; I yielded, however, and sat still in the saddle, looking out to the east.

Brown foot-hills, purple over their lower slopes with "fil-a-ree" blossoms, descended steeply to the plain of California, a great, inland, prairie sea, extending for five hundred miles, mountain-locked, between the Sierras and coast hills, and now a broad arabesque surface of colors. Miles of orange-colored flowers, cloudings of green and white, reaches of violet which looked like the shadow of a passing cloud, wandering in natural patterns over and through each other, sunny and intense along near our range, fading in the distance into pale bluish-pearl tones, and divided by long, dimly seen rivers, whose margins were edged by belts of bright emerald green. Beyond rose three hundred miles of Sierra half lost in light and cloud and mist, the summit in places sharply seen against a pale, beryl sky, and again buried in warm, rolling clouds. It was a mass of strong light, soft, fathomless shadows, and dark regions of forest. However, the three belts upon its front were tolerably clear. Dusky foot-hills rose over the plain with a coppery gold tone, suggesting the line of mining towns planted in its rusty ravines, — a suggestion I was glad to repel, and look higher into that cool, solemn realm where the pines stand, green-roofed, in infinite colonnade.   Lifted above the bustling industry of the plains and the melodramatic mining theatre of the foot-hills, it has a grand, silent life of its own, refreshing to contemplate even from a hundred miles away.

While I looked the sun descended ; shadows climbed the Sierras, casting a gloom over foot-hill and pine, until at last only the snow summits, reflecting the evening light, glowed like red lamps along the mountain wall for hundreds of miles.   The rest of the Sierra became invisible.   The snow burned for a moment in the violet sky, and at last went out.

II.

THROUGH THE FOREST.

1864.

VISALIA is the name of a small town embowered in oaks upon the Tulare Plain in Middle California, where we made our camp one May evening of 1864.

Professor Whitney, our chief, the State Geologist, had sent us out for a summer's campaign in the High Sierras, under the lead of Professor William H. Brewer, who was more sceptical than I as to the result of the mission.

Several times during the previous winter Mr. Hoffman and I, while on duty at the Mariposa gold-mines, had climbed to the top of Mount Bullion, and gained, in those clear January days, a distinct view of the High Sierra, ranging from the Mount Lyell group many miles south to a vast pile of white peaks, which, from our estimate, should lie near the heads of the King's and Kaweah rivers. Of their great height I was fully persuaded; and Professor Whitney, on the strength of these few observations, commissioned us to explore and survey the new Alps.

We numbered five in camp, — Professor Brewer; Mr. Charles F. Hoffman, chief topographer; Mr. James T. Gardner, assistant surveyor; myself, assistant geologist; and our man-of-all-work, to whom science already owes its debts.

When we got together our outfit of mules and equipments of all kinds, Brewer was going to re-engage, as general aid, a certain Dane, Jan Hoesch, who, besides being a

2

faultless mule-packer, was a rapid and successful financier, having twice, when the field-purse was low and remittances delayed, enriched us by what he called " dealing bottom stock " in his little evening games with the honest miners. Not ungrateful for that, I, however, detested the fellow with great cordiality.

"If I don't take him, will you be responsible for packing mules and for daily bread ? " said Brewer to me the morning of our departure from Oakland. " I will." "Then we 'll take your man Cotter; only, when the pack-saddles roll under the mules' bellies, I shall light my pipe and go botanizing. *Sabe ?* "

So my friend, Richard Cotter, came into the service, and the accomplished but filthy Jan opened a poker and rum shop on one of the San Francisco wharves, where he still mixes drinks and puts up jobs of "bottom stock." Secretly I longed for him as we came down the Pacheco Pass, the packs having loosened with provoking frequency. The animals of our small exploring party were upon a footing of easy social equality with us. All were excellent except mine. The choice of Hobson (whom I take to have been the youngest member of some company) falling naturally to me, I came to be possessed of the only hopeless animal in the band. Old Slum, a dignified roan mustang of a certain age, with the decorum of years and a conspicuous economy of force retained not a few of the affectations of youth, such as snorting theatrically, and shying, though with absolute safety to the rider, Professor Brewer. Hoffman's mount was a young half-breed, full of fire and gentleness. The mare Bess, my friend Gardner's pet, was a light bay creature, as full of spring and perception as her sex and species may be. A rare mule, Cate, carried Cotter. Nell and Jim, two old geological mules, branded with Mexican hieroglyphics from head to tail, were bearers of the loads.

My Buckskin was incorrigibly bad. To begin with, his anatomy was desultory and incoherent, the maximum of physical effort bringing about a slow, shambling gait quite unendurable. He was further cursed with a brain wanting the elements of logic, as evinced by such *non sequiturs* as shying insanely at wisps of hay, and stampeding beyond control when I tried to tie him to a load of grain. My sole amusement with Buckskin grew out of a psychological peculiarity of his, namely, the unusual slowness with which waves of sensation were propelled inward toward the brain from remote parts of his periphery. A dig of the spurs administered in the flank passed unnoticed for a period of time varying from twelve to thirteen seconds, till the protoplasm of the brain received the percussive wave, then, with a suddenness which I never wholly got over, he would dash into a trot, nearly tripping himself up with his own astonishment.

A stroke of good fortune completed our outfit and my happiness by bringing to Visalia a Spaniard who was under some manner of financial cloud. His horse was offered for sale, and quickly bought for me by Professor Brewer. We named him Kaweah, after the river and its Indian tribe. He was young, strong, fleet, elegant, a pattern of fine modelling in every part of his bay body and fine black legs ; every way good, only fearfully wild, with a blaze of quick electric light in his dark eye.

Shortly after sunrise one fresh morning we made a point of putting the packs on very securely, and, getting into our saddles, rode out toward the Sierras.

The group of farms surrounding Visalia is gathered within a belt through which several natural, and many more artificial, channels of the Kaweah flow. Groves of large, dark-foliaged oaks follow this irrigated zone ; the roads, nearly always in shadow, are flanked by small ranch-houses, fenced in with rank jungles of weeds and rows of decrepit pickets.

There is about these fresh ruins, these specimens of modern decay, an air of social decomposition not pleasant to perceive. Freshly built houses, still untinted by time, left in rickety disorder, half-finished windows, gates broken down or unhinged, and a kind of sullen neglect staring everywhere. What more can I say of the people than that they are chiefly Southern immigrants who subsist upon pork?

Rare exceptions of comfort and thrift shine out sometimes, with neat dooryards, well-repaired dwellings, and civilized-looking children. In these I never saw the mother of the family sitting cross-legged, smoking a corn-cob pipe, nor the father loafing about with a fiddle or shot-gun.

Our backs were now turned to this farm-belt, the road leading us out upon the open plain in our first full sight of the Sierras.

Grand and cool swelled up the forest; sharp and rugged rose the wave of white peaks, their vast fields of snow rolling over the summit in broad shining masses.

Sunshine, exuberant vegetation, brilliant plant life, occupied our attention hour after hour until the middle of the second day. At last, after climbing a long, weary ascent, we rode out of the dazzling light of the foot-hills into a region of dense woodland, the road winding through avenues of pines so tall that the late evening light only came down to us in scattered rays. Under the deep shade of these trees we found an air pure and grate-fully cool. Passing from the glare of the open country into the dusky forest, one seems to enter a door, and ride into a vast covered hall. The whole sensation is of being roofed and enclosed. You are never tired of gazing down

long vistas, where, in stately groups, stand tall shafts of
pine. Columns they are, each with its own characteristic
tinting and finish, yet all standing together with the air
of relationship and harmony. Feathery branches, trimmed
with living green, wave through the upper air, opening
broken glimpses of the far blue, and catching on their
polished surfaces reflections of the sun. Broad streams
of light pour in, gilding purple trunks and falling in bright
pathways along an undulating floor. Here and there are
wide open spaces around which the trees group themselves in majestic ranks.

Our eyes often ranged upward, the long shafts leading the vision up to green, lighted spires, and on to the
clouds. All that is dark and cool and grave in color,
the beauty of blue umbrageous distance, all the sudden
brilliance of strong local lights tinted upon green boughs
or red and fluted shafts, surround us in ever-changing
combination as we ride along these winding roadways of
the Sierra.

We had marched a few hours over high, rolling
wooded ridges, when in the late afternoon we reached the
brow of an eminence and began to descend. Looking
over the tops of the trees beneath us we saw a mountain
basin fifteen hundred feet deep surrounded by a rim of
pine-covered hills. An even unbroken wood covered
these sweeping slopes down to the very bottom, and in
the midst, open to the sun, lay a circular green meadow,
about a mile in diameter.

As we descended, side wood-tracks, marked by the
deep ruts of timber wagons, joined our road on either
side, and in the course of an hour we reached the basin
and saw the distant roofs of Thomas's Saw-Mill Ranch.
We crossed the level disk of meadow, fording a clear,
cold mountain stream, flowing, as the best brooks do,

over clean white granite sand, and near the northern margin of the valley, upon a slight eminence, in the edge of a magnificent forest, pitched our camp.

The hills to the westward already cast down a sombre shadow, which fell over the eastern hills and across the meadow, dividing the basin half in golden and half in azure green. The tall young grass was living with purple and white flowers. This exquisite carpet sweeps up over the bases of the hills in green undulations, and strays far into the forest in irregular fields. A little brooklet passed close by our camp and flowed down the smooth green *glacis* which led from our little eminence to the meadow. Above us towered pines two hundred and fifty feet high, their straight fluted trunks smooth and without a branch for a hundred feet. Above that, and on, to the very tops, the green branches stretched out and interwove, until they spread a broad leafy canopy from column to column.

Professor Brewer determined to make this camp a home for the week, during which we were to explore and study all about the neighborhood. We were on a great granite spur sixty miles from east to west by twenty miles wide, which lies between the Kaweah and King's River cañons. Rising in bold sweeps from the plain, this ridge joins the Sierra summit in the midst of a high group. Experience had taught us that the cañons are impassable by animals for any great distance; so the plan of campaign was to find a way up over the rocky crest of the spur as far as mules could go.

In the little excursions from this camp, which were made usually on horseback, we became acquainted with the forest, and got a good knowledge of the topography of a considerable region. On the heights above King's Cañon are some singularly fine assemblies of trees. Cot-

ter and I had ridden all one morning northeast from
camp under the shadowy roof of forest, catching but
occasional glimpses out over the plateau, until at last we
emerged upon the bare surface of a ridge of granite, and
came to the brink of a sharp precipice. Rocky crags
lifted just east of us. The hour devoted to climbing them
proved well spent.

A single little family of alpine firs growing in a niche
in the granite surface, and partly sheltered by a rock,
made the only shadow, and just shielded us from the
intense light as we lay down by their roots. North and
south, as far as the eye could reach, heaved the broad
green waves of plateau, swelling and merging through
endless modulation of slope and form.

Conspicuous upon the horizon, about due east of us, was
a tall pyramidal mass of granite, trimmed with buttresses
which radiated down from its crest, each one ornamented
with fantastic spires of rock. Between the buttresses
lay stripes of snow, banding the pale granite peak from
crown to base. Upon the north side it fell off, grandly
precipitous, into the deep upper cañon of King's River.
This gorge, after uniting a number of immense rocky
amphitheatres, is carved deeply into the granite two
and three thousand feet. In a slightly curved line from
the summit it cuts westward through the plateau, its
walls, for the most part, descending in sharp bare
slopes, or lines of ragged *débris*, the resting-place of processions of pines. We ourselves were upon the brink of
the south wall; three thousand feet below us lay the
valley, a narrow, winding ribbon of green, in which, here
and there, gleamed still reaches of the river. Wherever
the bottom widened to a quarter or half a mile, green
meadows and extensive groves occupied the level region.
Upon every niche and crevice of the walls, up and down

sweeping curves of easier descent, were grouped black companies of trees.

The behavior of the forest is observed most interestingly from these elevated points above the general face of the table-land. All over the gentle undulations of the more level country sweeps an unbroken covering of trees. Reaching the edge of the cañon precipices, they stand out in bold groups upon the brink, and climb all over the more ragged and broken surfaces of granite. Only the most smooth and abrupt precipices are bare. Here and there a little shelf of a foot or two in width, cracked into the face of the bluff, gives foothold to a family of pines, who twist their roots into its crevices and thrive. With no soil from which the roots may drink up moisture and absorb the slowly dissolved mineral particles, they live by breathing alone, moist vapors from the river below and the elements of the atmosphere affording them the substance of life.

I believe no one can study from an elevated lookout the length and depth of one of these great Sierra cañons without asking himself some profound geological questions. Your eyes range along one or the other wall. The average descent is immensely steep. Here and there side ravines break down the rim in deep lateral gorges. Again, the wall advances in sharp, salient precipices, rising two or three thousand feet, sheer and naked, with all the air of a recent fracture. At times the two walls approach each other, standing in perpendicular gateways. Toward the summits the cañon grows, perhaps, a little broader, and more and more prominent lateral ravines open into it, until at last it receives the snow drainage of the summit, which descends through broad, rounded amphitheatres, separated from each other by sharp, castellated snow-clad ridges.

Looking down the course of the river vertical precipices are seen to be less and less frequent, the walls inclining to each other more and more gently, until they roll out on the north and south in round wooded ridges. Solid, massive granite forms the material throughout its whole length. If you study the topography upon the plateaus above one of these cañons, you will see that the ridges upon one side are reproduced in the other, as if the outlines of wavy table-land topography had been determined before the great cañon was made.

It is not easy to propose a solution for this peculiar structure. I think, however, it is safe to say that actual rending asunder of the mountain mass determined the main outlines. Upon no other theory can we account for those blank walls. Where, in the upper course of the cañon, they descend in a smooth, ship-like curve, and the rocks bear upon their curved sides the markings and striations of glaciers, it is easy to see that those terrible ice-engines gradually modified their form; and toward the foot-hills the forces of aqueous erosion are clearly indicated in the rounded forms and broad undulations of the two banks.

Looking back from our isolated crag in the direction of our morning's ride, we saw the green hills break down into the basin of Thomas's Mill, but the disk of meadow lay too deep to be seen. Forests, dense and unbroken, grew to the base of our cliff. The southern sunlight reflected from its polished foliage gave to this whole sea of spiry tops a peculiar golden green, through which we looked down among giant red and purple trunks upon beds of bright mountain flowers. As the afternoon lengthened, the summit rank of peaks glowed warmer and warmer under inclined rays. The granite flushed with rosy brightness between the fields of glittering

2 *   c

golden snow. A mild, pearly haziness came gradually to obscure the ordinary cold-blue sky, and, settling into cañon depths and among the vast open corridors of the summit, veiled the savage sharpness of their details.

I lay several hours sketching the outlines of the summit, studying out the systems of alpine drainage, and getting acquainted with the long chain of peaks, that I might afterward know them from other points of view. I became convinced from the great apparent elevation and the wide fields of snow that we had not formerly deceived ourselves as to their great height. Warned at length by the deepening shadow in the King's Cañon, by the heightened glow suffusing the peaks, and the deep purple tone of the level expanse of forest, all forerunners of twilight, we quitted our eyry, crept carefully down over half-balanced blocks of *débris* to the horses, and, mounting, were soon headed homeward, in what seemed, by contrast, to be almost a nocturnal darkness.

Wherever the ground opened level before us we gave our horses the rein, and went at a free gallop through the forest; the animals realized that they were going home, and pressed forward with the greatest spirit. A good-sized log across our route seemed to be an object of special amusement to Kaweah, who seized the bits in his teeth and, dancing up, crouched, and cleared it with a mighty bound, in a manner that was indeed inspiring, yet left one with the impression that once was enough of that sort of thing. Fearing some manner of hostilities with him, I did my very best to quiet Kaweah, and by the end of an hour had gotten him down to a sensible, serious walk. I noticed that he insisted upon following his tracks of the morning's march, and was not contented unless I let him go on the old side of every tree. Thus I became so thoroughly convinced of his faculty to follow the morning's trail that I yielded all control of him, giving myself up to the enjoyment of the dimly lighted wood.

As the sun at last set, the shadow deepened into an impressive gloom; mighty trunks, rising into that dark region of interlocking boughs, only vaguely defined themselves against the twilight sky. We could no longer see our tracks, and the confused rolling topography looked alike whichever way we turned. Kaweah strode on in his confident way, and I was at last confirmed as to his sagacity by passing one after another the objects we had noted in the morning. Thus for a couple of hours we rode in the darkness. At length the rising moon poured down through broken tents of foliage its uncertain silvery light, which had the effect of deepening all the shadows, and lighting up in the strangest manner little local points. Here and there ahead of us the lighted trees rose like pillars of an ancient temple. The forest, which an hour before overpowered us with a sense of its dark enclosure, opened on in distant avenues as far as the eye could reach. As we rode through denser or more open passages the moon sailed into clear violet sky, or was obscured again by the sharply traced crests of the pines. Ravines, dark and unfathomable, yawned before us, their flanks half in shadow, half in weird uncertain light. Blocks of white granite gleamed here and there in contrast with the general depth of shade. At last, descending a hill, there shone before us a red light; the horses plunged forward at a gallop, and in a moment we were in camp. After this ride we supped, relishing our mountain fare, and then lay down upon blankets before a campfire for the mountaineer's short evening. One keeps awake under stimulus of the sparkling, frosty air for a while, and then turns in for the night, sleeping till daybreak with a light sound sleep.

The charm of this forest life, in spite of its scientific interest, and the constant succession of exquisite, highly colored scenes, would string one's feelings up to a high though monotonous key, were it not for the half-droll, half-pathetic *genre* picturesqueness which the Digger Indians introduce. Upon every stream and on all the finer camp-grounds throughout the whole forest are found these families of Indians who migrate up here during the hot weather, fishing, hunting, gathering pine-nuts, and lying off with that peculiar, bummerish ease, which, associated with natural mock dignity, throws about them a singular, and not unfrequently deep interest.

I never forget certain bright June sunrises when I have seen the Indian *paterfamilias* gather together his little tribe and address them in the heroic style concerning the vital importance of the grasshopper crop, and the reverence due to the Giver of manzanita berries. You come upon them as you travel the trails, proud-stepping " braves " leading the way, unhampered and free, followed by troops of submissive squaws loaded down with immense packages and baskets. Their death and burial customs too have elements of weird romantic interest.

I remember one morning when I was awakened before dawn by wild unearthly shrieks ringing through the forest and coming back again in plaintive echoes from the hills all about. Beyond description wild, these wails of violent grief followed each other with regular cadence, dying away in long despairing sobs. With a marvellous regularity they recurred, never varying the simple refrain. My curiosity was aroused so far as to get me out of my blankets, and, after a hurried bath in an icy stream, I joined my mountaineer acquaintance, Jerry, who was *en route* to the rancheria, " to see," as he expressed it, " them *tar-heads* howl." It seems my friend Buck, the Indian chief, had the night before lost his wife, Sally the Old, and the shouts came from professional mourners hired by her family to prepare the body and do up the necessary amount of grief. Old widows and superannuated wives who have outlived other forms of usefulness gladly enter this singular profession. They cut their hair short, and with each new death plaster on a fresh cap of pitch and ashes, daub the face with spots of tar, and, in general, array themselves as funeral experts.

The rancheria was astir when we arrived. It was a mere group of half a dozen smoky hovels, built of pine bark propped upon cones of poles, and arranged in a semicircle within the edge of the forest, fronting on a brook and meadow. Jerry and I leaned our backs against a large tree, and watched the group.

Buck's shanty was deserted, the body of his wife lying outside upon a blanket, being prepared by two of these funeral hags. Buck himself was quietly stuffing his stomach with a breakfast of venison and acorns, which were handed him at brief intervals by several sympathizing squaws.

Turning to Jerry with a countenance of stolid seriousness, he laconically remarked, " My woman she die! Very bad. To-night, sundown" (pointing to the sun), "she burn up." Meanwhile the tar-heads rolled Sally the Old over and over, all the while alternately howling the same dismal phrase. Indian relatives and friends, having the general air of animated rag-bags, arrived occasionally, and sat down in silence at a fire a little removed from the other Diggers, never once saluting them.

As we walked back to our camp, I remarked on the stolid, cruel expression of Buck's face, but Jerry, to my surprise, bade me not judge too hastily. He went on to explain that Indians have just as deep and tender attachments, just as much good sense, and, to wind up with, "as much human into 'em, as we edicated white folks."

His own squaw had instilled this into Jerry's naturally sentimental and credulous heart, so I refrained from expressing my convictions concerning Indians, which, I own, were formerly tinged with the most sanguinary Caucasian prejudice.

Jerry came for me by appointment just before sunset, and we walked leisurely across the meadow, and under lengthening pine shadows, to the rancheria. No one was stirring. Buck and the two vicarious mourners sat in his lodge door uttering low, half-audible groans. In the opening before the line of huts a low pile of dry logs had been carefully laid, upon which, outstretched, and wrapped in a red blanket, lay the dead form of Sally the Old, her face covered in careful folds. Upon her heart were a grass-woven water-bowl and her last pappoose basket.

Just as the sun sank to the horizon, one tar-head stepped out in front of the funeral pile, lifted up both hands, and gazed steadily and silently at the sun. She might have been five minutes in this statuesque position, her face full of strange, half-animal intensity of expression, her eyes glittering, the whole hard figure glowing with a deep bronze reflection. Suddenly she sprang back with the old wild shriek, seized a brand from one of the camp-fires, and lighted the funeral heap, when all the Indians came out, and grouped themselves in little knots around it. Sally the Old's children clung about an old mummy of a squaw, who squatted upon the ground and rocked her body to and fro, making a low cry as of an animal in pain. All the Indians looked serious; a group, who Jerry said were relatives, seemed stupefied with grief. Upon a few faces falling tears glistened in the light of the fire, which now shot up red tongues high in the air, lighting up with weird distinctness every feature of the whole group. Flames slowly lapped over, consuming the blanket, and caught the willow pappoose basket. When Buck saw this, the tears streamed from his eyes; he waved his hands eloquently, looking up to heaven, and uttered heart-broken sobs. The pappoose basket crackled for a moment, flashed into a blaze, and was gone. The two old women yelled their sharp death-cry, dancing, posturing, gesticulating toward the fire, and in slow measured chorus all the Indians intoned in pathetic measure, " Himalaya! Himalaya!" looking first at the mound of fire and then out upon the fading sunset.

It was all indescribably strange: monarch pines standing in solemn ranks far back into the dusky heart of the forest, glowing and brightening with pulsating reflections of firelight; the ring of Indians, crouching, standing fixed like graven images, or swaying mechanically to and fro; each tattered scarlet and white rag of their utterly squalid garments, every expression of barbaric grief or dull stolidity, were brought strongly out by the red flaming fire.

Buck watched with wet eyes that slow-consuming fire burn to ashes the body of his wife of many years, the mother of his group of poor frightened children. Not a stoical savage, but a despairing husband, stood before us. I felt him to be human. The body at last sank into a bed of flames which shot up higher than ever with fountains of sparks, and sucked together, hiding the remains forever from view. At this Buck sprang to the front and threw himself at the fire; but the two old women seized each a hand and dragged him back to his children, when he fell into a.fit of stupor.

As we walked home Jerry was quick to ask, "Did n't I tell you Injuns has feelings inside of 'em?" I answered promptly that I was convinced; and long after, as I lay awake through many night-hours listening to that shrill death-wail, I felt as if any policy toward the Indians based upon the assumption of their being brutes or devils was nothing short of a blot on this Christian century.

My sleep was light, and sunrise found me dressed, still listening, as under a kind of spell, to the mourners, who, though evidently exhausted, at brief intervals uttered the cry. Alone, and filled with serious reflections, I strolled over to the rancheria, finding every one there up and about his morning duties.

The tar-heads, withdrawn some distance into the forest, sat leaning against a stump, chatting and grinning together, now and then screeching by turns.

I asked Revenue Stamp, a good-natured, middle-aged Indian, where Buck was. He pointed to his hut, and replied, with an affable smile, "He whiskey drunk." "And who," I inquired, "is that fat girl with him?" "Last night he take her; new squaw," was the answer. I could hardly believe, but it was the actual truth; and I went back to camp an enlightened but disillusioned man. I left that day, and never had an opportunity to "free my mind" to Jerry. Since then I guardedly avoid all discussion of the "Indian question." When interrogated, I dodge, or protest ignorance; when pressed, I have been known to turn the subject; or, if driven to the wall, I usually confess my opinion that the Quakers will have to work a great reformation in the Indian before he is really fit to be exterminated.

The mill-people and Indians told us of a wonderful group of big trees (*Sequoia gigantea*), and about one particular tree of unequalled size. We found them easily, after a ride of a few miles in a northerly direction from our camp, upon a wide, flat-topped spur, where they grew, as is their habit elsewhere, in company with several other coniferous species, all grouped socially together, heightening each other's beauty by contrasts of form and color.

In a rather open glade, where the ground was for the most part green with herbage, and conspicuously starred with upland flowers, stood the largest shaft we observed. A fire had formerly burned off a small segment of its base, not enough, however, to injure the symmetrical appearance. It was a slowly tapering, regularly round column of about forty feet in diameter at the base, and rising two hundred and seventy-four feet, adorned with a few huge branches, which start horizontally from the trunk, but quickly turn down and spray out. The bark, thick but not rough, is scored up and down at considerable intervals with deep, smooth grooves, and is of brightest cinnamon color mottled in purple and yellow.

That which impresses one most after its vast bulk and grand, pillar-like stateliness, is the thin and inconspicuous foliage, which feathers out delicately on the boughs like a mere mist of pale apple-green. It would seem nothing when compared with the immense volume of tree for which it must do the ordinary respirative duty; but doubtless the bark performs a large share of this, its papery lamination and porous structure fitting it eminently for that purpose.

Near this "King of the Mountains" grew three other trees; one a sugar-pine (*Pinus Lambertiana*) of about eight feet in diameter, and hardly less than three hundred feet high (although we did not measure it, estimating simply by comparison of its rise above the *Sequoia*, whose height was quite accurately determined). For a

hundred and fifty feet the pine was branchless, and as
round as if turned, delicate bluish-purple in hue, and
marked with a network of scorings. The branches, in
nearly level poise, grew long and slenderly out from the
shaft, well covered with dark yellow-green needles. The
two remaining trees were firs (*Picea grandis*), which Abi
sprung from a common root, dividing slightly, as they
rose, a mass of feathery branches, whose load of polished
blue-green foliage, for the most part, hid the dark wood-
brown trunk. Grace, exquisite spire-like taper boughs,
whose plumes of green float lightly upon the air, elas-
ticity, and symmetry, are its characteristics.

In all directions this family continue grouping themselves always with attractive originality. There is something memorable in the harmonious yet positive colors of
this sort of forest. First, the foliage and trunk of each
separate tree contrasts finely, — cinnamon and golden
apple-green in the *Sequoia*, dark purple and yellowish-
green for the pine, deep wood-color and bluish-green of
fir.

The sky, which at this elevation of six thousand feet
is deep pure blue and often cloudless, is seen through
the tracery of boughs and tree-tops, which cast downward
fine and filmy shadows across the glowing trunks. Altogether, it is a wonderful setting for the *Sequoia*. The two
firs, judging by many of equal size whose age I have
studied, were about three hundred years old ; the pine,
still hale and vigorous, not less than five hundred ; and for
the " King of the Mountains " we cannot assign a probable age of less than two thousand years.

A mountain, a fossil from deepest geological horizon, a
ruin of human art, carry us back into the perspective of
centuries with a force that has become, perhaps, a little
conventional. No imperishableness of mountain-peak

or of fragment of human work, broken pillar or sand-worn image half lifted over pathetic desert, — none of these link the past and to-day with anything like the power of these monuments of living antiquity, trees that began to grow before the Christian era, and, full of hale vitality and green old age, still bid fair to grow broad and high for centuries to come. Who shall predict the limits of this unexampled life ? There is nothing which indicates suffering or degeneracy in the *Sequoia* as a species. I find pathological hints that several other far younger species in the same forest are gradually giving up their struggle for existence. That singular species *Pinus Sabiniana* appears to me to suffer death-pains from foot-hill extremes of temperature and dryness, and notably from ravenous parasites of the mistletoe type. At the other extreme the *Pinus flexilis* has about half given up the fight against cold and storms. Its young are dwarfed or huddled in thickets, with such mode of growth that they may never make trees of full stature; while higher up, standing among bare rocks and fields of ice, far above all living trees, are the stark white skeletons of noble dead specimens, their blanched forms rigid and defiant, preserved from decay by a marvellous hardness of fibre, and only wasted by the cutting of storm-driven crystals of snow. Still the *Sequoia* maintains perfect health.

It is, then, the vast respiring power, the atmosphere, the bland, regular climate, which give such long life, and not any richness or abundance of food received from the soil.

If one loves to gather the material for travellers' stories, he may find here and there a hollow fallen trunk through whose heart he may ride for many feet without bowing the head. But if he love the tree for its own grand nature, he may lie in silence upon the soft forest floor, in shadow or sunny warmth, if he please, and spend many days in wonder, gazing upon majestic shafts, following their gold and purple flutings from broad, firmly planted base up and on through the few huge branches, and among the pale clouds of filmy green traced in open network upon the deep blue of the sky.

Groups of this ancient race grow along the middle heights of the Sierra for almost two hundred miles, marking a line of groves through the forest of lesser trees, still retaining their power of reproduction, ripening cones with regularity, whose seed germinates, springs up, and grows with apparently as great vital power as the descendants of younger conifers. Nor are these their only remarkable characteristics. They possess hardly any roots at all. Several in each grove have been blown down, and lie slowly decomposing. They are found usually to have rested upon the ground with a few short pedestal-like feet penetrating the earth for a little way.

Too soon for my pleasure, the time came when we must turn our backs upon these stately groves and push up towards the snow.

Our route lay eastward, between the King's and Kaweah rivers, rising as we marched; the vegetation, as well as the barometer, accurately measuring the change.

We reached our camp on the Big Meadow plateau on the 22d of June, and that night the thermometer fell to 20° above zero. This cold was followed by a chilly, overcast morning, and about ten o'clock an old-fashioned snow-storm set in. Wind howled fiercely through the trees, coming down from the mountains in terribly powerful gusts. The green flower-covered meadow was soon buried under snow; and we explorers, who had no tent, hid ourselves under piles of brush, and on

the lee side of hospitable stones. Our scant supply
of blankets was a poor defence against such inclem-
ency; so we crawled out and made a huge camp-fire,
around which we sat for the rest of the day. During
the afternoon we were visited. A couple of hunters, with
their rifles over their shoulders, seeing the smoke of our
camp-fire, followed it through the woods and joined our
circle. They were typical mountaineers,— outcasts from
society, discontented with the world, comforting themselves in the solitude of nature by the occasional excitement of a bear-fight. One was a half-breed Cherokee,
rather over six feet high, powerfully built, and picturesquely dressed in buckskin breeches and green jacket; a
sort of Trovatore hat completed his costume, and gave him
an animated appearance. The other was unmistakably a
Pike-Countian, who had dangled into a pair of butternut
jeans. His greasy flannel shirt was pinned together with
thorns in lieu of buttons, and his hat fastened back in
the same way, having lost its stiffness by continual wetting. The Cherokee had a long manly stride, and the
Pike a rickety sort of shuffle. His anatomy was bad, his
physical condition worse, and I think he added to that a
sort of pride in his own awkwardness. Seeming to have
a principle of suspension somewhere about his shoulders,
which maintained his head at about the right elevation
above the ground, he kept up a good rate in walking
without apparently making an effort. His body swayed
with a peculiar corkscrew motion, and his long Missis-
sippi rifle waved to and fro through the air.

We all noticed the utter contrast between them as
these two men approached our fire. The hunter's taciturnity is a well-known *rôle*, but they had evidently
lived so long an isolated life that they were too glad of
any company to play it unfailingly; so it was they who

opened the conversation. We found that they were now camped only a half-mile from us, were hunting for deer-skins, and had already accumulated a very large number. They offered us plenty of venison, and were greatly inter-ested in our proposed journeys into the high mountains. From them we learned that they had themselves pene-trated farther than any others, and had only given up the exploration after wandering fruitlessly among the cañons for a month. They told us that not even Indians had crossed the Sierras to the east, and that if we did succeed in reaching this summit we would certainly be the first. We learned from them, also, that a mile to the northward was a great herd of cattle in charge of a party of Mex-icans. Fleeing before the continued drought of the plains, all the cattle-men of California drove the remains of their starved herds either to the coast or to the High Sierras, and grazed upon the summer pastures, descending in the autumn, and living upon the dry foot-hill grasses, until, under the influence of winter rains, the plains again clothe themselves with pasturage. The following morn-ing, having received a present of two deer from the hunt-ers, we packed our animals and started eastward, passing, after a few minutes' ride, the encampment of the Spaniards. About four thousand cattle roamed over the plateau, and were only looked after once or twice a week. The four Spaniards divided their time between drinking coffee and playing cards. They were engaged in the latter amuse-ment when we passed them ; and although we halted and tried to get some information, they only answered us in monosyllables, and continued their game. To the eastward the plateau rose toward the high mountains in immense granite steps. We rode pleasantly through the forest over these level tables, and climbed with difficulty the rugged rock-strewn fronts, each successive step bringing

us nearer the mountains, and giving us a far-reaching
view. Here and there the granite rose through the forest
in broad, smooth domes; and many times we were obliged
to climb these rocky slopes at the peril of our animals'
lives. After several days of marching and countermarch-
ing, we gave up the attempt to push farther in a southeast
direction, and turned north, toward the great cañon of
King's River, which we hoped might lead us up to the
Snow Group. Reaching the brink of this gorge, we
observed, about half-way down the slope, and standing
at equal levels on both flanks, singular embankments
— shelves a thousand feet in width — built at a height
of fifteen hundred feet above the valley bottom, their
smooth, evenly graded summits rising higher and
higher to the eastward on the cañon-wall until they
joined the snow. They were evidently the lateral moraines of a vast extinct glacier, and that opposite us
seemed to offer an easy ride into the heart of the mountains. With great difficulty we descended the long slope,
through chaparral and forest, reaching, at length, the
level, smooth glacier bottom. Here, threading its way
through alternate groves and meadows, was the King's
River, — a stream not over thirty feet in width, but rushing
with all the force of a torrent. Its icy temperature was
very refreshing after our weary climb down the wall. By
a series of long zigzags we succeeded in leading our animals up the flank to the top of the north moraine, and
here we found ourselves upon a forest-covered causeway,
almost as smooth as a railroad embankment. Its fluted
crest enclosed three separate pathways, each a hundred feet wide, divided from each other by roughly laid
trains of rocks, showing it evidently to be a compound
moraine. As we ascended toward the mountains, the
causeway was more and more isolated from the cliff,

until the depression between them widened to half a mile, and to at least five hundred feet deep. Throughout nearly a whole day we rode comfortably along at a gentle grade, reaching at evening the region of the snow, where, among innumerable huge granite blocks, we threaded our way in search of a camp-ground. The mountain amphitheatre which gave rise to the King's River opened to the east, a broad valley, into which we at length climbed; and, among scattered groves of alpine pines, and on patches of meadow, rode eastward till twilight, watching the high pyramidal peak which lay directly at the head of the gorge. By sunset we had gone as far as we could take the animals, and, in full view of our goal, camped for the night. The form of the mountain at the head of our ravine was purely Gothic.

A thousand upspringing spires and pinnacles pierce the sky in every direction, the cliffs and mountain-ridges are everywhere ornamented with countless needle-like turrets. Crowning the wall to the south of our camp were series of these jagged forms standing out against the sky like a procession of colossal statues. Whichever way we turned, we were met by some extraordinary fulness of detail. Every mass seemed to have the highest possible ornamental finish. Along the lower flanks of the walls, tall straight pines, the last of the forest, were relieved against the cliffs, and the same slender forms, although carved in granite, surmounted every ridge and peak.

Through this wide zone of forest we had now passed, and from its perpetual shadow had come out among the few black groves of fir into a brilliant alpine sunshine. The light, although surprisingly lively, was of a purity and refinement quite different from the strong glare of the plains.

III.

THE ASCENT OF MOUNT TYNDALL.

1864.

MORNING dawned brightly upon our bivouac among a cluster of dark firs in the mountain corridor opened by an ancient glacier of King's River into the heart of the Sierras. It dawned a trifle sooner than we could have wished, but Professor Brewer and Hoffman had breakfasted before sunrise, and were off with barometer and theodolite upon their shoulders, purposing to ascend our amphitheatre to its head and climb a great pyramidal peak which swelled up against the eastern sky, closing the view in that direction.

We who remained in camp spent the day in overhauling campaign materials and preparing for a grand assault upon the summits. For a couple of hours we could descry our friends through the field-glasses, their minute black forms moving slowly on among piles of giant *débris;* now and then lost, again coming into view, and at last disappearing altogether.

It was twilight of evening and almost eight o'clock when they came back to camp, Brewer leading the way, Hoffman following; and as they sat down by our fire without uttering a word, we read upon their faces terrible fatigue.

So we hastened to give them supper of coffee and soup, bread and venison, which resulted, after a time, in our getting in return the story of the day.

3   D

For eight whole hours they had worked up over granite and snow, mounting ridge after ridge, till the summit was made about two o'clock.

These snowy crests bounding our view at the eastward we had all along taken to be the summits of the Sierra, and Brewer had supposed himself to be climbing a dominant peak, from which he might look eastward over Owen's Valley and out upon leagues of desert. Instead of this a vast wall of mountains, lifted still higher than his peak, rose beyond a tremendous cañon which lay like a trough between the two parallel ranks of peaks. Hoffman showed us on his sketch-book the profile of this new range, and I instantly recognized the peaks which I had seen from Mariposa, whose great white pile had led me to believe them the highest points of California.

For a couple of months my friends had made me the target of plenty of pleasant banter about my "highest land," which they lost faith in as we climbed from Thomas's Mill, — I too becoming a trifle anxious about it ; but now that the truth had burst upon Brewer and Hoffman they could not find words to describe the terribleness and grandeur of the deep cañon, nor for picturing those huge crags towering in line at the east. Their peak, as indicated by the barometer, was in the region of thirteen thousand four hundred feet, and a level across to the farther range showed its crests to be at least fifteen hundred feet higher. They had spent hours upon the summit scanning the eastern horizon, and ranging downward into the labyrinth of gulfs below, and had come at last with reluctance to the belief that to cross this gorge and ascend the eastern wall of peaks was utterly impossible.

Brewer and Hoffman were old climbers, and their verdict of impossible oppressed me as I lay awake thinking of it ; but early next morning I had made up my mind, and, taking Cotter aside, I asked him in an easy manner whether he would like to penetrate the Terra Incognita with me at the risk of our necks, provided Brewer should consent. In a frank, courageous tone he answered after his usual mode, "Why not?" Stout of limb, stronger yet in heart, of iron endurance, and a quiet, unexcited temperament, and, better yet, deeply devoted to me, I felt that Cotter was the one comrade I would choose to face death with, for I believed there was in his manhood no room for fear or shirk.

It was a trying moment for Brewer when we found him and volunteered to attempt a campaign for the top of California, because he felt a certain fatherly responsibility over our youth, a natural desire that we should not deposit our triturated remains in some undiscoverable hole among the feldspathic granites; but, like a true disciple of science, this was at last over-balanced by his intense desire to know more of the unexplored region. He freely confessed that he believed the plan madness, and Hoffman, too, told us we might as well attempt to get on a cloud as to try the peak.

As Brewer gradually yielded his consent, I saw by his conversation that there was a possibility of success; so we spent the rest of the day in making preparations.

Our walking-shoes were in excellent condition, the hobnails firm and new. We laid out a barometer, a compass, a pocket-level, a set of wet and dry thermometers, note-books, with bread, cooked beans, and venison enough to last a week, rolled them all in blankets, making two knapsack-shaped packs strapped firmly together with loops for the arms, which, by Brewer's estimate, weighed forty pounds apiece.

Gardner declared he would accompany us to the summit of the first range to look over into the gulf we were

to cross, and at last Brewer and Hoffman also concluded
to go up with us.

Quite too early for our profit we all betook ourselves
to bed, vainly hoping to get a long refreshing sleep from
which we should arise ready for our tramp./

Never a man welcomed those first gray streaks in the
east gladder than I did, unless it may be Cotter, who has
in later years confessed that he did not go to sleep that
night. Long before sunrise we had done our breakfast
and were under way, Hoffman kindly bearing my pack,
and Brewer Cotter's.

Our way led due east up the amphitheatre and toward
Mount Brewer, as we had named the great pyramidal
peak.

Awhile after leaving camp, slant sunlight streamed in
among gilded pinnacles along the slope of Mount Brewer,
touching here and there, in broad dashes of yellow, the
gray walls, which rose sweeping up on either hand like
the sides of a ship.

Our way along the valley's middle ascended over a
number of huge steps, rounded and abrupt, at whose
bases were pools of transparent snow-water edged with
rude piles of erratic glacier blocks, scattered companies
of alpine firs, of red bark and having cypress-like darkness of foliage, with fields of snow under sheltering cliffs,
and bits of softest velvet meadow clouded with minute
blue and white flowers.

As we climbed, the gorge grew narrow and sharp, both
sides wilder; and the spurs which projected from them,
nearly overhanging the middle of the valley, towered
above us with more and more severe sculpture. We
frequently crossed deep fields of snow, and at last reached
the level of the highest pines, where long slopes of *débris*
swept down from either cliff, meeting in the middle.

Over and among these immense blocks, often twenty and thirty feet high, we were obliged to climb, hearing far below us the subterreanean gurgle of streams.

Interlocking spurs nearly closed the gorge behind us; our last view was out a granite gateway formed of two nearly vertical precipices, /sharp-edged, jutting buttress-like, and plunging down into a field of angular boulders which fill the valley bottom.

The eye ranged out from this open gateway overlooking the great King's Cañon with its moraine-terraced walls, the domes of granite upon Big Meadows, and the undulating stretch of forest which descends to the plain.

The gorge turning southward, we rounded a sort of mountain promontory, which, closing the view behind us, shut us up in the bottom of a perfect basin. In front lay a placid lake reflecting the intense black-blue of the sky. Granite, stained with purple and red, sank into it upon one side, and a broad spotless field of snow came down to its margin upon the other.

From a pile of large granite blocks, forty or fifty feet up above the lake margin, we could look down fully a hundred feet through the transparent water to where boulders and pebbles were strewn upon the stone bottom. We had now reached the base of Mount Brewer and were skirting its southern spurs in a wide open corridor surrounded in all directions by lofty granite crags from two to four thousand feet high ; above the limits of vegetation, rocks, lakes of deep heavenly blue, and white trackless snows were grouped closely about us. Two sounds, a sharp little cry of martens, and occasional heavy crashes of falling rock, saluted us.

Climbing became exceedingly difficult, light air — for we had already reached twelve thousand five hundred feet — beginning to tell upon our lungs to such an extent that my friend, who had taken turns with me in carrying my pack, was unable to do so any longer, and I adjusted it to my own shoulders for the rest of the day.

After four hours of slow laborious work we made the base of the *débris* slope which rose about a thousand feet to a saddle pass in the western mountain wall, that range upon which Mount Brewer is so prominent a point. We were nearly an hour in toiling up this slope over an uncertain footing which gave way at almost every step. At last, when almost at the top, we paused to take breath, and then all walked out upon the crest, laid off our packs, and sat down together upon the summit of the ridge, and for a few moments not a word was spoken.

The Sierras are here two parallel summit ranges. We were upon the crest of the western ridge, and looked down into a gulf five thousand feet deep, sinking from our feet in abrupt cliffs nearly or quite two thousand feet, whose base plunged into a broad field of snow lying steep and smooth for a great distance, but broken near its foot by craggy steps often a thousand feet high.

Vague blue haze obscured the lost depths, hiding details, giving a bottomless distance out of which, like the breath of wind, floated up a faint tremble, vibrating upon the senses, yet never clearly heard.

Rising on the other side, cliff above cliff, precipice piled upon precipice, rock over rock, up against sky, towered the most gigantic mountain-wall in America, culminating in a noble pile of Gothic-finished granite and enamel-like snow. How grand and inviting looked its white form, its untrodden, unknown crest, so high and pure in the clear strong blue! I looked at it as one contemplating the purpose of his life; and for just one moment I would have rather liked to dodge that purpose, or to have waited, or have found some excellent reason why I might not go; but all this quickly vanished, leaving a cheerful resolve to go ahead.

From the two opposing mountain-walls singular, thin, knife-blade ridges of stone jutted out, dividing the sides of the gulf into a series of amphitheatres, each one a labyrinth of ice and rock. Piercing thick beds of snow, sprang up knobs and straight isolated spires of rock, mere obelisks curiously carved by frost, their rigid, slender forms casting a blue, sharp shadow upon the snow. Embosomed in depressions of ice, or resting on broken ledges, were azure lakes, deeper in tone than the sky, which at this altitude, even at midday, has a violet duskiness.

To the south, not more than eight miles, a wall of peaks stood across the gulf, dividing the King's, which flowed north at our feet, from the Kern River, that flowed down the trough in the opposite direction.

I did not wonder that Brewer and Hoffman pronounced our undertaking impossible; but when I looked at Cotter there was such complete bravery in his eye that I asked him if he was ready to start. His old answer, "Why not?" left the initiative with me; so I told Professor Brewer that we would bid him good by. Our friends helped us on with our packs in silence, and as we shook hands there was not a dry eye in the party. Before he let go of my hand Professor Brewer asked me for my plan, and I had to own that I had but one, which was to reach the highest peak in the range.

After looking in every direction I was obliged to confess that I saw as yet no practicable way. We bade them a "good by," receiving their "God bless you" in return, and started southward along the range to look for some possible cliff to descend. Brewer, Gardner, and Hoffman turned north to push upward to the summit of Mount Brewer, and complete their observations. We saw them whenever we halted, until at last, on the very summit, their microscopic forms were for the last time discernible. With very great difficulty we climbed a peak which surmounted our wall just to the south of the pass, and, looking over the eastern brink, found that the precipice was still sheer and unbroken. In one place, where the snow lay against it to the very top, we went to its edge and contemplated the slide. About three thousand feet of unbroken white, at a fearfully steep angle, lay below us. We threw a stone over and watched it bound until it was lost in the distance; after fearful leaps we could only detect it by the flashings of snow where it struck, and as these were, in some instances, three hundred feet apart, we decided not to launch our own valuable bodies, and the still more precious barometer, after it.

There seemed but one possible way to reach our goal; that was to make our way along the summit of the cross ridge which projected between the two ranges. This divide sprang out from our Mount Brewer wall, about four miles to the south of us. To reach it we must climb up and down over the indented edge of the Mount Brewer wall. In attempting to do this we had a rather lively time scaling a sharp granite needle, where we found our course completely stopped by precipices four and five hundred feet in height. Ahead of us the summit continued to be broken into fantastic pinnacles, leaving us no hope of making our way along it; so we sought the most broken part of the eastern descent, and began to climb down. The heavy knapsacks, beside wearing our shoulders gradually into a black-and-blue state, overbalanced us terribly, and kept us in constant danger of pitching headlong. At last, taking them off, Cotter climbed down until he had found a resting-place upon a cleft of rock, then I lowered them to him with our lasso, afterwards

descending cautiously to his side, taking my turn in
pioneering downward, receiving the freight of knapsacks
by lasso as before.   In this manner we consumed more
than half the afternoon in descending a thousand feet of
broken, precipitous slope; and it was almost sunset when
we found ourselves upon the fields of level snow which
lay white and thick over the whole interior slope of
the amphitheatre.   The gorge below us seemed utterly
impassable.   At our backs the Mount Brewer wall either
rose in sheer cliffs or in broken, rugged stairway, such as
had offered us our descent.   From this cruel dilemma the
cross divide furnished the only hope, and the sole chance
of scaling that was at its junction with the Mount Brewer
wall.   Toward this point we directed our course, marching wearily over stretches of dense frozen snow, and
regions of *débris*, reaching about sunset the last alcove
of the amphitheatre, just at the foot of the Mount Brewer
wall.   It was evidently impossible for us to attempt to
climb it that evening, and we looked about the desolate
recesses for a sheltered camping-spot.   A high granite
wall surrounded us upon three sides, recurring to the
southward in long elliptical curves; no part of the summit being less than two thousand feet above us, the higher
crags not unfrequently reaching three thousand feet.   A
single field of snow swept around the base of the rock,
and covered the whole amphitheatre, except where a few
spikes and rounded masses of granite rose through it, and
where two frozen lakes, with their blue ice-disks, broke
the monotonous surface.   Through the white snow-gate
of our amphitheatre, as through a frame, we looked eastward upon the summit group; not a tree, not a vestige of
vegetation in sight, — sky, snow, and granite the only
elements in this wild picture.

   After searching for a shelter we at last found a granite

3 *

crevice near the margin of one of the frozen lakes, — a
sort of shelf just large enough for Cotter and me, — where
we hastened to make our bed, having first filled the canteen from a small stream that trickled over the ice, knowing that in a few moments the rapid chill would freeze it.
We ate our supper of cold venison and bread, and whittled
from the sides of the wooden barometer-case shavings
enough to warm water for a cup of miserably tepid tea,
and then, packing our provisions and instruments away at
the head of the shelf, rolled ourselves in our blankets and
lay down to enjoy the view.

After such fatiguing exercises the mind has an almost
abnormal clearness : whether this is wholly from within,
or due to the intensely vitalizing mountain air, I am not
sure ; probably both contribute to the state of exaltation
in which all alpine climbers find themselves. The solid
granite gave me a luxurious repose, and I lay on the edge
of our little rock niche and watched the strange yet brilliant scene.

All the snow of our recess lay in the shadow of the
high granite wall to the west, but the Kern divide which
curved around us from the southeast was in full light ; its
broken sky-line, battlemented and adorned with innumerable rough-hewn spires and pinnacles, was a mass of
glowing orange intensely defined against the deep violet
sky. At the open end of our horseshoe amphitheatre,
to the east, its floor of snow rounded over in a smooth
brink, overhanging precipices which sank two thousand
feet into the King's Cañon. Across the gulf rose the
whole procession of summit peaks, their lower halves
rooted in a deep sombre shadow cast by the western wall,
the heights bathed in a warm purple haze, in which the
irregular marbling of snow burned with a pure crimson
light. A few fleecy clouds, dyed fiery orange, drifted

slowly eastward across the narrow zone of sky which
stretched from summit to summit like a roof. At times
the sound of waterfalls, faint and mingled with echoes,
floated up through the still air. The snow near by lay
in cold ghastly shade, warmed here and there in strange
flashes by light reflected downward from drifting clouds.
The sombre waste about us; the deep violet vault overhead; those far summits, glowing with reflected rose;
the deep impenetrable gloom which filled the gorge, and
slowly and with vapor-like stealth climbed the mountain
wall extinguishing· the red light, combined to produce an
effect which may not be described; nor can I more than
hint at the contrast between the brilliancy of the scene·
under full light, and the cold, deathlike repose which followed when the wan cliffs and pallid snow were all over-
shadowed with ghostly gray.

A sudden chill enveloped us. Stars in a moment
crowded through the dark heaven, flashing with a frosty
splendor. The snow congealed, the brooks ceased to flow,
and, under the powerful sudden leverage of frost, immense
blocks were dislodged all along the mountain summits
and came thundering down the slopes, booming upon the
ice, dashing wildly upon rocks. Under the lee of our
shelf we felt quite safe, but neither Cotter nor I could
help being startled, and jumping just a little, as these
missiles, weighing often many tons, struck the ledge over
our heads and whizzed down the gorge, their stroke resounding fainter and fainter, until at last only a confused
echo reached us.

The thermometer at nine o'clock marked twenty degrees above zero. We set the " minimum" and rolled
ourselves together for the night. The longer I lay the
less I liked that shelf of granite; it grew hard in time,
and cold also, my bones seeming to approach actual con-

tact with the chilled rock; moreover, I found that even
so vigorous a circulation as mine was not enough to warm
up the ledge to anything like a comfortable temperature.
A single thickness of blanket is a better mattress than
none, but the larger crystals of orthoclase, protruding
plentifully, punched my back and caused me to revolve on
a horizontal axis with precision and frequency. How I
loved Cotter! how I hugged him and got warm, while
our backs gradually petrified, till we whirled over and
thawed them out together! The slant of that bed was
diagonal and excessive; down it we slid till the ice
chilled us awake, and we crawled back and chocked ourselves up with bits of granite inserted under my ribs and
shoulders. In this pleasant position we got dozing again,
and there stole over me a most comfortable ease. The
granite softened perceptibly. I was delightfully warm
and sank into an industrious slumber which lasted with
great soundness till four, when we rose and ate our breakfast of frozen venison.

The thermometer stood at two above zero; everything
was frozen tight except the canteen, which we had pru-
dently kept between us all night. Stars still blazed
brightly, and the moon, hidden from us by western cliffs,
shone in pale reflection upon the rocky heights to the
east, which rose, dimly white, up from the impenetrable
shadows of the cañon. Silence, — cold, ghastly dimness, in
which loomed huge forms, — the biting frostiness of the
air, wrought upon our feelings as we shouldered our packs
and started with slow pace to climb toward the " divide."

Soon, to our dismay, we found the straps had so chafed
our shoulders that the weight gave us great pain, and
obliged us to pad them with our handkerchiefs and
extra socks, which remedy did not wholly relieve us from
the constant wearing pain of the heavy load.

Directing our steps southward toward a niche in the wall which bounded us only half a mile distant, we travelled over a continuous snow-field frozen so densely as scarcely to yield at all to our tread, at the same time compressing enough to make· that crisp frosty sound which we all used to enjoy even before we knew from the books that it had something to do with the severe name of regelation.

As we advanced, the snow sloped more and more steeply up toward the crags, till by and by it became quite dangerous, causing us to cut steps with Cotter's large bowie-knife, — a slow, tedious operation, requiring patience of a pretty permanent kind. In this way we spent a quiet social hour or so. The sun had not yet reached us, being shut out by the high amphitheatre wall; but its cheerful light reflected downward from a number of higher crags, filling the recess with the brightness of day, and putting out of existence those shadows which so sombrely darkened the earlier hours. To look back when we stopped to rest was to realize our danger, — that smooth swift slope of ice carrying the eye down a thousand feet to the margin of a frozen mirror of ice; ribs and needles of rock piercing up through the snow, so closely grouped that, had we fallen, a miracle only might save us from being dashed. This led to rather deeper steps, and greater care that our burdens should be held more nearly over the centre of gravity, and a pleasant relief when we got to the top of the snow and sat down on a block of granite to breathe and look up in search of a way up the thousand-foot cliff of broken surface, among the lines of fracture and the galleries winding along the face.

It would have disheartened us to gaze up the hard, sheer front of precipices, and search among splintered projections, crevices, shelves, and snow-patches for an inviting route, had we not been animated by a faith that the mountains could not defy us.

Choosing what looked like the least impossible way, we started; but, finding it unsafe to work with packs on, resumed the yesterday's plan, — Cotter taking the lead, climbing about fifty feet ahead, and hoisting up the knapsacks and barometer as I tied them to the end of the lasso. Constantly closing up in hopeless difficulty before us, the way opened again and again to our gymnastics, till we stood together upon a mere shelf, not more than two feet wide, which led diagonally up the smooth cliff. Edging along in careful steps, our backs flattened upon the granite, we moved slowly to a broad platform, where we stopped for breath.

There was no foothold above us. Looking down over the course we had come, it seemed, and I really believe it was, an impossible descent; for one can climb upward with safety where he cannot downward. To turn back was to give up in defeat; and we sat at least half an hour, suggesting all possible routes to the summit, accepting none, and feeling disheartened. About thirty feet directly over our heads was another shelf, which, if we could reach, seemed to offer at least a temporary way upward. On its edge were two or three spikes of granite; whether firmly connected with the cliff, or merely blocks of *débris*, we could not tell from below. I said to Cotter, I thought of but one possible plan : it was to lasso one of these blocks, and to climb, sailor-fashion, hand over hand, up the rope. In the lasso I had perfect confidence, for I had seen more than one Spanish bull throw his whole weight against it without parting a strand. The shelf was so narrow that throwing the coil of rope was a very difficult undertaking. I tried three times, and Cotter spent five minutes vainly whirling the loop up at the granite spikes. At last I made a lucky throw, and it tightened upon one of the smaller protuberances. I drew the noose close, and very gradually threw my hundred and fifty pounds upon the rope; then Cotter joined me, and, for a moment, we both hung our united weight upon it. Whether the rock moved slightly or whether the lasso stretched a little we were unable to decide; but the trial must be made, and I began to climb slowly. The smooth precipice-face against which my body swung offered no foothold, and the whole climb had therefore to be done by the arms, an effort requiring all one's determination. When about half-way up I was obliged to rest, and, curling my feet in the rope, managed to relieve my arms for a moment. In this position I could not resist the fascinating temptation of a survey downward.

Straight down, nearly a thousand feet below, at the foot of the rocks, began the snow, whose steep, roof-like slope, exaggerated into an almost vertical angle, curved down in a long white field, broken far away by rocks and polished, round lakes of ice.

Cotter looked up cheerfully and asked how I was making it; to which I answered that I had plenty of wind left. At that moment, when hanging between heaven and earth, it was a deep satisfaction to look down at the wild gulf of desolation beneath, and up to unknown dangers ahead, and feel my nerves cool and unshaken.

A few pulls hand over hand brought me to the edge of the shelf, when, throwing an arm around the granite spike, I swung my body upon the shelf and lay down to rest, shouting to Cotter that I was all right, and that the prospects upward were capital. After a few moments' breathing I looked over the brink and directed my comrade to tie the barometer to the lower end of the lasso, which he did, and that precious instrument was hoisted

to my station, and the lasso sent down twice for knapsacks, after which Cotter came up the rope in his very
muscular way without once stopping to rest. We took
our loads in our hands, swinging the barometer over my
shoulder, and climbed up a shelf which led in a zigzag
direction upward and to the south, bringing us out at last
upon the thin blade of a ridge which connected a short
distance above with the summit. It was formed of huge
blocks, shattered, and ready, at a touch, to fall.

So narrow and sharp was the upper slope, that we
dared not walk, but got astride, and worked slowly along
with our hands, pushing the knapsacks in advance, now
and then holding our breath when loose masses rocked
under our weight.

Once upon the summit, a grand view burst upon us.
Hastening to step upon the crest of the divide, which was
never more than ten feet wide, frequently sharpened to a
mere blade, we looked down the other side, and were
astonished to find we had ascended the gentler slope, and
that the rocks fell from our feet in almost vertical precipices for a thousand feet or more. A glance along the
summit toward the highest group showed us that any
advance in that direction was impossible, for the thin
ridge was gashed down in notches three or four hundred
feet deep, forming a procession of pillars, obelisks, and
blocks piled upon each other, and looking terribly insecure.

We then deposited our knapsacks in a safe place, and,
finding that it was already noon, determined to rest a
little while and take a lunch at over thirteen thousand
feet above the sea.

West of us stretched the Mount Brewer wall with its
succession of smooth precipices and amphitheatre ridges.
To the north the great gorge of the King's River yawned

down five thousand feet. To the south the valley of the Kern, opening in the opposite direction, was broader, less deep, but more filled with broken masses of granite. Clustered about the foot of the divide were a dozen alpine lakes; the higher ones blue sheets of ice, the lowest completely melted. Still lower in the depths of the two cañons we could see groups of forest trees; but they were so dim and so distant as never to relieve the prevalent masses of rock and snow. Our divide cast its shadow for a mile down King's Cañon in dark blue profile upon the broad sheets of sunny snow, from whose brightness the hard splintered cliffs caught reflections and wore an aspect of joy. Thousands of rills poured from the melting snow, filling the air with a musical tinkle as of many accordant bells. The Kern Valley opened below us with its smooth oval outline, the work of extinct glaciers, whose form and extent were evident from worn cliff-surface and rounded wall; snow-fields, relics of the former *névé*, hung in white tapestries around its ancient birthplace; and, as far as we could see, the broad, corrugated valley, for a breadth of fully ten miles, shone with burnishings wherever its granite surface was not covered with lakelets or thickets of alpine vegetation.

Through a deep cut in the Mount Brewer wall we gained our first view to the westward, and saw in the distance the wall of the South King's Cañon, and the granite point which Cotter and I had climbed a fortnight before. But for the haze we might have seen the plain; for above its farther limit were several points of the Coast Ranges, isolated like islands in the sea.

The view was so grand, the mountain colors so brilliant, immense snow-fields and blue alpine lakes so charming, that we almost forgot we were ever to move, and it was

E

only after a swift hour of this delight that we began to consider our future course.

The King's Cañon, which headed against our wall, seemed untraversable, — no human being could climb along the divide; we had then but one hope of reaching the peak, and our greatest difficulty lay at the start. If we could climb down to the Kern side of the divide, and succeed in reaching the base of the precipices which fell from our feet, it really looked as if we might travel without difficulty among the *roches moutonnées* to the other side of the Kern Valley, and make our attempt upon the southward flank of the great peak. One look at the sublime white giant decided us. We looked down over the precipice, and at first could see no method of descent. Then we went back and looked at the road we had come up, to see if that were not possibly as bad; but the broken surface of the rocks was evidently much better climbing-ground than anything ahead of us. Cotter, with danger, edged his way along the wall to the east, and I to the west, to see if there might not be some favorable point; but we both returned with the belief that the precipice in front of us was as passable as any of it. Down it we must.

After lying on our faces, looking over the brink, ten or twenty minutes, I suggested that by lowering ourselves on the rope we might climb from crevice to crevice; but we saw no shelf large enough for ourselves and the knapsacks too. However, we were not going to give it up without a trial; and I made the rope fast round my breast, and, looping the noose over a firm point of rock, let myself slide gradually down to a notch forty feet below. There was only room beside me for Cotter, so I made him send down the knapsacks first. I then tied these together by the straps with my silk handkerchiefs, and hung them off as far to the left as I could reach without losing my balance, looping the handkerchiefs over a point of rock. Cotter then slid down the rope, and, with considerable difficulty, we whipped the noose off its resting-place above, and cut off our connection with the upper world.

"We 're in for it now, King," remarked my comrade, as he looked aloft, and then down; but our blood was up, and danger added only an exhilarating thrill to the nerves.

The shelf was hardly more than two feet wide, and the granite so smooth that we could find no place to fasten the lasso for the next descent; so I determined to try the climb with only as little aid as possible. Tying it round my breast again, I gave the other end into Cotter's hands, and he, bracing his back against the cliff, found for himself as firm a foothold as he could, and promised to give me all the help in his power. I made up my mind to bear no weight unless it was absolutely necessary; and for the first ten feet I found cracks and protuberances enough to support me, making every square inch of surface do friction duty, and hugging myself against the rocks as tightly as I could. When within about eight feet of the next shelf, I twisted myself round upon the face, hanging by two rough blocks of protruding feldspar, and looked vainly for some further hand-hold; but the rock, beside being perfectly smooth, overhung slightly, and my legs dangled in the air. I saw that the next cleft was over three feet broad, and I thought, possibly, I might, by a quick slide, reach it in safety without endangering Cotter. I shouted to him to be very careful and let go in case I fell, loosened my hold upon the rope, and slid quickly down. My shoulder struck against the rock and threw me out of balance; for an instant I reeled over upon the verge, in danger of falling, but, in the excitement, I thrust out my hand and seized a small alpine gooseberry-bush, the first piece of vegetation we had seen. Its roots were so firmly fixed in the crevice that it held my weight and saved me.

I could no longer see Cotter, but I talked to him, and heard the two knapsacks come bumping along till they slid over the eaves above me, and swung down to my station, when I seized the lasso's end and braced myself as well as possible, intending, if he slipped, to haul in slack and help him as best I might. As he came slowly down from crack to crack, I heard his hobnailed shoes grating on the granite; presently they appeared dangling from the eaves above my head. I had gathered in the rope until it was taut, and then hurriedly told him to drop. He hesitated a moment, and let go. Before he struck the rock I had him by the shoulder, and whirled him down upon his side, thus preventing his rolling overboard, which friendly action he took quite coolly.

The third descent was not a difficult one, nor the fourth; but when we had climbed down about two hundred and fifty feet, the rocks were so glacially polished and water-worn that it seemed impossible to get any farther. To our right was a crack penetrating the rock perhaps a foot deep, widening at the surface to three or four inches, which proved to be the only possible ladder. As the chances seemed rather desperate, we concluded to tie ourselves together, in order to share a common fate; and with a slack of thirty feet between us, and our knapsacks upon our backs, we climbed into the crevice, and began descending with our faces to the cliff. This had to be done with unusual caution, for the foothold was about as good as none, and our fingers slipped annoyingly on the smooth stone; besides, the knapsacks and instruments kept a steady backward pull, tending to overbalance us. But we took pains to descend one at a time, and rest wherever the niches gave our feet a safe support. In this way we got down about eighty/feet of smooth, nearly vertical wall, reaching the top of a rude granite stairway, which led to the snow; and here we sat down to rest, and found to our astonishment that we had been three hours from the summit.

After breathing a half-minute we continued down, jumping from rock to rock, and, having, by practice, become very expert in balancing ourselves, sprang on, never resting long enough to lose the *aplomb*, and in this manner made a quick descent over rugged *débris* to the crest of a snow-field, which, for seven or eight hundred feet more, swept down in a smooth, even slope, of very high angle, to the borders of a frozen lake.

Without untying the lasso which bound us together, we sprang upon the snow with a shout, and glissaded down splendidly, turning now and then a somersault, and shooting out like cannon-balls almost to the middle of the frozen lake; I upon my back, and Cotter feet first, in a swimming position. The ice cracked in all directions. It was only a thin, transparent film, through which we could see deep into the lake. Untying ourselves, we hurried ashore in different directions, lest our combined weight should be too great a strain upon any point.

With curiosity and wonder we scanned every shelf and niche of the last descent. It seemed quite impossible we could have come down there, and now it actually was beyond human power to get back again. But what cared we? "Sufficient unto the day — " We were bound for that still distant, though gradually nearing, summit; and we had come from a cold shadowed cliff into deliciously warm sunshine, and were jolly, shouting, singing songs, and calling out the companionship of a hundred echoes.

Six miles away, with no grave danger, no great difficulty, between us, lay the base of our grand mountain.   Upon its skirts we saw a little grove of pines, an ideal bivouac, and toward this we bent our course.

After the continued climbing of the day, walking was a delicious rest, and forward we pressed with considerable speed, our hobnails giving us firm footing on the glittering glacial surface.   Every fluting of the great valley was in itself a considerable cañon, into which we descended, climbing down the scored rocks, and swinging from block to block, until we reached the level of the pines.   Here, sheltered among *roches moutonnées,* began to appear little fields of alpine grass, pale yet sunny, soft under our feet, fragrantly jewelled with flowers of fairy delicacy, holding up amid thickly clustered blades chalices of turquoise and amethyst, white stars, and fiery little globes of red. Lakelets, small but innumerable, were held in glacial basins, the striæ and grooves of that old dragon's track ornamenting their smooth bottoms.

One of these, a sheet of pure beryl hue, gave us much pleasure from its lovely transparency, and because we · lay down in the necklace of grass about it and smelled flowers, while tired muscles relaxed upon warm beds of verdure, and the pain in our burdened shoulders went away, leaving us delightfully comfortable.

After the stern grandeur of granite and ice, and with the peaks and walls still in view, it was relief to find ourselves again in the region of life.   I never felt for trees and flowers such a sense of intimate relationship and sympathy.   When we had no longer excuse for resting, I invented the palpable subterfuge of measuring the altitude of the spot, since the few clumps of low, wide-boughed pines near by were the highest living trees.   So we lay longer with less and less will to rise, and when resolution called us to our feet the getting-up was sorely like Rip Van Winkle's in the third act.

The deep glacial cañon-flutings across which our march then lay proved to be great consumers of time; indeed it was sunset when we reached the eastern ascent, and began to toil up through scattered pines, and over trains of moraine rocks, toward the great peak. Stars were already flashing brilliantly in the sky, and the low glowing arch in the west had almost vanished when we reached the upper trees, and threw down our knapsacks to camp. The forest grew on a sort of plateau-shelf with a precipitous front to the west, — a level surface which stretched eastward and back to the foot of our mountain, whose lower spurs reached within a mile of camp. Within the shelter lay a huge fallen log, like all these alpine woods one mass of resin, which flared up when we applied a match, illuminating the whole grove. By contrast with the darkness outside, we seemed to be in a vast, many-pillared hall. The stream close by afforded water for our blessed teapot; venison frizzled with mild, appetizing sound upon the ends of pine sticks; matchless beans allowed themselves to become seductively crisp upon our tin plates. That supper seemed to me then the quintessence of gastronomy, and I am sure Cotter and I must have said some very good *après-dîner* things, though I long ago forgot them all. Within the ring of warmth, on elastic beds of pine-needles, we curled up, and fell swiftly into a sound sleep.

I woke up once in the night to look at my watch, and observed that the sky was overcast with a thin film of cirrus cloud to which the reflected moonlight lent the appearance of a glimmering tent, stretched from mountain to mountain over cañons filled with impenetrable darkness, only the vaguely lighted peaks and white snow-fields distinctly seen. I closed my eyes and slept soundly until Cotter woke me at half past three, when we arose, breakfasted by the light of our fire, which still blazed brilliantly, and, leaving our knapsacks, started for the mountain with only instruments, canteens, and luncheon.

In the indistinct moonlight climbing was very difficult at first, for we had to thread our way along a plain which was literally covered with glacier boulders, and the innumerable brooks which we crossed were frozen solid. However, our march brought us to the base of the great mountain, which, rising high against the east, shut out the coming daylight, and kept us in profound shadow. From base to summit rose a series of broken crags, lifting themselves from a general slope of *débris*. Toward the left the angle seemed to be rather gentler, and the surface less ragged; and we hoped, by a long *détour* round the base, to make an easy climb up this gentler face. So we toiled on for an hour over the rocks, reaching at last the bottom of the north slope. Here our work began in good earnest. The blocks were of enormous size, and in every stage of unstable equilibrium, frequently rolling over as we jumped upon them, making it necessary for us to take a second leap and land where we best could. To our relief we soon surmounted the largest blocks, reaching a smaller size, which served us as a sort of stairway.

The advancing daylight revealed to us a very long, comparatively even snow-slope, whose surface was pierced by many knobs and granite heads, giving it the aspect of an ice-roofing fastened on with bolts of stone. It stretched in far perspective to the summit, where already the rose of sunrise reflected gloriously, kindling a fresh enthusiasm within us.

Immense boulders were partly embedded in the ice just above us, whose constant melting left them trembling on the edge of a fall. It communicated no very pleasant sensation to see above you these immense missiles hanging by a mere band, and knowing that, as soon as the sun rose, you would be exposed to a constant cannonade.

The east side of the peak, which we could now partially see, was too precipitous to think of climbing. The slope toward our camp was too much broken into pinnacles and crags to offer us any hope, or to divert us from the single way, dead ahead, up slopes of ice and among fragments of granite. The sun rose upon us while we were climbing the lower part of this snow, and in less than half an hour, melting, began to liberate huge blocks, which thundered down past us, gathering and growing into small avalanches below.

We did not dare climb one above another, according to our ordinary mode, but kept about an equal level, a hundred feet apart, lest, dislodging the blocks, one should hurl them down upon the other.

We climbed alternately up smooth faces of granite, clinging simply by the cracks and protruding crystals of feldspar, and then hewed steps up fearfully steep slopes of ice, zigzagging to the right and left to avoid the flying boulders. When midway up this slope we reached a place where the granite rose in perfectly smooth bluffs on either side of a gorge, — a narrow cut, or walled way, leading up to the flat summit of the cliff. This we scaled by cutting ice steps, only to find ourselves fronted again by a still higher wall. Ice sloped from its front at too steep an angle for us to follow, but had melted in contact with it, leaving a space three feet wide between the ice and the rock. We entered this crevice and climbed along its

4

bottom, with a wall of rock rising a hundred feet above us on one side, and a thirty-foot face of ice on the other, through which light of an intense cobalt-blue penetrated.

Reaching the upper end, we had to cut our footsteps upon the ice again, and, having braced our backs against the granite, climb up to the surface. We were now in a dangerous position : to fall into the crevice upon one side was to be wedged to death between rock and ice ; to make a slip was to be shot down five hundred feet, and then hurled over the brink of a precipice. In the friendly seat which this wedge gave me, I stopped to take wet and dry observations with the thermometer, — this being an absolute preventive of a scare, — and to enjoy the view.

The wall of our mountain sank abruptly to the left, opening for the first time an outlook to the eastward. Deep — it seemed almost vertically — beneath us we could see the blue water of Owen's Lake, ten thousand feet down. The summit peaks to the north were piled in titanic confusion, their ridges overhanging the eastern slope with terrible abruptness. Clustered upon the shelves and plateaus below were several frozen lakes, and in all directions swept magnificent fields of snow. The summit was now not over five hundred feet distant, and we started on again with the exhilarating hope of success. But if Nature had intended to secure the summit from all assailants, she could not have planned her defences better; for the smooth granite wall which rose above the snow-slope continued, apparently, quite round the peak, and we looked in great anxiety to see if there was not one place where it might be climbed. It was all blank except in one place; quite near us the snow bridged across the crevice, and rose in a long point to the summit of the wall, — a great icicle-column frozen in a niche of the bluff, — its base about ten feet wide, narrowing to two feet at the top. We climbed to the base of this spire of ice, and, with the utmost care, began to cut our stairway. The material was an exceedingly compacted snow, passing into clear ice as it neared the rock. We climbed the first half of it with comparative ease; after that it was almost vertical, and so thin that we did not dare to cut the footsteps deep enough to make them absolutely safe. There was a constant dread lest our ladder should break off, and we be thrown either down the snow-slope or into the bottom of the crevasse. At last, in order to prevent myself from falling over backwards, I was obliged to thrust my hand into the crack between the ice and the wall, and the spire became so narrow that I could do this on both sides; so that the climb was made as upon a tree, cutting mere toe-holes and embracing the whole column of ice in my arms. At last I reached the top, and, with the greatest caution, wormed my body over the brink, and, rolling out upon the smooth surface of the granite, looked over and watched Cotter make his climb. He came steadily up, with no sense of nervousness, until he got to the narrow part of the ice, and here he stopped and looked up with a forlorn face to me; but as he climbed up over the edge the broad smile came back to his face, and he asked me if it had occurred to me that we had, by and by, to go down again.

We had now an easy slope to the summit, and hurried up over rocks and ice, reaching the crest at exactly twelve o'clock. I rang my hammer upon the topmost rock; we grasped hands, and I reverently named the grand peak MOUNT TYNDALL.

IV.

THE DESCENT OF MOUNT TYNDALL.

1864.

To our surprise, upon sweeping the horizon with my level, there appeared two peaks equal in height with us, and two rising even higher. That which looked highest of all was a cleanly cut helmet of granite upon the same ridge with Mount Tyndall, lying about six miles south, and fronting the desert with a bold square bluff which rises to the crest of the peak, where a white fold of snow trims it gracefully.

Mount Whitney, as we afterwards called it in honor of our chief, is probably the highest land within the United States. Its summit looked glorious, but inaccessible.

The general topography overlooked by us may be thus simply outlined. Two parallel chains, enclosing an intermediate trough, face each other. Across this deep enclosed gulf, from wall to wall, juts the thin, but lofty and craggy ridge, or " divide," before described, which forms an important water-shed, sending those streams which enter the chasm north of it into King's River, those south forming the most important sources of the Kern, whose straight, rapidly deepening valley stretches south, carved profoundly in granite, while the King's, after flowing longitudinally in the opposite course for eight or ten miles, turns abruptly west around the base of Mount Brewer, cuts across the western ridge, opening a gate of its own, and carves a rock channel transversely down the Sierra to the California plain.

Fronting us stood the west chain, a great mural ridge watched over by two dominant heights, Kaweah Peak and Mount Brewer, its wonderful profile defining against the western sky a multitude of peaks and spires. Bold buttresses jut out through fields of ice, and reach down stone arms among snow and *débris*. North and south of us the higher, or eastern, summit stretched on in miles and miles of snow-peaks, the farthest horizon still crowded with their white points. East the whole range fell in sharp, hurrying abruptness to the desert, where, ten thousand feet below, lay a vast expanse of arid plain intersected by low parallel ranges, traced from north to south. Upon the one side a thousand sculptures of stone, hard, sharp, shattered by cold into infiniteness of fractures and rift, springing up, mutely severe, into the dark, austere blue of heaven ; scarred and marked, except where snow or ice, spiked down by ragged granite bolts, shields with its pale armor these rough mountain shoulders ; storm-tinted at summit, and dark where, swooping down from ragged cliff, the rocks plunge over cañon-walls into blue, silent gulfs.

Upon the other hand, reaching out to horizons faint and remote, lay plains clouded with the ashen hues of death; stark, wind-swept floors of white, and hill-ranges, rigidly formal, monotonously low, all lying under an unfeeling brilliance of light, which, for all its strange, unclouded clearness, has yet a vague half-darkness, a suggestion of black and shade more truly pathetic than fading twilight. No greenness soothes, no shadow cools the glare. Owen's Lake, an oval of acrid water, lies dense blue upon the brown sage-plain, looking like a plate of hot metal. Traced in ancient beach-lines, here and there upon hill and plain, relics of ancient lake-shore outline the memory of a cooler past, — a period of life and verdure when the stony chains were green islands among basins of wide, watery expanse.

The two halves of this view, both in sight at once, express the highest, the most acute, aspects of desolation,— inanimate forms out of which something living has gone forever. From the desert have been dried up and blown away its seas. Their shores and white, salt-strewn bottoms lie there in the eloquence of death. Sharp white light glances from all the mountain-walls, where in marks and polishings has been written the epitaph of glaciers now melted and vanished into air. Vacant cañons lie open to the sun, bare, treeless, half shrouded with snow, cumbered with loads of broken *débris*, still as graves, except when flights of rocks rush down some chasm's throat, startling the mountains with harsh, dry rattle, their fainter echoes from below followed too quickly by dense silence.

The serene sky is grave with nocturnal darkness. The earth blinds you with its light. That fair contrast we love in lower lands between bright heavens and dark cool earth here reverses itself with terrible energy. You look up into an infinite vault, unveiled by clouds, empty and dark, from which no brightness seems to ray, an expanse with no graded perspective, no tremble, no vapory mobility, only the vast yawning of hollow space.

With an aspect of endless remoteness burns the small white sun, yet its light seems to pass invisibly through the sky, blazing out with intensity upon mountain and plain, flooding rock details with painfully bright reflections, and lighting up the burnt sand and stone of the desert with a strange blinding glare. There is no sentiment of beauty in the whole scene ; no suggestion, however far remote, of sheltered landscape; not even the air of virgin hospitality that greets us explorers in so many

uninhabited spots which by their fertility and loveliness
of grove or meadow seem to offer man a home, or us
nomads a pleasant camp-ground.   Silence and desolation
are the themes which nature has wrought out under this
eternally serious sky.   A faint suggestion of life clings
about the middle altitudes of the eastern slope, where
black companies of pine, stunted from breathing the hot
desert air, group themselves just beneath the bottom of
perpetual snow, or grow in patches of cloudy darkness
over the moraines, those piles of wreck crowded from
their pathway by glaciers long dead.   Something there is
pathetic in the very emptiness of these old glacier valleys,
these imperishable tracks of unseen engines.   One's eye
ranges up their broad, open channel to the shrunken white
fields surrounding hollow amphitheatres which were once
crowded with deep burdens of snow, — the birthplace of
rivers of ice now wholly melted ; the dry, clear heavens
overhead, blank of any promise of ever rebuilding them.
I have never seen Nature when she seemed so little
" Mother Nature " as in this place of rocks and snow,
echoes and emptiness.   It impresses me as the ruins of
some bygone geological period, and no part of the present
order, like a specimen of chaos which has defied the
finishing hand of Time.

Of course I see its bearings upon climate, and could
read a lesson quite glibly as to its usefulness as a con-
denser, and tell you gravely how much California has for
which she may thank these heights, and how little Nevada ; but looking from this summit with all desire to
see everything, the one overmastering feeling is desolation, desolation !

Next to this, and more pleasing to notice, is the interest and richness of the granite forms ; for the whole
region, from plain to plain, is built of this dense solid

rook, and is sculptured under chisel of cold in shapes of
great variety, yet all having a common spirit, which is
purely Gothic.

In the much discussed origin of this order of building,
I never remember to have seen, though it can hardly have
escaped mention, any suggestion of the possibility of the
Gothic having been inspired by granite forms. Yet, as I
sat on Mount Tyndall, the whole mountains shaped themselves like the ruins of cathedrals, — sharp roof-ridges,
pinnacled and statued; buttresses more spired and ornamented than Milan's; receding doorways with pointed
arches carved into blank façades of granite, doors never
to be opened, innumerable jutting points with here and
there a single cruciform peak, its frozen roof and granite
spires so strikingly Gothic I cannot doubt that the Alps
furnished the models for early cathedrals of that order.

I thoroughly enjoyed the silence, which, gratefully contrasting with the surrounding tumult of form, conveyed
to me a new sentiment. I have lain and listened through
the heavy calm of a tropical voyage, hour after hour,
longing for a sound ; and in desert nights the dead stillness has many a time awakened me from sleep. For
moments, too, in my forest life, the groves made absolutely
no breath of movement; but there is around these summits the soundlessness of a vacuum. The sea stillness
is that of sleep. The desert of death, this silence is
like the waveless calm of space.

All the while I made my instrumental observations
the fascination of the view so held me that I felt no surprise at seeing water boiling over our little fagot blaze
at a temperature of one hundred and ninety-two degrees
F., nor in observing the barometrical column stand at
17.99 inches ; and it was not till a week or so after
that I realized we had felt none of the conventional sen-

sations of nausea, headache, and I don't know what all, that people are supposed to suffer at extreme altitudes; but these things go with guides and porters, I believe, and with coming down to one's hotel at evening there to scold one's picturesque *aubergiste* in a French which strikes upon his ear as a foreign tongue; possibly all that will come to us with advancing time, and what is known as "doing America." They are already shooting our buffaloes; it cannot be long before they will cause themselves to be honorably dragged up and down our Sierras, with perennial yellow gaiter, and ostentation of bathtub.

Having completed our observations, we packed up the instruments, glanced once again around the whole field of view, and descended to the top of our icicle ladder. Upon looking over, I saw to my consternation that during the day the upper half had broken off. Scars traced down upon the snow-field below it indicated the manner of its fall, and far below, upon the shattered *debris*, were strewn its white relics. I saw that nothing but the sudden gift of wings could possibly take us down to the snow-ridge. We held council and concluded to climb quite round the peak in search of the best mode of descent.

As we crept about the east face, we could look straight down upon Owen's Valley, and into the vast glacier gorges, and over piles of moraines and fluted rocks, and the frozen lakes of the eastern slope. When we reached the southwest front of the mountain we found that its general form was that of an immense horseshoe, the great eastern ridge forming one side, and the spur which descended to our camp the other, we having climbed up the outer part of the toe. Within the curve of the horseshoe was a gorge, cut almost perpendicularly down two thousand feet, its side rough-hewn walls of rocks and snow, its narrow bottom almost a continuous chain of deep blue lakes with loads of ice and *débris* piles. The stream which flowed through them joined the waters from our home grove, a couple of miles below the camp. If we could reach the level of the lakes, I believed we might easily climb round them, and out of the upper end of the horseshoe, and walk upon the Kern plateau round to our bivouac.

It required a couple of hours of very painstaking deliberate climbing to get down the first descent, which we did, however, without hurting our barometer, and fortunately without the fatiguing use of the lasso ; reaching finally the uppermost lake, a granite bowlful of cobalt-blue water, transparent and unrippled. So high and enclosing were the tall walls about us, so narrow and shut in the cañon, so flattened seemed the cover of sky, we felt oppressed after the expanse and freedom of our hours on the summit.

The snow-field we followed, descending farther, was irregularly honeycombed in deep pits, circular or irregular in form, and melted to a greater or less depth, holding each a large stone embedded in the bottom. It seems they must have fallen from the overhanging heights with sufficient force to plunge into the snow.

Brilliant light and strong color met our eyes at every glance, — the rocks of a deep purple-red tint, the pure alpine lakes of a cheerful sapphire blue, the snow glitteringly white. The walls on either side for half their height were planed and polished by glaciers, and from the smoothly glazed sides the sun was reflected as from a mirror.

Mile after mile we walked cautiously over the snow, and climbed around the margins of lakes, and over piles of *débris* which marked the ancient terminal moraines.

At length we reached the end of the horseshoe, where the walls contracted to a gateway, rising on either side in immense vertical pillars a thousand feet high. Through this gateway we could look down the valley of the Kern, and beyond to the gentler ridges where a smooth growth of forest darkened the rolling plateau. Passing the last snow, we walked through this gateway and turned westward round the spur toward our camp. The three miles which closed our walk were alternately through groves of *Pinus flexilis* and upon plains of granite.

The glacier sculpture and planing are here very beautiful, the large crystals of orthoclase with which the granite is studded being cut down to the common level, their rosy tint making with the white base a beautiful burnished porphyry.

The sun was still an hour high when we reached camp, and with a feeling of relaxation and repose we threw ourselves down to rest by the log, which still continued blazing. We had accomplished our purpose.

During the last hour or two of our tramp Cotter had complained of his shoes, which were rapidly going to pieces. Upon examination we found to our dismay that there was not over half a day's wear left in them, a calamity which gave to our difficult homeward climb a new element of danger. The last nail had been worn from my own shoes, and the soles were scratched to the quick, but I believed them stout enough to hold together till we should reach the main camp.

We planned a pair of moccasins for Cotter, and then spent a pleasant evening by the camp-fire, rehearsing our climb to the detail, sleep finally overtaking us and holding us fast bound until broad daylight next morning, when we woke with a sense of having slept for a week, quite bright and perfectly refreshed for our homeward journey.

After a frugal breakfast, in which we limited ourselves to a few cubic inches of venison, and a couple of stingy slices of bread, with a single meagre cup of diluted tea, we shouldered our knapsacks, which now sat lightly upon toughened shoulders, and marched out upon the granite plateau.

We had concluded that it was impossible to retrace our former way, knowing well that the precipitous divide could not be climbed from this side ; then, too, we had gained such confidence in our climbing powers, from constant victory, that we concluded to attempt the passage of the great King's Cañon, mainly because this was the only mode of reaching camp, and since the geological section of the granite it exposed would afford us an exceedingly instructive study.

The broad granite plateau which forms the upper region of the Kern Valley slopes in general inclination up to the great divide.   This remarkably pinnacled ridge, where it approaches the Mount Tyndall wall, breaks down into a broad depression where the Kern Valley sweeps northward, until it suddenly breaks off in precipices three thousand feet down into the King's Canon.

The morning was wholly consumed in walking up this gently inclined plane of granite, our way leading over the glacier-polished foldings and along graded undulations among labyrinths of alpine garden and wildernesses of erratic boulders, little lake-basins, and scattered clusters of dwarfed and sombre pine.

About noon we came suddenly upon the brink of a precipice which sunk sharply from our feet into the gulf of the King's Cañon.   Directly opposite us rose Mount Brewer and up out of the depths of those vast sheets

of frozen snow swept spiry buttress-ridges, dividing the
upper heights into those amphitheatres over which we
had struggled on our outward journey. Straight across
from our point of view was the chamber of rock and ice
where we had camped on the first night. The wall at
our feet fell sharp and rugged, its lower two-thirds hidden
from our view by the projections of a thousand feet of
crags. Here and there, as we looked down, small patches
of ice, held in rough hollows, rested upon the steep surface, but it was too abrupt for any great fields of snow.
I dislodged a boulder upon the edge and watched it
bound down the rocky precipice, dash over eaves a thousand feet below us, and disappear; the crash of its fall coming up to us from the unseen depths fainter and fainter,
until the air only trembled with confused echoes.

A long look at the pass to the south of Mount Brewer,
where we had parted from our friends, animated us with
courage to begin the descent, which we did with utmost
care, for the rocks, becoming more and more glacier-
smoothed, afforded us hardly any firm footholds. When
down about eight hundred feet we again rolled rocks ahead
of us, and saw them disappear over the eaves, and only
heard the sound of their stroke after many seconds, which
convinced us that directly below lay a great precipice.

At this juncture the soles came entirely off Cotter's
shoes, and we stopped upon a little cliff of granite to
make him moccasins of our provision bags and slips of
blanket, tying them on as firmly as we could with the
extra straps and buckskin thongs.

Climbing with these proved so insecure that I made
Cotter go behind me, knowing that under ordinary circumstances I could stop him if he fell.

Here and there in the clefts of the rocks grew stunted
pine bushes, their roots twisted so firmly into the crevices

that we laid hold of them with the utmost confidence whenever they came within our reach. In this way we descended to within fifty feet of the brink, having as yet no knowledge of the cliffs below, except our general memory of their aspect from the Mount Brewer wall.

The rock was so steep that we descended in a sitting posture, clinging with our hands and heels.

I heard Cotter say, " I think I must take off these moccasins and try it barefooted, for I don't believe I can make it." These words were instantly followed by a startled cry, and I looked round to see him slide quickly toward me, struggling and clutching at the smooth granite. As he slid by I made a grab for him with my right hand, catching him by the shirt, and, throwing myself as far in the other direction as I could, seized with my left hand a little pine tuft, which held us. I asked Cotter to edge along a little to the left, where he could get a brace with his feet and relieve me of his weight, which he cautiously did. I then threw a couple of turns with the lasso round the roots of the pine bush, and we were safe, though hardly more than twenty feet from the brink. The pressure of curiosity to get a look over that edge was so strong within me, that I lengthened out sufficient lasso to reach the end, and slid slowly to the edge, where, leaning over, I looked down, getting a full view of the wall for miles. Directly beneath, a sheer cliff of three or four hundred feet stretched down to a pile of *débris* which rose to unequal heights along its face, reaching the very crest not more than a hundred feet south of us. From that point to the bottom of the cañon broken rocks, ridges rising through vast sweeps of *débris*, tufts of pine and frozen bodies of ice, covered the further slope.

I returned to Cotter, and, having loosened ourselves from the pine bush, inch by inch crept along the granite until we supposed ourselves to be just over the top of the *débris* pile, where I found a firm brace for my feet, and lowered Cotter to the edge. He sang out "All right!" and climbed over on the uppermost *débris*, his head only remaining in sight of me; when I lay down upon my back, making knapsack and body do friction duty, and, letting myself move, followed Cotter and reached his side.

From that point the descent required us two hours of severe constant labor, which was monotonous of itself, and would have proved excessively tiresome but for the constant interest of glacial geology beneath us. When at last we reached bottom and found ourselves upon a velvety green meadow, beneath the shadow of wide-armed pines, we realized the amount of muscular force we had used up, and threw ourselves down for a rest of half an hour, when we rose, not quite renewed, but fresh enough to finish the day's climb.

In a few minutes we stood upon the rocks just above King's River, — a broad white torrent fretting its way along the bottom of an impassable gorge. Looking down the stream, we saw that our right bank was a continued precipice, affording, so far as we could see, no possible descent to the river's margin, and indeed, had we gotten down, the torrent rushed with such fury that we could not possibly have crossed it. To the south of us, a little way up stream, the river flowed out from a broad oval lake, three quarters of a mile in length, which occupied the bottom of the granite basin. Unable to cross the torrent, we must either swim the lake or climb round its head. Upon our side the walls of the basin curved to the head of the lake in sharp smooth precipices, or broken slopes of *débris;* while on the opposite side its margin was a beautiful shore of emerald meadow, edged with a continuous grove of coniferous trees. Once upon this

other side, we should have completed the severe part of
our journey, crossed the gulf, and have left all danger behind us ; for the long slope of granite and ice which rose
upon the west side of the cañon and the Mount Brewer
wall opposed to us no trials save those of simple fatigue.

Around the head of the lake were crags and precipices
in singularly forbidding arrangement. As we turned
thither we saw no possible way of overcoming them. At
its head the lake lay in an angle of the vertical wall, sharp
and straight like the corner of a room ; about three hundred feet in height, and for two hundred and fifty feet of
this, a pyramidal pile of blue ice rose from the lake, rested against the corner, and reached within forty feet of
the top. Looking into the deep blue water of the lake, I
concluded that in our exhausted state it was madness
to attempt to swim it. The only other alternative was to
scale that slender pyramid of ice and find some way to
climb the forty feet of smooth wall above it ; a plan we
chose perforce, and started at once to put into execution,
determined that if we were unsuccessful we would fire a
dead log which lay near, warm ourselves thoroughly, and
attempt the swim. At its base the ice mass overhung
the lake like a roof, under which the water had melted
its way for a distance of not less than a hundred feet, a
thin eave overhanging the water. To the very edge of
this I cautiously went, and, looking down into the lake,
saw though its beryl depths the white granite blocks
strewn upon the bottom at least one hundred feet below
me. It was exceedingly transparent, and, under ordinary
circumstances, would have been a most tempting place for
a dive ; but at the end of our long fatigue, and with the
still unknown tasks ahead, I shrunk from a swim in such
a chilly temperature.

We found the ice-angle difficultly steep, but made our

way successfully along its edge, clambering up the crevices melted between its body and the smooth granite to a point not far from the top, where the ice had considerably narrowed, and rocks overhanging it encroached so closely that we were obliged to leave the edge and make our way with cut steps out upon its front. Streams of water, dropping from the overhanging rock-eaves at many points, had worn circular shafts into the ice, three feet in diameter and twenty feet in depth. Their edges offered us our only foothold, and we climbed from one to another, equally careful of slipping upon the slope itself, or falling into the wells. Upon the top of the ice we found a narrow, level platform, upon which we stood together, resting our backs in the granite corner, and looked down the awful pathway of King's Cañon, until the rest nerved us up enough to turn our eyes upward at the forty feet of smooth granite which lay between us and safety.

Here and there were small projections from its surface, little protruding knobs of feldspar, and crevices riven into its face for a few inches.

As we tied ourselves together, I told Cotter to hold himself in readiness to jump down into one of these in case I fell, and started to climb up the wall, succeeding quite well for about twenty feet. About two feet above my hands was a crack, which, if my arms had been long enough to reach, would probably have led me to the very top; but I judged it beyond my powers, and, with great care, descended to the side of Cotter, who believed that his superior length of arm would enable him to make the reach.

I planted myself against the rock, and he started cautiously up the wall. Looking down the glare front of ice, it was not pleasant to consider at what velocity a slip would send me to the bottom, or at what angle, and to what probable depth, I should be projected into the ice-water. Indeed, the idea of such a sudden bath was so annoying that I lifted my eyes toward my companion. He reached my farthest point without great difficulty, and made a bold spring for the crack, reaching it without an inch to spare, and holding on wholly by his fingers. He thus worked himself slowly along the crack toward the top, at last getting his arms over the brink, and gradually drawing his body up and out of sight. It was the most splendid piece of slow gymnastics I ever witnessed. For a moment he said nothing; but when I asked if he was all right cheerfully repeated, " All right." It was only a moment's work to send up the two knapsacks and barometer, and receive again my end of the lasso. As I tied it round my breast, Cotter said to me, in an easy, confident tone, " Don't be afraid to bear your weight." I made up my mind, however, to make that climb without his aid, and husbanded my strength as I climbed from crack to crack. I got up without difficulty to my former point, rested there a moment, hanging solely by my hands, gathered every pound of strength and atom of will for the reach, then jerked myself upward with a swing, just getting the tips of my fingers into the crack. In an instant I had grasped it with my right hand also. I felt the sinews of my fingers relax a little, but the picture of the slope of ice and the blue lake affected me so strongly that I redoubled my grip, and climbed slowly along the crack until I reached the angle and got one arm over the edge as Cotter had done. As I rested my body upon the edge and looked up at Cotter, I saw that, instead of a level top, he was sitting upon a smooth roof-like slope, where the least pull would have dragged him over the brink. He had no brace for his feet, nor hold for his hands, but had seated himself calmly, with the rope tied round his breast, knowing that my only safety lay in being able to make the climb entirely unaided; certain that the least waver in his tone would have disheartened me, and perhaps made it impossible. The shock I received on seeing this affected me for a moment, but not enough to throw me off my guard, and I climbed quickly over the edge. When we had walked back out of danger we sat down upon the granite for a rest.

In all my experience of mountaineering I have never known an act of such real, profound courage as this of Cotter's. It is one thing, in a moment of excitement, to make a gallant leap, or hold one's nerves in the iron grasp of will, but to coolly seat one's self in the door of death, and silently listen for the fatal summons, and this all for a friend, — for he might easily have cast loose the lasso and saved himself, — requires as sublime a type of courage as I know.

But a few steps back we found a thicket of pine overlooking our lake, by which there flowed a clear rill of snow-water. Here, in the bottom of the great gulf, we made our bivouac ; for we were already in the deep evening shadows, although the mountain-tops to the east of us still burned in the reflected light. It was the luxury of repose which kept me awake half an hour or so, in spite of my vain attempts at sleep. To listen for the pulsating sound of waterfalls and arrowy rushing of the brook by our beds was too deep a pleasure to quickly yield up.

Under the later moonlight I rose and went out upon the open rocks, allowing myself to be deeply impressed by the weird Dantesque surroundings ; — darkness, out of which to the sky towered stern, shaggy bodies of rock ; snow, uncertainly moonlit with cold pallor ; and at my feet the basin of the lake, still, black, and gemmed with

reflected stars, like the void into which Dante looked
through the bottomless gulf of Dis.   A little way off
there appeared upon the brink of a projecting granite
cornice two dimly seen forms ; pines I knew them to be,
yet their motionless figures seemed bent forward, gazing
down the cañon ; and I allowed myself to name them
Mantuan and Florentine, thinking at the same time how
grand and spacious the scenery, and how powerful their
attitude, how infinitely more profound the mystery of
light and shade, than any of those hard, theatrical concep-
tions with which Doré has sought to shut in our imagination.   That artist, as I believe, has reached a conspicuous
failure from an overbalancing love of solid, impenetrable
darkness.   There is in all his Inferno landscape a certain
sharp boundary between the real and unreal, and never the
infinite suggestiveness of great regions of half-light, in
which everything may be seen, nothing recognized.   Without waking Cotter, I crept back to my blankets, and to sleep.

The morning of our fifth and last day's tramp must
have dawned cheerfully ; at least, so I suppose from its
aspect when we first came back to consciousness, surprised
to find the sun risen from the eastern mountain-wall and
the whole gorge flooded with its direct light.   Rising as
good as new from our mattress of pine twigs, we hastened
to take breakfast, and started up the long, broken slope of
the Mount Brewer wall.   To reach the pass where we had
parted from our friends required seven hours of slow,
laborious climbing, in which we took advantage of every
outcropping spine of granite and every level expanse of
ice to hasten at the top of our speed.   Cotter's feet were
severely cut ; his tracks upon the snow were marked by
stains of blood, yet he kept on with undiminished spirit,
never once complaining.   The perfect success of our journey so inspired us with happiness that we forgot danger
and fatigue, and chatted in liveliest strain.

It was about two o'clock when we reached the summit
and rested a moment to look back over our new Alps,
which were hard and distinct under direct unpoetic light;
yet with all their dense gray and white reality, their long,
sculptured ranks, and cold, still summits, we gave them a
lingering farewell look, which was not without its deep
fulness of emotion, then turned our backs and hurried
down the *débris* slope into the rocky amphitheatre at the
foot of Mount Brewer, and by five o'clock had reached
our old camp-ground. We found here a note pinned to a
tree informing us that the party had gone down into the
lower cañon, five miles below, that they might camp in
better pasturage.

The wind had scattered the ashes of our old camp-fire,
and banished from it the last sentiment of home. We
hurried on, climbing among the rocks which reached down
to the crest of the great lateral moraine, and then on in
rapid stride along its smooth crest, riveting our eyes upon
the valley below, where we knew the party must be camped.

At last, faintly curling above the sea of green tree-tops,
a few faint clouds of smoke wafted upward into the air.
We saw them with a burst of strong emotion, and ran
down the steep flank of the moraine at the top of our
speed. Our shouts were instantly answered by the three
voices of our friends, who welcomed us to their camp-fire
with tremendous hugs.

After we had outlined for them the experience of our
days, and as we lay outstretched at our ease, warm in the
blaze of the glorious camp-fire, Brewer said to me, "King,
you have relieved me of a dreadful task. For the last
three days I have been composing a letter to your family,
but somehow I did not get beyond 'It becomes my painful duty to inform you.'"

V.

THE NEWTYS OF PIKE.

1864.

OUR return from Mount Tyndall to such civilization as flourishes around the Kaweah outposts was signalized by us chiefly as to our *cuisine*, which offered now such bounties as the potato, and once a salad, in which some middle-aged lettuce became the vehicle for a hollow mockery of dressing. Two or three days, during which we dined at brief intervals, served to completely rest us, and put in excellent trim for further campaigning all except Professor Brewer, upon whom a constant toothache wore painfully, — my bullet-mould failing even upon the third trial to extract the unruly member.

It was determined we should ride together to Visalia, seventy miles away, and, the more we went, the impatienter became my friend, till we agreed to push ahead through day and night, and reached the village at about sunrise in a state of reeling sleepiness quite indescribably funny.

At evening, when it became time to start back for our mountain camp my friend at last yielded consent to my project of climbing the Kern Sierras to attempt Mount Whitney; so I parted from him, and, remaining at Visalia, outfitted myself with a pack-horse, two mounted men, and provisions enough for a two weeks' trip.

I purposely avoid telling by what route I entered the Sierras, because there lingers in my breast a desire to see once more that lovely region, and failing, as I do, to confide in the people, I fear lest, if the camp I am going to describe should be recognized, I might, upon revisiting the scene, suffer harm, or even come to an untimely end. I refrain, then, from telling by what road I found myself entering the region of the pines one lovely twilight evening, two days after leaving Visalia. Pines, growing closer and closer, from sentinels gathered to groups, then stately groves, and at last, as the evening wore on, assembled in regular forest, through whose open tops the stars shone cheerfully.

I came upon an open meadow, hearing in front the rush of a large brook, and directly reached two camp-fires, where were a number of persons. My two hirelings caught and unloaded the pack-horse, and set about their duties, looking to supper and the animals, while I prospected the two camps. That just below me, on the same side of the brook, I found to be the bivouac of a company of hunters, who, in the ten minutes of my call, made free with me, hospitably offering a jug of whiskey, and then went on in their old eternal way of making bear-stories out of whole cloth.

I left them with a belief that my protoplasm and theirs must be different, in spite of Mr. Huxley, and passed across the brook to the other camp. Under noble groups of pines smouldered a generous heap of coals, the ruins of a mighty log. A little way from this lay a confused pile of bedclothes, partly old and half-bald buffalo-robes, but, in the main, thick strata of what is known to irony as comforters, upon which, outstretched in wretched awkwardness of position, was a family, all with their feet to the fire, looking as if they had been blown over in one direction, or knocked down by a single bombshell. On the extremities of this common bed, with the air of having gotten as far from each other as possible, the mother and father of the Pike family reclined; between them were two small children — a girl and boy — and a huge girl, who, next the old man, lay flat upon her back, her mind absorbed in the simple amusement of waving one foot (a cowhide eleven) slowly across the fire, squinting, with half-shut eye, first at the vast shoe and thence at the fire, alternately hiding bright places and darting the foot quickly in the direction of any new display of heightening flame. The mother was a bony sister, in the yellow, shrunken, of sharp visage, in which were prominent two cold eyes and a positively poisonous mouth; her hair, the color of faded hay, tangled in a jungle around her head. She rocked jerkily to and· fro, removing at intervals a clay pipe from her mouth in order to pucker her thin lips up to one side, and spit with precision upon a certain spot in the fire, which she seemed resolved to prevent from attaining beyond a certain faint glow.

I have rarely felt more in difficulty for an overture to conversation, and was long before venturing to propose, "You seem to have a pleasant camp-spot here." The old woman sharply, and in almost a tone of affront, answered, "They 's wus, and then again they 's better."

"Doos well for our hogs," inserted the old man. "We 've a band of pork that make out to find feed."

"Oh! how many have you?" I asked.

"Nigh three thousand."

"Won't you set?" asked Madame; then, turning, "You, Susan, can't you try for to set up, and not spread so? Hain't you no manners, say?"

At this the massive girl got herself somewhat together, and made room for me, which I declined, however.

"Prospecting?" inquired Madame.

"I say huntin'," suggested the man.

"Maybe he 's a cattle-feller," interrupted the little girl.

" Goin' somewhere, ain't yer ? " was Susan's guess.

I gave brief account of myself, evidently satisfying the social requirements of all but the old woman, who at once classified me as not up to her standard. Susan saw this, so did her father, and it became evident to me in ten minutes' conversation that they two were always at one, and made it their business to be in antagonism to the mother. They were then allies of mine from nature, and I felt at once at home. I saw too that Susan, having slid back to her horizontal position when I declined to share her rightful ground, was watching with subtle solicitude that fated spot in the fire, opposing sympathy and squints accurately aligned by her shoe to the dull spot in the embers, which slowly went out into blackness before the well-directed fire of her mother's saliva.

The shouts which I heard proceeding from the direction of my camp were easily translatable into summons for supper. Mr. Newty invited me to return later and be sociable, which I promised to do, and, going to my camp, supped quickly and left the men with orders about picketing the animals for the night, then, strolling slowly down to the camp of my friends, seated myself upon a log by the side of the old gentleman. Feeling that this somewhat formal attitude unfitted me for partaking to the fullest degree the social ease around me, and knowing that my buckskin trousers were impervious to dirt, I slid down in a reclined posture with my feet to the fire, in absolute parallelism with the rest of the family.

The old woman was in the exciting *dénouement* of a coon-story, directed to her little boy, who sat clinging to her skirt and looking in her face with absorbed curiosity. " And when Johnnie fired," she said, " the coon fell and busted open." The little boy had misplaced his sympathies with the raccoon, and having inquired plain-

5   G

tively, "Did it hurt him?" was promptly snubbed with
the reply, "Of course it hurt him. What do you suppose coons is made for?" Then turning to me she put
what was plainly enough with her a test-question: "I
allow you have killed your coon in your day?" I saw at
once that I must forever sink beneath the horizon of her
standards, but, failing in real experience or accurate
knowledge concerning the coon, knew no subterfuges
would work with her. Instinct had taught her that I
had never killed a coon, and she had asked me thus ostentatiously to place me at once and forever before the
family in my true light. "No, ma'am," I said; "now you
speak of it, I realize that I never have killed a coon."
This was something of a staggerer to Susan and her
father, yet as the mother's pleasurable dissatisfaction with
me displayed itself by more and more accurate salivary
shots at the fire, they rose to the occasion, and began to
palliate my past. "Maybe," ventured Mr. Newty, "that
they don't have coon round the city of York"; and I felt
that I needed no self-defence when Susan firmly and
defiantly suggested to her mother that perhaps I was in
better business.

Driven in upon herself for some time, the old woman
smoked in silence, until Susan, seeing that her mother
gradually quenched a larger and larger circle upon the
fire, got up and stretched herself, and giving the coals a
vigorous poke swept out of sight the quenched spot, thus
readily obliterating the result of her mother's precise and
prolonged expectoration; then flinging a few dry boughs
upon the fire illumined the family with the ruddy blaze,
and sat down again, leaning upon her father's knee with
a faint light of triumph in her eye.

I ventured a few platitudes concerning pigs, not penetrating the depths of that branch of rural science enough

to betray my ignorance. Such sentiments as "A little piece of bacon well broiled for breakfast is very good," and "Nothing better than cold ham for lunch," were received by Susan and her father in the spirit I meant, — of entire good-will toward pork generically. I now look back in amusement at having fallen into this weakness, for the Mosaic view of pork has been mine from infancy, and campaigning upon government rations has, in truth, no tendency to dim this ancient faith.

By half past nine the gates of conversation were fairly open, and our part of the circle enjoyed itself socially, — taciturnity and clouds of Virginia plug reigning supreme upon the other. The two little children crept under comforters somewhere near the middle of the bed, and subsided pleasantly to sleep. The old man at last stretched sleepily, finally yawning out, "Susan, I do believe I am too tired out to go and see if them corral bars are down. I guess you 'll have to go. I reckon there ain't no bears round to-night." Susan rose to her feet, stretched herself with her back to the fire, and I realized for the first time her amusing proportions. In the region of six feet, tall, square-shouldered, of firm iron back and heavy mould of limb, she yet possessed that suppleness which enabled her as she rose to throw herself into nearly all the attitudes of the Niobe children. As her yawn deepened, she waved nearly down to the ground, and then, rising upon tiptoe, stretched up her clinched fists to heaven with a groan of pleasure. Turning to me, she asked, "How would you like to see the hogs?" The old man added, as an extra encouragement, "Pootiest band of hogs in Tulare County! There 's littler of the real sissor-bill nor Mexican racer stock than any band I have ever seen in the State. I driv the original outfit from Pike County to Oregon in '51 and '52." By this time I was actually interested in them, and joining Susan we passed out into the forest.

The full moon, now high in the heavens, looked down over the whole landscape of clustered forest and open meadow with tranquil silvery light. It whitened measurably the fine spiry tips of the trees, fell luminous upon broad bosses of granite which here and there rose through the soil, and glanced in trembling reflections from the rushing surface of the brook. Far in the distance moonlit peaks towered in solemn rank against the sky.

We walked silently on four or five minutes through the woods, coming at last upon a fence which margined a wide circular opening in the wood. The bars, as her father had feared, were down. We stepped over them, quietly entered the enclosure, put them up behind us, and proceeded to the middle, threading our way among sleeping swine to where a lonely tree rose to the height of about two hundred feet. Against this we placed our backs, and Susan waved her hand in pride over the two acres of tranquil pork. The eye, after accustoming itself to the darkness, took cognizance of a certain ridgyness of surface which came to be recognized as the objects of Susan's pride.

Quite a pretty effect was caused by the shadow of the forest, which, cast obliquely downward by the moon, divided the corral into halves of light and shade.

The air was filled with heavy breathing, interrupted by here and there a snore, and at times by crescendos of tumult, caused by forty or fifty pigs doing battle for some favorite bed-place.

I was informed that Susan did not wish me to judge of them by dark, but to see them again in the full light of day. She knew each individual pig by its physiognomy, having, as she said, " growed with 'em."

As we strolled back toward the bars a dusky form disputed our way, — two small, sharp eyes and a wild crest of bristles were visible in the obscure light. "That's Old Arkansas," said Susan; "he's eight year old come next June, and I never could get him to like me." I felt for my pistol, but Susan struck a vigorous attitude, ejaculating, " S-S-oway, Arkansas !" She made a dash in his direction; a wild scuffle ensued, in which I heard the dull thud of Susan's shoe, accompanied by, "Take that, dog-on-you !" a cloud of dust, one shrill squeal, and Arkansas retreated into the darkness at a business-like trot.

When quite near the bars the mighty girl launched herself into the air, alighting with her stomach across the topmost rail, where she hung a brief moment, made a violent muscular contraction, and alighted upon the ground outside, communicating to it a tremor quite perceptible from where I stood. I climbed over after her, and we sauntered under the trees back to camp.

The family had disappeared, a few dry boughs, however, thrown upon the coals, blazed up, and revealed their forms in the corrugated topography of the bed.

I bade Susan good night, and before I could turn my back she kicked her number-eleven shoes into the air, and with masterly rapidity turned in, as Minerva is said to have done, in full panoply.

I fled precipitately to my camp, and sought my blankets, lying awake in a kind of half-revery, in which Susan and Arkansas, the old woman and her coons, were the prominent figures. Later I fell asleep, and lay motionless until the distant roar of swine awoke me before sunrise next morning.

Seated upon my blankets, I beheld Susan's mother drag forth the two children, one after another, by the napes of their necks, and, shaking the sleep out of them, propel them spitefully toward the brook; then taking her pipe from her mouth she bent low over the sleeping form of her huge daughter, and in a high, shrill, nasal key, screeched in her ear, "Yew Suse!"

No sign of life on the part of the daughter.

"Susan, *are* you a-going to get up?"

Slight muscular contraction of the lower limbs.

"Will you hear me, *Susan?*"

"Marm," whispered the girl, in low, sleepy tones.

"Get up and let the *hogs* out!"

The idea had at length thrilled into Susan's brain, and with a violent suddenness she sat bolt upright, brushing her green-colored hair out of her eyes, and rubbing those valuable but bleared organs with the ponderous knuckles of her forefingers.

By this time I started for the brook for my morning toilet, and the girl and I met upon opposite banks, stooping to wash our faces in the same pool. As I opened my dressing-case her lower jaw fell, revealing a row of ivory teeth rounded out by two well-developed "wisdoms," which had all that dazzling grin one sees in the show-windows of certain dental practitioners. It required but a moment to gather up a quart or so of water in her broad palms, and rub it vigorously into a small circle upon the middle of her face, the moisture working outward to a certain high-water mark, which, along her chin and cheeks, defined the limits of former ablution; then, baring her large red arms to the elbow, she washed her hands, and stood resting them upon her hips, dripping freely, and watching me with intense curiosity.

When I reached the towel process, she herself twisted her body after the manner of the Belvidere torso, bent low her head, gathered up the back breadths of her petticoat, and wiped her face vigorously upon it, which had the effect of tracing concentric streaks irregularly over her countenance.

I parted my hair by the aid of a small dressing-glass, which so fired Susan that she crossed the stream with a mighty jump, and stood in ecstasy by my side. She borrowed the glass, and then my comb, rewashed her face, and fell to work diligently upon her hair.

All this did not so limit my perception as to prevent my watching the general demeanor of the family. The old man lay back at his ease, puffing a cloud of smoke; his wife, also emitting volumes of the vapor of "navy plug," squatted by the camp-fire, frying certain lumps of pork, and communicating, an occasional spiral jerk to the coffee-pot, with the purpose, apparently, of stirring the grounds. The two children had gotten upon the back of a contemplative ass, who stood by the upper side of the bed quietly munching the corner of a comforter.

My friend was in no haste. She squandered much time upon the arrangement of her towy hair, and there was something like a blush of conscious satisfaction when she handed me back my looking-glass and remarked ironically, " O no, I guess not, — no, sir."

I begged her to accept the comb and glass, which she did with maidenly joy.

This unusual toilet had stimulated with self-respect Susan's every fibre, and as she sprung back across the brook and approached her mother's camp-fire, I could not fail to admire the magnificent turn of her shoulders and the powerful, queenly poise of her head. Her full, grand form and heavy strength reminded me of the statues of Ceres, yet there was withal a very unpleasant suggestion of fighting trim, a sort of prize-ring manner of swinging the arms, and hitching of the shoulders. She suddenly spied the children upon the jackass, and with one wide sweep of her right arm projected them over the creature's head, and planted her left eleven firmly in the ribs of the donkey, who beat a precipitate retreat in the direction of the hog-pens, leaving her executing a *pas seul*, — a kind of slow, stately jig, something between the minuet and the *juba*, accompanying herself by a low-hummed air and a vigorous beating of time upon her slightly lifted knee.

It required my Pike County friends but ten minutes to swallow their pork and begin the labors of the day.

The mountaineers' camp was not yet astir. These children of the forest were well chained in slumber; for, unless there is some special programme for the day, it requires the leverage of a high sun to arouse their faculties, dormant enough by nature, and soothed into deepest quiet by whiskey. About eight o'clock they breakfasted, and by nine had engaged my innocent camp-men in a game of social poker.

I visited my horses, and had them picketed in the best possible feed, and congratulated myself that they were recruiting finely for the difficult ride before me.

Susan, after a second appeal from her mother, ran over to the corral and let out the family capital, who streamed with exultant grunt through the forest, darkening the fair green meadow gardens, and happily passing out of sight.

When I had breakfasted I joined Mr. Newty in his trip to the corral, where we stood together for hours, during which I had mastered the story of his years since, in 1850, he left his old home in Pike of Missouri.

It was one of those histories common enough through this wide West, yet never failing to startle me with its horrible lesson of social disintegration, of human retrograde.

That brave spirit of Westward Ho ! which has been the
pillar of fire and cloud leading on the weary march of
progress over stretches of desert, lining the way with
graves of strong men; of new-born lives; of sad, patient
mothers, whose pathetic longing for the new home died
with them; of the thousand old and young whose last
agony came to them as they marched with eyes strained
on after the sunken sun, and whose shallow barrows
scarcely lift over the drifting dust of the desert; that restless spirit which has dared to uproot the old and plant
the new, kindling the grand energy of California, laying
foundations for a State to be, that is admirable, is poetic,
is to fill an immortal page in the story of America; but
when, instead of urging on to wresting from new lands
something better than old can give, it degenerates into
mere weak-minded restlessness, killing the power of
growth, the ideal of home, the faculty of repose, it results
in that race of perpetual emigrants who roam as dreary
waifs over the West, losing possessions, love of life, love
of God, slowly dragging from valley to valley till they fall
by the wayside, happy if some chance stranger performs
for them the last rites, — often less fortunate, as blanched
bones and fluttering rags upon too many hillsides plainly
tell.

The Newtys were of this dreary brotherhood. In 1850,
with a small family of that authentic strain of high-bred
swine for which Pike County is widely known, as Mr. Newty avers, they bade Missouri and their snug farm good by,
and, having packed their household goods into a wagon
drawn by two spotted oxen, set out with the baby Susan
for Oregon, where they came after a year's march, tired,
and cursed with a permanent discontent. There they
had taken up a rancho, a quarter-section of public domain,
which at the end of two years was "improved" to the

5 *

extent of the "neatest little worm fence this side of
Pike," a barn, and a smoke-house. "In another year,"
said my friend, "I'd have dug for a house, but we tuck
ager and the second baby died." One day there came a
man who "let on that he knowd" land in California much
fairer and more worthy tillage than Oregon's best, so the
poor Newtys harnessed up the wagon and turned their
backs upon a home nearly ready for comfortable life, and
swept south with pigs and plunder. Through all the
years this story had repeated itself, new homes gotten to
the edge of completion, more babies born, more graves
made, more pigs, who replenished as only the Pike
County variety may, till it seemed to me the mere mul-
tiplication of them must reach a sufficient dead weight to
anchor the family; but this was dispelled when Newty
remarked: "These yer hogs is awkward about moving,
and I've pretty much made my mind to put 'em all
into bacon this fall, and sell out and start for Montana."

Poor fellow! at Montana he will probably find a man
from Texas who in half an hour will persuade him that
happiness lies there.

As we walked back to their camp, and when Dame
Newty hove in sight, my friend ventured to say, "Don't
you mind the old woman and her coons. She's from
Arkansas. She used to say no man could have Susan
who could n't show coonskins enough of his own killing
to make a bedquilt, but she's over that mostly." In
spite of this assurance my heart fell a trifle when, the
first moment of our return, she turned to her husband
and asked, "Do you mind what a dead-open-and-shut
on coons our little Johnny was when he was ten years
old?" I secretly wondered if the dead-open-and-shut
had anything to do with his untimely demise at eleven,
but kept silence.

Regarding her as a sad product of the disease of chronic emigration, her hard thin nature, all angles and stings, became to me one of the most depressing and pathetic spectacles, and the more when her fever-and-ague boy, a mass of bilious lymph, came and sat by her, looking up with great haggard eyes as if pleading for something, he knew not what, but which I plainly saw only death could bestow.

Noon brought the hour of my departure. Susan and her father talked apart a moment, then the old man said the two would ride along with me for a few miles, as he had to go in that direction to look for new hog-feed.

I despatched my two men with the pack-horse, directing them to follow the trail, then saddled my Kaweah and waited for the Newtys. The old man saddled a shaggy little mountain pony for himself, and for Susan strapped a sheepskin upon the back of a young and fiery mustang colt.

While they were getting ready, I made my horse fast to a stake and stepped over to bid good by to Mrs. Newty. I said to her, in tones of deference, " I have come to bid you good by, madam, and when I get back this way I hope you will be kind enough to tell me one or two really first-rate coon-stories. I am quite ignorant of that animal, having been raised in countries where they are extremely rare, and I would like to know more of what seems to be to you a creature of such interest." The wet, gray eyes relaxed, as I fancied, a trifle of their asperity ; a faint kindle seemed to light them for an instant as she asked, " You never see coons catch frogs in a spring branch ? "

" No, Madam," I answered.

" Well, I wonder ! Well, take care of yourself, and when you come back this way stop along with us, and we 'll kill a yearlin' and I 'll tell you about a coon that used to live under grandfather's barn." She actually offered me her hand, which I grasped and shook in a friendly manner, chilled to the very bone with its damp coldness.

Mr. Newty mounted, and asked me if I was ready. Susan stood holding her prancing mustang. To put that girl on her horse after the ordinary plan would have required the strength of Samson, or the use of a step-ladder, neither of which I possessed; so I waited for events to develop themselves. The girl stepped to the left side of her horse, twisted one hand in the mane, laying the other upon his haunches, and, crouching for a jump, sailed through the air, alighting upon the sheepskin. The horse reared, and Susan, twisting herself around, came right side up with her knee upon the sheepskin, shouting, as she did so, " I guess you don't get me off, sir!" I jumped upon Kaweah, and our two horses sprang forward together, Susan waving her hand to her father, and crying, " Come along after, old man !" and to her mother, " Take care of yourself!" which is the Pike County for *Au revoir!* Her mustang tugged at the bit, and bounded wildly into the air. We reached a stream bank at full gallop, the horses clearing it at a bound, sweeping on over the green floor, and under the magnificent shadow of the forest. Newty, following us at an humble trot, slopped through the creek, and when I last looked he had nearly reached the edge of the wood.

I could but admire the unconscious excellence of Susan's riding, her firm, immovable seat, and the perfect coolness with which she held the fiery horse. This quite absorbed me for five minutes, when she at last broke the silence by the laconic inquiry, " Does yourn buck?" To which I added the reply that he had only occasionally been

guilty of that indiscretion. She then informed me that
the first time she had mounted the colt he had "nearly
bucked her to pieces; he had jumped and jounced till
she was plum tuckered out" before he had given up.
Gradually reining the horses down and inducing them to
walk, we rode side by side through the most magnificent
forest of the Sierras, and I determined to probe Susan
to see whether there were not, even in the most latent
condition, some germs of the appreciation of nature. I
looked from base to summit of the magnificent shafts, at
the green plumes which traced themselves against the
sky, the exquisite fall of purple shadows and golden
light upon trunks, at the labyrinth of glowing flowers, at
the sparkling whiteness of the mountain brook, and up to
the clear matchless blue that vaulted over us, then turned
to Susan's plain, honest face, and gradually introduced
the subject of trees. Ideas of lumber and utilitarian
notions of fence-rails were uppermost in her mind; but I
briefly penetrated what proved to be only a superficial
stratum of the materialistic, and asked her point-blank
if she did not admire their stately symmetry. A strange,
new light gleamed in her eye as I described to her the
growth and distribution of forests, and the marvellous
change in their character and aspects as they approached
the tropics. The palm and the pine, as I worked them
up to her, really filled her with delight, and prompted
numerous interested and intelligent queries, showing that
she thoroughly comprehended my drift.

In the pleasant hour of our chat I learned a new lesson
of the presence of undeveloped seed in the human mind.

Mr. Newty at last came alongside and remarked that
he must stop about here; "but," he added, "Susan will go
on with you about half a mile, and come back and join
me here after I have taken a look at the feed." As he

rode out into the forest a little way, he called me to him, and I was a little puzzled at what seemed to be the first traces of embarrassment I had seen in his manner.

" You 'll take care of yourself, now, won't you ? " he asked. I tried to convince him that I would.

A slight pause.

" You 'll take care of yourself, won't you ?"

He might rely on it, I was going to say.

He added, " Thet — thet — thet man what gits Susan *has half the hogs !* "

Then turning promptly away, he spurred the pony, and his words as he rode into the forest were, " Take good care of yourself ! "

Susan and I rode on for half a mile, until we reached the brow of a long descent, which she gave me to understand was her limit.

We shook hands and I bade her good by, and as I trotted off these words fell sweetly upon my ear, " Say, you 'll take good care of yourself, won't you, say ? "

I took pains not to overtake my camp-men, wishing to be alone ; and as I rode for hour after hour the picture of this family stood before me in all its deformity of outline, all its poverty of detail, all its darkness of future, and I believe I thought of it too gravely to enjoy as I might the subtle light of comedy which plays about these hard, repulsive figures.

In conversation I had caught the clew of a better past. Newty's father was a New-Englander, and he spoke of him as a man of intelligence and, as I should judge, of some education. Mrs. Newty's father had been an Arkansas judge, not perhaps the most enlightened of men, but still very far in advance of herself. The conspicuous retrograde seemed to me an example of the most hopeless phase of human life. If, as I suppose, we may all sooner or later give in our adhesion to the Darwinian view of development, does not the same law which permits such splendid scope for the better open up to us also possible gulfs of degradation, and are not these chronic emigrants whose broken-down wagons and weary faces greet you along the dusty highways of the far West melancholy examples of beings who have forever lost the conservatism of home and the power of improvement ?

VI.

KAWEAH'S RUN.

1864.

AFTER trying hard to climb Mount Whitney without success, and having returned to the plains, I enjoyed my two days' rest in hot Visalia, where were fruits and people, and where I at length thawed out the last traces of alpine cold, and recovered from hard work and the sinful bread of my fortnight's campaign.   I considered it happiness to spend my whole day on the quiet hotel veranda accustoming myself again to such articles as chairs and newspapers, and watching with unexpected pleasure the few village girls who flitted about during the day, and actually found time after sunset to chat with favored fellows beneath the wide oaks of the street-side.   Especially interesting seemed the rustic sister of whom I bought figs at a garden gate, thinking her, as I did, *comme il faut*, though recollecting later that her gown was of forgotten mode, and that she carried a suggestion of ancient history in the obsolete style of her back hair.   Everybody was of interest to me, not excepting the two Mexican mountaineers who monopolized the agent at Wells, Fargo, & Co.'s office, causing me delay.   They were transacting some little item of business, and stood loafing by the counter, mechanically jingling huge spurs and shrugging their shoulders as they chatted in a dull, sleepy way. At the door they paused, keeping up quite a lively dispute, without apparently noticing me as I drew a small bag of gold and put it in my pocket.   There was no

especial reason why I should remark the stolid, brutal
cast of their countenances, as I thought them not worse
than the average Californian greaser; but it occurred to me
that one might as well guess at a geological formation as
to attempt to judge the age of mountaineers, because they
get very early in life a fixed expression, which is deepened
by continual rough weathering and undisturbed accumulations of dirt. I observed them enough to see that the
elder was a man of middle height, of wiry, light figure
and thin hawk visage; a certain angular sharpness making itself noticeable about the shoulders and arms, which
tapered to small almost refined hands. A mere fringe of
perfectly straight black beard followed the curve of his
chin, tangling itself at the ear with shaggy unkempt
locks of hair. He wore an ordinary stiff-brimmed
Spanish sombrero, and the inevitable greasy red sash
performed its rather difficult task of holding together
flannel shirt and buckskin breeches, besides half covering
with folds a long narrow knife.

His companion struck me as a half-breed Indian, somewhere about eighteen years of age, his beardless face
showing deep brutal lines, and a mouth which was a mere
crease between hideously heavy lips. Blood stained the
rowels of his spurs; an old felt hat, crumpled and
ragged, slouched forward over his eyes, doing its best to
hide the man.

I thought them a hard couple, and summed up their
traits as stolidity and utter cruelty.

I was pleased that the stable-man who saddled Kaweah
was unable to answer their inquiry where I was going,
and annoyed when I heard the hotel-keeper inform them
that I started that day for Millerton.

Leaving behind us people and village, Kaweah bore me
out under the grateful shade. of oaks, among rambling

settlements and fields of harvested grain, whose pale
Naples-yellow stubble and stacks contrasted finely with
the deep foliage, and served as a pretty groundwork for
stripes of vivid green which marked the course of numberless irrigating streams.   Low cottages, overarched with
boughs and hemmed in with weed jungles, margined my
road.   I saw at the gate many children who looked me
out of countenance with their serious, stupid stare; they
were the least self-conscious of any human beings I have
seen.

Trees and settlements and children were soon behind
us, an open plain stretching on in front without visible limit, — a plain slightly browned with the traces of
dried herbaceous plants, and unrelieved by other object than distant processions of trees traced from some
cañon gate of the Sierras westward across to the middle
valley, or occasional bands of restless cattle marching
solemnly about in search of food.   It was not pleasant to
realize that I had one hundred and twenty miles of this
lonely sort of landscape ahead of me, nor that my only
companion was Kaweah; for with all his splendid powers
and rare qualities of instinct there was not the slightest evidence of response or affection in his behavior.
Friendly toleration was the highest gift he bestowed
on me, though I think he had great personal enjoyment
in my habits as a rider.   The only moments that we ever
seemed thoroughly *en rapport* were when I crowded him
down to a wild run, using the spur and shouting at him
loudly, or when in our friendly races homeward toward
camp, through the forest, I put him at a leap where he
even doubted his own power.   At such times I could
communicate ideas to him with absolute certainty.   He
would stop, or turn, or gather himself for a leap, at my
will, as it seemed to me, by some sort of magnetic com-

munication; but I always paid dearly for this in long, tiresome efforts to calm him.

With the long level road ahead of me, I dared not attack its monotony by any unusual riding, and having settled him at our regular travelling trot, — a gait of about six miles an hour, — I forgot all about the dreary expanse of plain, and gave myself up to quiet revery. About dusk we had reached the King's River Ferry.

An ugly, unpainted house, perched upon the bluff, and flanked by barns and outbuildings of disorderly aspect, overlooked the ferry. Not a sign of green vegetation could be seen, except certain half-dried willows standing knee-deep along the river's margin, and that dark pine zone lifted upon the Sierras in eastern distance.

It is desperate punishment to stay through a summer at one of these plain ranches, there to be beat upon by an unrelenting sun, in the midst of a scorched landscape, and forced to breathe sirocco and sand; yet there are found plenty of people who are glad to become master of one of these ferries or stage stations, their life for the most part silent, and as unvaried as its outlook, given over wholly to permanent and vacant loafing.

Supper was announced by a business-like youth, who came out upon the veranda and vigorously rung a tavern bell, although I was the only auditor, and, likely enough, the only person within twenty miles.

I envy my horse at such times; the graminivorous have us at a disadvantage, for one revolts at the *cuisine*, although disliking to insult the house by quietly shying the food out the window. I arose hungry from the table, remembering that some eminent hygeist has avowed that by so doing one has achieved sanitary success.

As I walked over to see Kaweah at the corral, I glanced down the river, and saw, perhaps a quarter of a mile below, two horsemen ride down our bank, spur their horses into the stream, swim to the other side, and struggle up a steep bank, disappearing among bunches of cottonwood trees near the river.

So dangerous and unusual a proceeding could not have been to save the half-dollar ferriage. There was something about their seat, and the cruel way they drove home their spurs, that, in default of better reasons, made me think them Mexicans.

The whole Tulare plain is the home of nomadic ranchers, who, as pasturage changes, drive about their herds of horses and cattle from range to range; and as the wolves prowl around for prey, so a class of Mexican highwaymen rob and murder them from one year's end to the other.

I judged the swimmers were bent on some such errand, and lay down on the ground by Kaweah, to guard him, rolling myself in my soldier's great-coat, and slept with saddle for a pillow.

Once or twice the animal waked me up by stamping restively, but I could perceive no cause for alarm, and slept on comfortably until a little before sunrise, when I rose, took a plunge in the river, and hurriedly dressed myself for the day's ride; the ferryman, who had promised to put me across the river at dawn, was already at his post, and, after permitting Kaweah to drink a deep draught, I rode him out on the ferry-boat, and was quickly at the other side.

The road for two or three miles ascends the right bank of the river, approaching in places quite closely to the edge of its bluffs. I greatly enjoyed my ride, watching the Sierra sky-line high and black against a golden circle of dawn, and seeing it mirrored faithfully in still reaches of river, and pleasing myself with the continually changing foreground, as group after group of tall motionless

cottonwoods were passed. The willows, too, are pleasing
in their entire harmony with the scene, and the air they
have of protecting bank and shore from torrent and sun.
The plain stretched off to my left into dusky distance,
and ahead, in a bare, smooth expanse, dreary by its
monotony, yet not altogether repulsive in the pearly obscurity of the morning. In midsummer these plains are
as hot as the Sahara through the long blinding day; but
after midnight there comes a delicious blandness upon the
air, a suggestion of freshness and upspringing life, which
renews vitality within you.

Kaweah showed the influence of this condition in the
sensitive play of ears and toss of head, and in his free,
spirited stride. I was experimenting on his sensitiveness
to sounds, and had found that his ears turned back at the
faintest whisper, when suddenly his head rose, he looked
sharply forward toward a clump of trees on the river-
bank, one hundred and fifty yards in front of us, where a
quick glance revealed to me a camp-fire and two men
hurrying saddles upon their horses, — a gray and a sorrel.

They were Spaniards, — the same who had swum
King's River the afternoon before, and, as it flashed on
me finally, the two whom I had studied so attentively at
Visalia. Then I at once saw their purpose was to way-
lay me, and made up my mind to give them a lively run.
The road followed the bank up to their camp in an
easterly direction, and then, turning a sharp right angle
to the north, led out upon the open plain, leaving the
river finally.

I decided to strike across, and threw Kaweah into a
sharp trot.

I glanced at my girth and then at the bright copper
upon my pistol, and settled myself firmly in the saddle.

Finding that they could not saddle quickly enough to

attack me mounted, the older villain grabbed a shot-gun, and sprung out to head me off, his comrade meantime tightening the cinches.

I turned Kaweah farther off to the left, and tossed him a little more rein, which he understood and sprung out into a gallop.

The robber brought his gun to his shoulder, covered me, and yelled in good English, "Hold on, you ——!" At that instant his companion dashed up leading the other horse. In another moment they were mounted and after me, yelling, "Hu-hla" to the mustangs, plunging in the spurs, and shouting occasional volleys of oaths.

By this time I had regained the road, which lay before me traced over the blank objectless plain in vanishing perspective. Fifteen miles lay between me and a station; Kaweah and pistol were my only defence, yet at that moment I felt a thrill of pleasure, a wild moment of inspiration, almost worth the danger to experience.

I glanced over my shoulder and found that the Spaniards were crowding their horses to the fullest speed; their hoofs rattling on the dry plain were accompanied by inarticulate noises, like the cries of bloodhounds. Kaweah comprehended the situation. I could feel his grand legs gather under me, and the iron muscles contract with excitement; he tugged at the bit, shook his bridle-chains, and flung himself impatiently into the air.

It flashed upon me that perhaps they had confederates concealed in some ditch far in advance of me, and that the plan was to crowd me through at fullest speed, giving up the chase to new men and fresh horses; and I resolved to save Kaweah to the utmost, and only allow him a speed which should keep me out of gunshot. So I held him firmly, and reserved my spur for the last emergency. Still we fairly flew over the plain, and I said to myself, as the clatter of hoofs and din of my pursuers rang in my ears now and then, as the freshening breeze hurried it forward, that, if those brutes got me, there was nothing in blood and brains; for Kaweah was a prince beside their mustangs, and I ought to be worth two villains.

For the first twenty minutes the road was hard and smooth and level; after that gentle, shallow undulations began, and at last, at brief intervals, were sharp narrow arroyos (ditches eight or nine feet wide). I reined Kaweah in, and brought him up sharply on their bottoms, giving him the bit to spring up on the other side; but he quickly taught me better, and, gathering, took them easily, without my feeling it in his stride.

The hot sun had arisen. I saw with anxiety that the tremendous speed began to tell painfully on Kaweah. Foam tinged with blood fell from his mouth, and sweat rolled in streams from his whole body, and now and then he drew a deep-heaving breath. I leaned down and felt of the cinch to see if it had slipped forward, but, as I had saddled him with great care, it kept its true place, so I had only to fear the greasers behind, or a new relay ahead. I was conscious of plenty of reserved speed in Kaweah, whose powerful run was already distancing their fatigued mustangs.

As we bounded down a roll of the plain, a cloud of dust sprung from a ravine directly in front of me, and two black objects lifted themselves in the sand. I drew my pistol, cocked it, whirled Kaweah to the left, plunging by and clearing them by about six feet; a thrill of relief came as I saw the long white horns of Spanish cattle gleam above the dust.

Unconsciously I restrained Kaweah too much, and in a moment the Spaniards were crowding down upon me at a fearful rate. On they came, the crash of their spurs and the clatter of their horses distinctly heard; and as I had so often compared the beats of chronometers, I unconsciously noted that while Kaweah's, although painful, yet came with regular power, the mustang's respiration was quick, spasmodic, and irregular. I compared the intervals of the two mustangs, and found that one breathed better than the other, and then upon counting the best mustang with Kaweah, found that he breathed nine breaths to Kaweah's seven. In two or three minutes I tried it again, finding the relation ten to seven; then I felt the victory, and I yelled to Kaweah. The thin ears shot back flat upon his neck; lower and lower he lay down to his run; I flung him a loose rein, and gave him a friendly pat on the withers. It was a glorious burst of speed; the wind rushed by and the plain swept under us with dizzying swiftness. I shouted again, and the thing of nervous life under me bounded on wilder and faster, till I could feel his spine thrill as with shocks from a battery. I managed to look round, — a delicate matter at speed, — and saw, far behind, the distanced villains, both dismounted, and one horse fallen.

In an instant I drew Kaweah in to a gentle trot, looking around every moment, lest they should come on me unawares. In a half-mile I reached the station, and I was cautiously greeted by a man who sat by the barn door, with a rifle across his knees. He had seen me come over the plain, and had also seen the Spanish horse fall. Not knowing but he might be in league with the robbers, I gave him a careful glance before dismounting, and was completely reassured by an expression of terror which had possession of his countenance.

I sprung to the ground and threw off the saddle, and after a word or two with the man, who proved to be the

sole occupant of this station, we fell to work together
upon Kaweah, my cocked pistol and his rifle lying close
at hand. We sponged the creature's mouth, and, throwing a sheet over him, walked him regularly up and down
for about three quarters of an hour, and then taking him
upon the open plain, where we could scan the horizon in.
all directions, gave him a thorough grooming. I never
saw him look so magnificently as when we led him down
to the creek to drink; his skin was like satin, and the
veins of his head and neck stood out firm and round like
whip-cords.

In the excitement of taking care of Kaweah I had
scarcely paid any attention to my host, but after two
hours, when the horse was quietly munching his hay, I
listened attentively to his story.

The two Spaniards had lurked round his station during the night, guns in hand, and had made an attempt to
steal a pair of stage-horses from the stable, but, as he had
watched with his rifle, they finally rode away.

By his account, I knew them to be my pursuers; they
had here, however, ridden two black mustangs, and had
doubtless changed their mount for the sole purpose of
waylaying me.

About eleven o'clock, it being my turn to watch the
horizon, I saw two horsemen making a long *détour* round
the station, disappearing finally in the direction of Millerton. By my glass I could only make out that they
were men riding in single file on a sorrel and a gray
horse; but this, with the fact of the long *détour* which
finally brought them back into the road again, convinced
me that they were my enemies. The uncomfortable prob-
ability of their raising a band, and returning to make
sure of my capture, filled me with disagreeable foreboding,
and all day long, whether my turn at sentinel duty or

not, I did little else than range my eye over the valley in all directions.

Twice during the day I led Kaweah out and paced him to and fro, for fear his tremendous exertion would cause a stiffening of the legs ; but each time he followed close to my shoulder with the same firm, proud step, and I gloried in him.

Shortly after dark I determined to mount and push forward to Millerton, my friend, the station-man, having given me careful directions as to its position ; and I knew from the topography of the country, that, by abandoning the road and travelling by the stars, I could not widely miss my mark ; so at about nine o'clock I saddled up Kaweah, and, mounting, bade good by to my friend.

The air was bland, the heavens cloudless and starlit ; in the west a low arch of light out of which had faded the last traces of sunset color ; in the east a silver dawn shone mild and pure above the Sierras, brightening as the light in the west faded, till at last one jetty crag was cut upon the disk of rising moon.

Upon the light gray tone of the plain every object might be seen, and as I rode on the memory of danger passed away, leaving me in full enjoyment of companionship with the hour and with my friend Kaweah, whose sturdy, easy stride was in itself a delight. There is a charm peculiar to these soft, dewless nights. It seems the perfection of darkness in which you get all the rest of sleep while riding, or lying wide awake on your blankets. Now and then an object, vague and unrecognized, loomed out of dusky distance, arresting our attention, for Kaweah's quick eye usually found them first : dead carcasses of starved cattle, a blanched skull, or stump of aged oak, were the only things seen, and we gradually got accustomed to these, passing with no more than a glance.

At last we approached a region of low, rolling sand-hills, where Kaweah's tread became muffled, and the silence so oppressive as to call out from me a whistle. That instrument proved excellent in Traviata solos; but when I attempted some of Chopin, failed so painfully that I was glad to be diverted by arriving at the summit of the zone of hills, and looking out upon the wide, shallow valley of the San Joaquin, a plain dotted with groves, and lighted here and there by open reaches of moonlit river.

I looked up and down, searching for lights which should mark Millerton. I had intended to strike the river above the settlement, and should now, if my reckoning was correct, be within half a mile of it.

Riding down to the river-bank, I dismounted, and allowed Kaweah to quench his thirst. The cool mountain water, fresh from the snow, was delicious to him. He drank, stopped to breathe, and drank again and again. I allowed him also to feed a half-moment on the grass by the river-bank, and then remounting headed down the river, and rode slowly along under the shadow of trees, following a broad, well-beaten trail which led, as I believed to the village.

While in a grove of oaks, jingling spurs suddenly sounded ahead, and directly I heard voices. I quickly turned Kaweah from the trail, and tied him a few rods off, behind a thicket, then crawled back into a bunch of buckeye bushes, disturbing some small birds, who took flight. In a moment two horsemen, talking Spanish, neared, and as they passed I recognized their horses and then the men. The impulse to try a shot was so strong that I got out my revolver, but upon second thought put it up. As they rode on into the shadow, the younger, as I judged by his voice, broke out in a delicious melody, one of those passionate Spanish songs with a peculiar throbbing cadence, which he emphasized by sharply ringing his spurs.

These Californian scoundrels are invariably light-hearted ; crime cannot overshadow the exhilaration of outdoor life, remorse and gloom are banished like clouds before this perennially sunny climate. They make amusement out of killing you, and regard a successful plundering time as a sort of pleasantry.

As the soft full tones of my bandit died in distance, I went for Kaweah, and rode rapidly westward in the opposite direction, bringing up soon in the outskirts of Millerton, just as the last gamblers were closing up their little games, and about the time the drunk were conveying one another home. Kaweah being stabled, I went to the hotel, an excellent and orderly establishment, where a colored man of mild manners gave me supper and made me at home by gentle conversation, promising at last to wake me early, and bidding me good night at my room door with the tones of an old friend. I think his soothing spirit may partly account for the genuinely profound sleep into which I quickly fell, and which held me fast bound, until his hand on my shoulder and " Half past four, sir," called me back, and renewed the currents of consciousness.

After we had had our breakfast Kaweah and I forded the San Joaquin, and I at once left the road, determined to follow a mountain trail which led toward Mariposa. The trail proved a good one to travel, of smooth, soft surface, and pleasant in its diversity of ups and downs, and with rambling curves which led through open regions of brown hills, whose fern and grass were ripened to a common yellow-brown, then among park-like slopes, crowned with fine oaks, and occasional pine woods, the ground

frequently covering itself with clumps of such shrubs
as chaparral, and the never-enough-admired manzanita.
Yet I think I never saw such facilities for an ambuscade.
I imagined the path went out of its way to thread every
thicket, and the very trees grouped themselves with a
view to highway robbery.

I soon, though, got tired looking out for my Spaniards,
and became assured of having my ride to myself when I
studied the trail, and found that Kaweah's were the first
tracks of the day.

Riding thus in the late summer along the Sierra foot-
hills, one is constantly impressed with the climatic peculiarities of the region. With us in the East, plant life
seems to continue until it is at last put out by cold, the
trees appear to grow till the first frosts ; but in the Sierra
foot-hills growth and active life culminate in June and
early July, and then follow long months of warm storm-
less autumn wherein the hills grow slowly browner, and
the whole air seems to ripen into a fascinating repose, —
a rich, dreamy quiet, with distance lost behind pearly
hazes, with warm tranquil nights, dewless and silent.
This period is wealthy in yellows and russets and browns,
in great overhanging masses of oak, whose olive hue is
warmed into umber depth, in groves of serious pines, red
of bark, and cool in the dark greenness of their spires.
Nature wears an aspect of patient waiting for a great
change ; ripeness, existence beyond the accomplishment
of the purpose of life, a long, pleasant, painless waiting for
death, — these are the conditions of the vegetation ; and
it is vegetation more than the peculiar appearance of the
air which impresses the strange · character of the season.
It is as if our August should grow rich and ripe, through
cloudless days and glorious warm nights, on till February,
and then wake as from sleep, to break out in the bloom
of May.

I was delighted to ride thus alone, and expose myself, as one uncovers a sensitized photographic plate, to be influenced ; for this is a respite from scientific work, when through months you hold yourself accountable for seeing everything, for analyzing, for instituting perpetual comparison, and as it were sharing in the administering of the physical world. No tongue can tell the relief to simply withdraw scientific observation, and let Nature impress you in the dear old way with all her mystery and glory, with those vague indescribable emotions which tremble between wonder and sympathy.

Behind me in distance stretched the sere plain where Kaweah's run saved me. To the west, fading out into warm blank distance, lay the great valley of San Joaquin, into which, descending by sinking curves, were rounded hills, with sunny brown slopes softened as to detail by a low clinging bank of milky air. Now and then out of the haze to the east indistinct rosy peaks, with dull, silvery snow-marblings, stood dimly up against the sky, and higher yet a few sharp summits lifted into the clearer heights seemed hung there floating. Quite in harmony with this was the little group of Dutch settlements I passed, where an antique-looking man and woman sat together on a veranda sunning their white hair, and silently smoking old porcelain pipes.

Nor was there any element of incongruity at the "rancheria" where I dismounted to rest shortly after noon. A few sleepy Indians lay on their backs dreaming ; the good-humored stout squaws, nursing pappooses, or lying outstretched upon red blankets. The agreeable harmony was not alone from the Indian summer in their blood, but in part as well from the features of their dress and facial expression. Their clothes, of Caucasian origin, quickly fade out into utter barbarism, toning down to

warm dirty umbers, never failing to be relieved, here and
there, by ropes of blue and white beads, or head-band
and girdle of scarlet cloth. I saw one woman, of splendid
mould, soundly sleeping upon her back, a blanket covering her from the waist down in ample folds, her bare
body and large full breasts kindled into bronze under
streaming light; the arms flung out wide and relaxed;
the lips closed with grave compression, and about the
eyes and full throat an air of deep, eternal sleep. She
might have been a casting in metal but for the rich hot
color in her lips and cheeks.

Toward the late afternoon, trotting down a gentle forest
slope, I came in sight of a number of ranch buildings
grouped about a central open space. A small stream
flowed by the outbuildings, and wound among chaparral-
covered spurs below. Considerable crops of grain had
been gathered into a corral, and a number of horses were
quietly straying about. Yet with all the evidences of
considerable possessions the whole place had an air of
suspicious mock-sleepiness. Riding into the open square,
I saw that one of the buildings was a store, and to this I
rode, tying Kaweah to the piazza post.

I thought the whole world slumbered when I beheld
the sole occupant of this country store, a red-faced man
in pantaloons and shirt, who lay on his back upon a
counter fast asleep, the handle of a revolver grasped in
his right hand. It seemed to me if I were to wake him
up a little too suddenly he might misunderstand my
presence and do some accidental damage; so I stepped
back and poked Kaweah, making him jump and clatter
his hoofs, and at once the proprietor sprung to the door,
looking flustered and uneasy.

I asked him if he could accommodate me for the afternoon and night, and take care of my horse; to which he

replied, in a very leisurely manner, that there was a bed, and something to eat, and hay, and that if I was inclined to take the chances I might stay.

Being in mind to take the chances, I did stay, and my host walked out with me to the corral, and showed me where to get Kaweah's hay and grain.

I loafed about for an hour or two, finding that a Chinese cook was the only other human being in sight, and then concluded to pump the landlord. A half-hour's trial thoroughly disgusted me, and I gave it up as a bad job. I did, however, learn that he was a man of Southern birth, of considerable education, which a brutal life and depraved mind had not been able to fully obliterate. He seemed to care very little for his business, which indeed was small enough, for during the time I spent there not a single customer made his appearance. The stock of goods I observed on examination to be chiefly fire-arms, every manner of gambling apparatus, and liquors; the few pieces of stuffs, barrels, and boxes of groceries appeared to be disposed rather as ornaments than for actual sale.

From each of the man's trousers' pockets protruded the handle of a derringer, and behind his counter were arranged in convenient position two or three double-barrelled shot-guns.

I remarked to him that he seemed to have a handily arranged arsenal, at which he regarded me with a cool, quiet stare, polished the handle of one of his derringers upon his trousers, examined the percussion-cap with great deliberation, and then with a nod of the head intended to convey great force, said, "You don't live in these parts," —a fact for which I felt not unthankful.

The man drank brandy freely and often, and at intervals of about half an hour called to his side a plethoric

old cat named " Gospel," stroked her with nervous rapidity, swearing at the same time in so *distrait* and unconscious a manner that he seemed mechanically talking to
himself.

Whoever has travelled on the West Coast has not
failed to notice the fearful volleys of oaths which the
oxen-drivers hurl at their teams, but for ingenious flights
of fancy profanity I have never met the equal of my
host. With the most perfect good-nature and in· un-
moved continuance he uttered florid blasphemies, which,
I think, must have taken hours to invent. I was glad,
when bedtime came, to be relieved of his presence, and
especially pleased when he took me to the little separate
building in which was a narrow single bed. Next this
building on the left was the cook-house and dining-
room, and upon the right lay his own sleeping apartment.
Directly across the square, and not more than sixty feet
off, was the gate of the corral, which creaked on its rusty
hinges, when moved, in the most dismal manner.

As I lay upon my bed I could hear Kaweah occasionally stamp ; the snoring of the Chinaman on one side,
and the low mumbled conversation of my host and his
squaw on the other. I felt no inclination to sleep, but
lay there in half-doze, quite conscious, yet withdrawn
from the present.

I think it must have been about eleven o'clock when I
heard the clatter of a couple of horsemen, who galloped
up to my host's building and sprang to the ground, their
Spanish spurs ringing on the stone. I sat up in bed,
grasped my pistol, and listened. The peach-tree next my
window rustled. The horses moved about so restlessly
that I heard but little of the conversation, but that little
I found of personal interest to myself.

I give as nearly as I can remember the fragments of

6 *   I

dialogue between my host and the man whom I recognized as the older of my two robbers.

"When did he come?"

"Wall, the sun might have been about four hours."

"Has his horse give out?"

I failed to hear the answer, but was tempted to shout
out "No!"

"Gray coat, buckskin breeches."   (My dress.)

"Going to Mariposa at seven in the morning."

"I guess I would n't round here."

A low muttered soliloquy in Spanish wound up with
a growl.

"No, Antone, not within a mile of the place. "'Sta
buen'."

Out of the compressed jumble of the final sentence I
got but the one word, "buckshot."

The Spaniards mounted and the sound of their spurs
and horses' hoofs soon died away in the north, and I lay
for half an hour revolving all sorts of plans. The safest
course seemed to be to slip out in the darkness and fly
on foot to the mountains, abandoning my good Kaweah;
but I thought of his noble run, and it seemed to me so
wrong to turn my back on him that I resolved to unite
our fate. I rose cautiously, and, holding my watch up to
the moon, found that twelve o'clock had just passed, then
taking from my pocket a five-dollar gold piece, I laid it
upon the stand by my bed, and in my stocking feet, with
my clothes in my hands, started noiselessly for the corral.
A fierce bull-dog, who had shown no disposition to make
friends with me, bounded from the open door of the proprietor to my side. Instead of tearing me, as I had expected, he licked my hands and fawned about my feet.

Reaching the corral gate, I dreaded opening it at once,
remembering the rusty hinges, so I hung my clothes upon

an upper bar of the fence, and, cautiously lifting the latch, began to push back the gate, inch by inch, an operation which required me eight or ten minutes; then I walked up to Kaweah and patted him. His manger was empty; he had picked up the last kernel of barley. The creature's manner was full of curiosity, as if he had never been approached in the night before. Suppressing his ordinary whinnying, he preserved a motionless, statue-like silence. I was in terror lest by a neigh, or some nervous movement, he should waken the sleeping proprietor and expose my plan.

The corral and the open square were half covered with loose stones, and when I thought of the clatter of Kaweah's shoes I experienced a feeling of trouble, and again meditated running off on foot, until the idea struck me of muffling the iron feet. Ordinarily Kaweah would not allow me to lift his forefeet at all. The two blacksmiths who shod him had done so at the peril of their lives, and whenever I had attempted to pick up his hind feet he had warned me away by dangerous stamps; so I approached him very timidly, and was surprised to find that he allowed me to lift all four of his feet without the slightest objection. As I stooped down he nosed me over, and nibbled playfully at my hat. In constant dread lest he should make some noise, I hurried to muffle his forefeet with my trousers and shirt, and then, with rather more care, to tie upon his hind feet my coat and drawers.

Knowing nothing of the country ahead of me, and fearing that I might again have to run for it, I determined at all cost to water him. Groping about the corral and barn, and at last finding a bucket, and descending through the darkness to the stream, I brought him a full draught, which he swallowed eagerly, when I tied my shoes on the saddle pommel, and led the horse slowly out of the corral gate, holding him firmly by the bit, and feeling his nervous breath pour out upon my hand.

When we had walked perhaps a quarter of a mile, I stopped and listened. All was quiet, the landscape lying bright and distinct in full moonlight. I unbound the wrappings, shook from them as much dust as possible, dressed myself, and then mounting, started northward on the Mariposa trail with cocked pistol.

In the soft dust we travelled noiselessly for a mile or so, passing from open country into groves of oak and thickets of chaparral.

Without warning, I suddenly came upon a smouldering fire close by the trail, and in the shadow descried two sleeping forms, one stretched on his back snoring heavily, the other lying upon his face, pillowing his head upon folded arms.

I held my pistol aimed at one of the wretches, and rode by without wakening them, guiding Kaweah in the thickest dust.

It keyed me up to a high pitch. I turned around in the saddle, leaving Kaweah to follow the trail, and kept my eyes riveted on the sleeping forms, until they were lost in distance, and then I felt safe.

We galloped over many miles of trail, enjoying a sunrise, and came at last to Mariposa, where I deposited my gold, and then went to bed and made up my lost sleep.

VII.

AROUND YOSEMITE WALLS.

1864.

LATE in the afternoon of October 5, 1864, a party of us reached the edge of Yosemite, and, looking down into the valley, saw that the summer haze had been banished from the region by autumnal frosts and wind. We looked in the gulf through air as clear as a vacuum, discerning small objects upon valley-floor and cliff-front.

That splendid afternoon shadow which divides the face of El Capitan was projected far up and across the valley, cutting it in halves, — one a mosaic of russets and yellows with dark pine and glimpse of white river; the other a cobalt-blue zone, in which the familiar groves and meadows were suffused with shadow-tones. It is hard to conceive a more pointed contrast than this same view in October and June. Then, through a slumberous yet transparent atmosphere, you look down upon emerald freshness of green, upon arrowy rush of swollen river, and here and there, along pearly cliffs, as from the clouds, tumbles white silver dust of cataracts. The voice of full soft winds swells up over rustling leaves, and, pulsating, throbs like the beating of far-off surf. All stern sublimity, all geological terribleness, are veiled away behind magic curtains of cloud-shadow and broken light. Misty brightness, glow of cliff and sparkle of foam, wealth of beautiful details, the charm of pearl and emerald, cool gulfs of violet shade stretching back in deep recesses of the walls, — these are the features which lie under the June sky.

Now all that has gone. The shattered fronts of walls stand out sharp and terrible, sweeping down in broken crag and cliff to a valley whereon the shadow of autumnal death has left its solemnity. There is no longer an air of beauty. In this cold, naked strength, one has crowded on him the geological record of mountain work, of granite plateau suddenly rent asunder, of the slow, imperfect manner in which Nature has vainly striven to smooth her rough work and bury the ruins with thousands of years' accumulation of soil and *débris.*

Already late, we hurried to descend the trail, and were still following it when darkness overtook us; but ourselves and the animals were so well acquainted with every turn, that we found no difficulty in continuing our way to Longhurst's house, and here we camped for the night.

By an Act of Congress the Yosemite Valley had been segregated from the public domain, and given — " donated," as they call it — to the State of California, to be held inalienable for all time as a public pleasure-ground. The Commission into whose hands this trust devolved, had sent Mr. Gardner and myself to make a survey defining the boundaries of the new grant. It was necessary to execute this work before the Legislature should meet in December, and we undertook the work, knowing very well that we must use the utmost haste in order to escape a three months' imprisonment, — for in early winter the immense Sierra snow-falls would close the doors of mountain trails, and we should be unable to reach the lowlands until the following spring.

The party consisted of my companion, Mr. Gardner; Mr. Frederick A. Clark, who had been detailed from the service of the Mariposa Company to assist us ; Longhurst, an *habitué* of the valley, — a weather-beaten round-the-worlder, whose function in the party was to tell yarns, sing songs, and feed the inner man ; Cotter and Wilmer, chainmen ; and two mules, — one who was blind, and the other who, I aver, would have discharged his duty very much better without eyes.

We had chosen, as the head-quarters of the survey, two little cabins under the pine-trees near Black's Hotel. They were central ; they offered us a shelter; and from their doors, which. opened almost upon the Merced itself, we obtained a most delightful sunrise view of the Yosemite.

Next morning, in spite of early outcries from Longhurst, and a warning solo of his performed with spoon and fry-pan, we lay in our comfortable blankets pretending to enjoy the effect of sunrise light upon the Yosemite cliff and fall, all of us unwilling to own that we were tired out and needed rest. Breakfast had waited an hour or more when we got a little weary of beds and yielded to the temptation of appetite.

A family of Indians, consisting of two huge girls and their parents, sat silently waiting for us to commence, and, after we had begun, watched every mouthful from the moment we got it successfully impaled upon the camp forks, a cloud darkening their faces as it disappeared forever down our throats.

But we quite lost our spectators when Longhurst came upon the boards as a flapjack-frier, — a *rôle* to which he bent his whole intelligence, and with entire success. Scorning such vulgar accomplishment as turning the cake over in mid-air, he slung it boldly up, turning it three times, — ostentatiously greasing the pan with a fine centrifugal movement, and catching the flapjack as it fluttered down, — and spanked it upon the hot coals with a touch at once graceful and masterly.

I failed to enjoy these products, feeling as if I were

breakfasting in sacrilege upon works of art. Not so our Indian friends, who wrestled affectionately for frequent unfortunate cakes which would dodge Longhurst and fall into the ashes.

By night we had climbed to the top of the northern wall, camping at the head-waters of a small brook, named by emotional Mr. Hutchings, I believe, the Virgin's Tears, because from time to time from under the brow of a cliff just south of El Capitan there may be seen a feeble waterfall. I suspect this sentimental pleasantry is intended to bear some relation to the Bridal Veil Fall opposite. If it has any such force at all, it is a melancholy one, given by unusual gauntness and an aged aspect, and by the few evanescent tears which this old virgin sheds.

A charming camp-ground was formed by bands of russet meadow wandering in vistas through a stately forest of dark green fir-trees unusually feathered to the base. Little mahogany-colored pools surrounded with sphagnum lay in the meadows, offering pleasant contrast of color. Our camp-ground was among clumps of thick firs, which completely walled in the fire, and made close overhanging shelters for table and beds.

Gardner, Cotter, and I felt thankful to our thermometer for owning up frankly the chill of the next morning, as we left a generous camp-fire and marched off through fir forest and among brown meadows and bare ridges of rock toward El Capitan. This grandest of granite precipices is capped by a sort of forehead of stone sweeping down to level, severe brows, which jut out a few feet over the edge. A few weather-beaten, battle-twisted, and black pines cling in clefts, contrasting in force with the solid white stone.

We hung our barometer upon a stunted tree quite near the brink, and, climbing cautiously down, stretched ourselves out upon an overhanging block of granite, and looked over into the Yosemite Valley.

The rock fell under us in one sheer sweep thirty-two hundred feet; upon its face we could trace the lines of fracture and all prominent lithological changes. Directly beneath, outspread like a delicately tinted chart, lay the lovely park of Yosemite, winding in and out about the solid white feet of precipices which sunk into it on either side; its sunlit surface invaded by the shadow of the south wall; its spires of pine, open expanses of buff and drab meadow, and families of umber oaks rising as background for the vivid green river-margin and flaming orange masses of frosted cottonwood foliage.

Deep in front the Bridal Veil brook made its way through the bottom of an open gorge and plunged off the edge of a thousand-foot cliff, falling in white water-dust and drifting in pale translucent clouds out over the tree-tops of the valley.

Directly opposite us, and forming the other gate-post of the valley's entrance, rose the great mass of Cathe-dral Rocks, — a group quite suggestive of the Florence Duomo.

But our grandest view was eastward, above the deep sheltered valley and over the tops of those terrible granite walls, out upon rolling ridges of stone and wonderful granite domes. Nothing in the whole list of irruptive products, except volcanoes themselves, is so wonderful as these domed mountains. They are of every variety of conoidal form, having horizontal sections accurately ellip-tical, ovoid, or circular, and profiles varying from such semicircles as the cap behind the Sentinel to the grace-ful infinite curves of the North Dome. Above and be-yond these stretch back long bare ridges connecting with sunny summit peaks.

The whole region is one solid granite mass, with here and there shallow soil layers, and a thin variable forest which grows in picturesque mode, defining the leading lines of erosion as an artist deepens here and thère a line to hint at some structural peculiarity.

A complete physical exposure of the range, from summit to base, lay before us. At one extreme stand sharpened peaks, white in fretwork of glistening ice-bank, or black where tower straight bolts of snowless rock; at the other stretch away plains smiling with a broad honest brown under autumn sunlight. They are not quite lovable even in distant tranquillity of hue, and just escape being interesting in spite of their familiar rivers and associated belts of oaks. Nothing can ever render them quite charming, for in the startling splendor of flower-clad April you are surfeited with an embarrassment of beauty, at all other times stunned by their poverty. Not so the summits; forever new, full of individuality, rich in detail, and coloring themselves anew under every cloud change or hue of heaven, they lay you under their spell.

From them the eye comes back over granite waves and domes to the sharp precipice-edges overhanging Yosemite. We look down those vast, hard, granite fronts, cracked and splintered, scarred and stained, down over gorges crammed with *débris*, or dark with files of climbing pines. Lower the precipice-feet are wrapped in meadow and grove, and beyond, level and sunlit, lies the floor,—that smooth river-cut park, with exquisite perfection of finish.

The dome-like cap of Capitan is formed of concentric layers like the peels of an onion, each one about two or three feet thick. Upon the precipice itself, either from our station on an overhanging crevice, or from any point of opposite cliff or valley bottom, this structure is seen to be superficial, never descending more than a hundred feet.

In returning to camp we followed a main ridge, smooth and white under foot, but shaded by groves of alpine-firs. Trees which here reach mature stature, and in apparent health, stand rooted in white gravel, resulting from surface decomposition. I am sure their foliage is darker than can be accounted for by effect of white contrasting earth. Wherever, in deep depressions, enough wash soil and vegetable mould have accumulated, there the trees gather in thicker groups, lift themselves higher, spread out more and finer feathered branches ; sometimes, however, richness of soil and perfection of condition prove fatal through overcrowding. They are wonderfully like human communities. One may trace in an hour's walk nearly all the laws which govern the physical life of men.

Upon reaching camp we found Longhurst in a deep religious calm, happy in his mind, happy, too, in the posture of his body, which was reclining at ease upon a comfortable blanket-pile before the fire ; a verse of the hymn " Coronation " escaped murmurously from his lips, rising at times in shaky crescendos, accompanied by a waving and desultory movement of the forefinger. He had found among our medicines a black bottle of brandy, contrived to induce a mule to break it, and, just to save as much as possible while it was leaking, drank with freedom. Anticipating any possible displeasure of ours, Longhurst had collected his wits and arrived at a most excellent dinner, crowning the repast with a duff, accurately globular, neatly brecciated with abundant raisins, and drowned with a foaming sauce, to which the last of the brandy imparted an almost pathetic flavor.

The evening closed with moral remark and spiritual

song from Longhurst, and the morning introduced us to
our prosaic labor of running the boundary line, — a task
which consumed several weeks, and occupied nearly all of
our days. I once or twice found time to go down to the
cliff-edges again for the purpose of making my geological
studies.

An excursion which Cotter and I made to the top of
the Three Brothers proved of interest. A half-hour's
walk from camp, over rolling granite country, brought us
to a ridge which jutted boldly out from the plateau to the
edge of the Yosemite wall. Upon the southern side of
this eminence heads a broad *débris*-filled ravine, which
descends to the valley bottom ; upon the other side the
ridge sends down its waters along a steep declivity into
a lovely mountain basin, where, surrounded by forest,
spreads out a level expanse of emerald meadow, with a
bit of blue lakelet in the midst. The outlet of this little
valley is through a narrow rift in the rocks leading down
into the Yosemite fall. Along the crest of our jutting
ridge we found smooth pathway, and soon reached the
summit. Here again we were upon the verge of a precipice, this time four thousand two hundred feet high.
Beneath us the whole upper half of the valley was as
clearly seen as the southern half had been from Capitan. The sinuosities of the Merced, those narrow silvery
gleams which indicated the channel of the Yosemite
creek, the broad expanse of meadow, and *débris* trains
which had bounded down the Sentinel slope, were all
laid out under us, though diminished by immense depth.

The loftiest and most magnificent parts of the walls
crowded in a semicircle in front of us ; above them the
domes, lifted even higher than ourselves, swept down to
the precipice-edges. Directly to our left we overlooked
the goblet-like recess into which the Yosemite tumbles,

and could see the white torrent leap through its granite lip, disappearing a thousand feet below, hidden from our view by projecting crags; its roar floating up to us, now resounding loudly, and again dying off in faint reverberations like the sounding of the sea.

Looking up upon the falls from the valley below, one utterly fails to realize the great depth of the semicircular alcove into which it descends.

Looking back at El Capitan, its sharp vertical front was projected against far blue foot-hills, the creamy whiteness of sunlit granite cut upon aerial distance, clouds and cold blue sky shutting down over white crest and jetty pine-plumes, which gather helmet-like upon its upper dome. Perspective effects are marvellously brought out by the stern, powerful reality of such rock bodies as Capitan. Across their terrible blade-like precipice-edges you look on and down over vistas of cañon and green hill-swells, the dark color of pine and fir broken by bare spots of harmonious red or brown, and changing with distance into purple, then blue, which reaches on farther into the brown monotonous plains. Beyond, where the earth's curve defines its horizon, dim serrations of Coast Range loom indistinctly on the hazy air. From here those remarkable fracture results, the Royal Arches, a series of recesses carved into the granite front, beneath the North Dome, are seen in their true proportions.

The concentric structure which covers the dome with a series of plates penetrates to a greater depth than usual. The Arches themselves are only fractured edges of these plates, resulting from the intersection of a cliff-plane with the conoidal shells.

We had seen the Merced group of snow-peaks heretofore from the west, but now gained a more oblique view, which began to bring out the thin obelisk form of Mount

Clark, a shape of great interest from its marvellous thin-
ness. Mount Starr King, too, swelled up to its commanding height, the most elevated of the domes.

Looking in the direction of the Half-Dome, I was constantly impressed with the inclination of the walls, with
the fact that they are never vertical for any great depth.
This is observed, too, remarkably, in the case of El Capitan, whose apparently vertical profile is very slant, the
actual base standing twelve hundred feet in advance of
the brow.

For a week the boundary survey was continued northeast and parallel to the cliff wall, about a mile back from
its brink, following through forests and crossing granite
spurs until we reached the summit of that high bare
chain which divides the Virgin's Tears from Yosemite
Creek, and which, projecting southward, ends in the Three
Brothers. East of this the declivity falls so rapidly to
the valley of the upper Yosemite Creek that chaining was
impossible, and we were obliged to throw our line across
the cañon, a little over a mile, by triangulation. This
completed, we resumed it on the North Dome spur, trans-
ferring our camp to a bit of alpine meadow south of the
Mono trail, and but a short distance from the North
Dome itself.

After the line was finished here, and a system of triangles determined by which we connected our northern
points with those across the chasm of the Yosemite, we
made several geological excursions along the cliffs, studying the granite structure, working out its lithological
changes, and devoting ourselves especially to the system
of moraines and glacier marks which indicate direction
and volume of the old ice-flow.

An excursion to the summit of the North Dome was
exceedingly interesting. From the rear of our camp we

entered immediately a dense forest of conifers, which
stretch southward along the summit of the ridge until
solid granite, arresting erosion, afforded but little foothold. As usual, among the cracks, and clinging round
the bases of boulders, a few hardy pines manage to live,
almost to thrive; but as we walked groups became scarcer,
trees less healthy, all at last giving way to bare solid
stone. The North Dome itself, which is easily reached,
affords an impressive view up the Illilluette and across
upon the fissured front of the Half-Dome. It is also one
of the most interesting specimens of conoidal structure,
since its mass is not only divided by large spherical shells,
but each of these is subdivided by a number of lesser
divisional planes. No lithological change is, however,
noticeable between the different shells. The granite is
composed chiefly of orthoclase, transparent vitreous
quartz, and about an equal proportion of black mica and
hornblende. Here and there adularia occurs, and, very
sparingly, albite.

With no difficulty, but some actual danger, I climbed
down a smooth granite roof-slope to where the precipice
of Royal Arches makes off, and where, lying upon a
sharp neatly fractured edge, I was able to look down and
study those purple markings which are vertically striped
upon so many of these granite cliffs. I found them to
be bands of lichen growth which follow the curves of
occasional water-flow. During any great rain-storm, and
when snow upon the uplands is suddenly melted, innumerable streams, many of them of considerable volume,
find their way to the precipice-edge, and pour down its
front. Wherever this is the case, a deep purple lichen
spreads itself upon the granite, and forms those dark
cloudings which add so greatly to the variety and interest of the cliffs.

I found it extremest pleasure to lie there alone on the dizzy brink, studying the fine sculpture of cliff and crag, overlooking the arrangement of *débris* piles, and watching that slow grand growth of afternoon shadows. Sunset found me there, still disinclined to stir, and repaid my laziness by a glorious spectacle of color. At this hour there is no more splendid contrast of light and shade than one sees upon the western gateway itself, — dark-shadowed Capitan upon one side profiled against the sunset sky, and the yellow mass of Cathedral Rocks rising opposite in full light, while the valley is divided equally between sunshine and shade. Pine groves and oaks, almost black in the shadow, are brightened up to clear red-browns where they pass out upon the lighted plain. The Merced, upon its mirror-like expanses, here reflects deep blue from Capitan, and there the warm Cathedral gold. The last sunlight reflected from some curious smooth surfaces upon rocks east of the Sentinel, and about a thousand feet above the valley. I at once suspected them to be glacier marks, and booked them for further observation.

My next excursion was up to Mount Hoffmann, among a group of snow-fields, whose drainage gathers at last through lakes and brooklets to a single brook (the Yosemite), and flows twelve miles in a broad arc to its plunge over into the valley. From the summit, which is of a remarkably bedded conoidal mass of granite, sharply cut down in precipices fronting the north, is obtained a broad commanding view of Sierras from afar, by the heads of several San Joaquin branches, up to the ragged volcanic piles about Silver Mountain.

From the top I climbed along slopes, and down by a wide *détour* among frozen snow-banks and many little basins of transparent blue water, amid black shapes of stunted fir, and over the confused wreck of rock and tree-

trunk thrown rudely in piles by avalanches whose tracks
were fresh enough to be of interest.

Upon reaching the bottom of a broad, open glacier-
valley, through whose middle flows the Yosemite Creek
and its branches, I was surprised to find the streams
nearly all dry; that the snow itself, under influence of
cold, was a solid ice mass, and the Yosemite Creek, even
after I had followed it down for miles, had entirely ceased
to flow. At intervals the course of the stream was carried over slopes of glacier-worn granite, ending almost
uniformly in shallow rock basins, where were considerable ponds of water, in one or two instances expanding
to the dignity of lakelets.

The valley describes an arc whose convexity is in the
main turned to the west, the stream running nearly due
west for about four miles, turning gradually to the southward, and, having crossed the Mono trail, bending again
to the southeast, after which it discharges over the verge
of the cliff. An average breadth of this valley is about
half a mile; its form a shallow elliptical trough, rendered
unusually smooth by the erosive action of old glaciers.
Roches moutonnées break its surface here and there, but in
general the granite has been planed down into remarkable smoothness. All along its course a varying rubbish
of angular boulders has been left by the retiring ice,
whose material, like that of the whole country, is of granite; but I recognized prominently black sienitic granite
from the summit of Mount Hoffmann, which, from superior
hardness, has withstood disintegration, and is perhaps the
most frequent material of glacier-blocks. The surface
modelling is often of the most finished type; especially is
this the case wherever the granite is highly silicious, its
polish becoming then as brilliant as a marble mantel. In
very feldspathic portions, and particularly where ortho-

7   J

clase predominates, the polished surface becomes a crust, usually about three quarters of an inch thick, in which the ordinary appearance of the minerals has been somewhat changed, the rock-surface by long pressure rendered extremely dense, and in a measure separated from the underlying material. This smooth crust is constantly breaking off in broad flakes. The polishing extended up the valley sides to a height of about seven hundred feet. The average section of the old glacier was perhaps six hundred feet thick by half a mile in width. I followed its whole course from Mount Hoffmann down as far as I could ride, and then tying my horse only a little way from the brink of the cliff I continued downward on foot, walking upon the dry stream-bed. I found here and there a deep pit-hole, sometimes twenty feet deep, was carved in mid-channel, and was often full of water. Just before reaching the cliff verge the stream enters a narrow, sharp cut about one hundred and twenty feet in depth, and probably not over thirty feet wide. The bottom and sides of this granite lip, here and there, are evidently glacier-polished, but the greater part of the scorings have been worn away by the attrition of sands. A peculiar brilliant polish, which may be seen there to-day, is wholly the result of recent sand friction.

It was noon when I reached the actual lip, and crept with extreme caution down over smooth rounded granite, between towering walls, to where the Yosemite Fall makes its wonderful leap. Polished rock curved over too dangerously for me to lean out and look down over the cliff-front itself. A stone gate dazzlingly gilded with sunlight formed the frame through which I looked down upon that lovely valley.

Contrast with the strength of yellow rock and severe adamantine sculpture threw over the landscape beyond a strange unreality, a soft aerial depth of purple tone quite as new to me as it was beautiful beyond description. There, twenty-six hundred feet below, lay meadow and river, oak and pine, and a broad shadow-zone cast by the opposite wall. Over it all, even through the dark sky overhead, there seemed to be poured some absolute color, some purple air, hiding details, and veiling with its soft amethystine obscurity all that hard, broken roughness of the Sentinel cliffs. In this strange, vacant, stone corridor, this pathway for the great Yosemite torrent, this sounding-gallery of thunderous tumult, it was a strange sensation to stand, looking in vain for a drop of water, listening vainly, too, for the faintest whisper of sound, and I found myself constantly expecting some sign of the returning flood.

From the lip I climbed a high point just to the east, getting a grand view down the cliff, where a broad purple band defined the Yosemite spray line. There, too, I found unmistakable ice-striæ, showing that the glacier of Mount Hoffmann had actually poured over the brink. At the moments of such discovery, one cannot help restoring in imagination pictures of the past. When we stand by river-bank or meadow of that fair valley, looking up at the torrent falling bright under fulness of light,. and lovely in its graceful wind-swayed airiness, we are apt to feel its enchantment; but how immeasurably grander must it have been when the great, living, moving glacier, with slow invisible motion, crowded its huge body over the brink, and launched blue ice-blocks down through the foam of the cataract into that gulf of wild rocks and eddying mist!

The one-eyed mule, Bonaparte, I found tied where I had left him; and, as usual, I approached him upon his blind side, able thus to get successfully into my saddle, without danger to life or limb. I could never become attached to the creature, although he carried me faithfully many difficult and some dangerous miles, and for the reason that he made a pretext of his half-blindness to commit excesses, such as crowding me against trees and refusing to follow trails. Realizing how terrible under reinforcement of hereditary transmission· the peculiarly mulish traits would have become, one is more than thankful to Nature for depriving this singular hybrid of the capacity of handing them down.

Rather tired, and not a little bruised by untimely collision with trees, I succeeded at last in navigating Bonaparte safely to camp, and turning him over to his fellow, Pumpkinseed.

The nights were already very cold, our beds on frozen ground none of the most comfortable; in fact, enthusiasm had quite as much to do with our content as the blankets or Longhurst's culinary art, which, enclosed now by the narrow limit of bacon, bread, and beans, failed to produce such dainties as thrice-turned slapjacks or plum-duffs of solemnizing memory.

One more geological trip finished my examination of this side of the great valley. It was a two days' ramble all over the granite ridges, from the North Dome up to Lake Tenaya, during which I gathered ample evidence that a broad sheet of glacier, partly derived from Mount Hoffmann and in part from the Mount Watkins Ridge and Cathedral Peak, but mainly from the great Tuolumne glacier, gathered and flowed down into the Yosemite Valley. Where it moved over the cliffs there are well-preserved scarrings. The facts which attest this are open to observation, and seem to me important in making up a statement of past conditions.

We were glad to get back at last to our two little cabins

in the valley, although our serio-comic hangers-on, the Diggers, were gone, and the great fall was dry.

A rest of one day proved refreshing enough for us to leave camp and ascend by Mariposa trail to Meadow Brook, where we made a bivouac, from which Gardner began his southern boundary line, and I renewed my geological studies east of Inspiration Point.

I always go swiftly by this famous point of view now, feeling somehow that I don't belong to that army of literary travellers who have here planted themselves and burst into rhetoric. Here all who make California books, down to the last and most sentimental specimen who so much as meditates a letter to his or her local paper, dismount and inflate. If those firs could recite half the droll *mots* they have listened to, or if I dared tell half the delicious points I treasure, it would sound altogether too amusing among these dry-enough chapters.

I had always felt a desire to examine Bridal Veil cañon and the southwest Cathedral slope. Accordingly one fine morning I set out alone, and descended through chaparral and over rough *débris* slopes to the stream, which at this time, unlike the other upland brooks, flowed freely, though with far less volume than in summer. At this altitude only such streams as derive their volume wholly from melting snow dry up in the cold autumnal and winter months; spring-fed brooks hold their own, and rather increase as cold weather advances.

It was a wild gorge down which I tramped, following the stream-bed, often jumping from block to block, or letting myself down by the chaparral boughs that overhung my way. Splendid walls on either side rose steep and high, for the most part bare, but here and there on shelf or crevice bearing clusters of fine conifers, their lower slopes one vast wreck of boulders and thicket of chaparral plants.

Not without some difficulty I at length got to the brink and sat down to rest, looking over at the valley, whose meadows were only a thousand feet below; a cool stirring breeze blew up the Merced Cañon, swinging the lace-like scarf of foam which fell from my feet, and, floating now against the purple cliff, again blew out gracefully to the right or left. While I looked a gust came roaming around the Cathedral Rocks, impinging against our cliff near the fall, and apparently got in between it and the cliff, carrying the whole column of falling water straight out in a streamer through the air.

I went back to camp by way of the Cathedral Rocks, finding much of interest in the conoidal structure, which is yet perfectly apparent, and unobscured by erosion or the terrible splitting asunder they have suffered. Upon a ridge connecting these rocks with the plateaus just south there were many instructive and delightful points of view, especially the crag just above the Cathedral Spires, from which I overlooked a large part of valley and cliff, with the two sharp slender minarets of granite close beneath me. That great block forming the plateau between the Yosemite and Illilluette cañons afforded a fine field for studying granite, pine, and many remarkably characteristic views of the gorge below and peaks beyond. From our camp I explored every ravine and climbed each eminence, reaching at last, one fine afternoon, the top of that singular hemispherical mass, the Sentinel Dome. From this point one sweeps the horizon in all directions. You stand upon the crest of half a globe, whose smooth white sides, bearing here and there stunted pines, slope away regularly in all directions from your feet. Below, granite masses, blackened here and there with densely clustered forest, stretch through varied undulations toward you. At a little distance from the foot of the Half-

Dome trees hold upon sharp brinks, and precipices plunge off into Yosemite upon one side, and the dark rocky cañon of Illilluette upon the other. Eastward, soaring into clouds, stands the thin vertical mass of the Half-Dome.

From this view the snowy peak of the Obelisk, flattened into broad dome-like outline, rises, shutting out the more distant Sierra summits. This peak, from its peculiar position and thin tower-like form, offers one of the most tempting summits of the region. From that slender top one might look into the Yosemite, and into that basin of ice and granite between the Merced and Mount Lyell groups. I had longed for it through the last month's campaign, and now made up my mind, with this inspiring view, to attempt it at all hazards.

A little way to the east, and about a thousand feet below the brink of the Glacier Point, the crags appeared to me particularly tempting; so in the late afternoon I descended, walking over a rough, gritty surface of granite, which gave me secure foothold. Upon the very edge the immense splintered blocks lay piled one upon another; here a mass jutting out and overhanging upon the edge, and here a huge slab pointed out like a barbette gun. I crawled out upon of one these projecting blocks and rested myself, while studying the view.

From here the one very remarkable object is the Half-Dome. You see it now edgewise and in sharp profile, the upper half of the conoid fronting the north with a sharp, sheer fracture-face of about two thousand feet vertical. From the top of this a most graceful helmet curve sweeps over to the south, and descends almost perpendicularly into the valley of the Little Yosemite; and here from the foot springs up the block of Mount Broderick,—a single, rough-hewn pyramid, three thousand feet from summit to base, trimmed upon its crest with a few pines, and spreading out its southern base into a precipice, over which plunges the white Nevada torrent. Observation had taught me that a glacier flowed over the Yosemite brink. As I looked over now I could see its shallow valley, and the ever-rounded rocks over which it crowded itself and tumbled into the icy valley below. Up the Yosemite gorge, which opened straight before me, I knew that another great glacier had flowed; and also that the valley of the Illilluette and the Little Yosemite had been the bed of rivers of ice; a study, too, of the markings upon the glacier cliff above Hutchings's house, had convinced me that a glacier no less than a thousand feet deep had flowed through the valley, occupying its entire bottom.

It was impossible for me, as I sat perched upon this jutting rock mass, in full view of all the cañons which had led into this wonderful converging system of ice-rivers, not to imagine a picture of the glacier period. Bare or snow-laden cliffs overhung the gulf; streams of ice, here smooth and compacted into a white plain, there riven into innumerable crevasses, or tossed into forms like the waves of a tempest-lashed sea, crawled through all the gorges. Torrents of water and avalanches of rock and snow spouted at intervals all along the cliff walls. Not a tree nor a vestige of life was in sight, except far away upon ridges below, or out upon the dimly expanding plain. Granite and ice and snow, silence broken only by the howling tempest and the crash of falling ice or splintered rock, and a sky deep freighted with cloud and storm,— these were the elements of a period which lasted immeasurably long, and only in comparatively the most recent geological times have given way to the present marvellously changed condition. Nature in her present aspects, as well as in the records of her past, here constantly

AROUND YOSEMITE WALLS.   153

offers the most vivid and terrible contrasts. Can anything be more wonderfully opposite than that period of
leaden sky, gray granite, and desolate stretches of white,
and the present, when of the old order we have only left
the solid framework of granite, and the indelible inscriptions of glacier work? To-day their burnished pathways
are legibly traced with the history of the past. Every
ice-stream is represented by a feeble river, every great
glacier cascade by a torrent of white foam dashing itself
down rugged walls, or spouting from the brinks of upright
cliffs. The very avalanche tracks are darkened by clustered woods, and over the level pathway of the great
Yosemite glacier itself is spread a park of green, a mosaic of forest, a thread of river.

7 *

VIII.

A SIERRA STORM.

1864.

FROM every commanding eminence around the Yosemite no distant object rises with more inspiring greatness than the Obelisk of Mount Clark. Seen from the west it is a high isolated peak, having a dome-like outline very much flattened upon its west side, the precipice sinking deeply down to an old glacier ravine. From the north this peak is a slender single needle, jutting two thousand feet from a rough-hewn pedestal of rocks and snow-fields. Forest-covered heights rise to its base from east and west. To the south it falls into a deep saddle, which rises again, after a level outline of a mile, sweeping up in another noble granite peak. On the north the spur drops abruptly down, overhanging an edge of the great Merced gorge, its base buried beneath an accumulation of morainal matter deposited by ancient Merced glaciers. From the region of Mount Hoffmann looming in most impressive isolation, its slender needle-like summit had long fired us with ambition ; and having finished my agreeable climb round the Yosemite walls, I concluded to visit the mountain with Cotter, and, if the weather should permit, to attempt a climb. We packed our two mules with a week's provisions and a single blanket each, and on the 10th of November left our friends at the head-quarters' camp in Yosemite Valley and rode out upon the Mariposa trail, reaching the plateau by noon. Having passed Meadow Brook, we left the path and bore off in the direction of

Mount Clark, spending the afternoon in riding over granite ridges and open stretches of frozen meadow, where the ground was all hard, and grass entirely cropped off by numerous herds of sheep that had ranged here during summer. The whole earth was bare, and rang under our mules' hoofs almost as clearly as the granite itself.

We camped for the night on one of the most eastern affluents of Bridal Veil Creek, and were careful to fill our canteens before the bitter night-chill should freeze it over. By our camp was a pile of pine logs swept together by some former tempest; we lighted them, and were quickly saluted by a magnificent bonfire. The animals were tied within its ring of warmth, and our beds laid where the rain of sparks could not reach. As we were just going to sleep, our mules pricked up their ears and looked into the forest. We sprang to our feet, picked up our pistols, expecting an Indian or a grizzly, but were surprised to see, riding out of the darkness, a lonely mountaineer, mounted upon a little mustang, carrying his long rifle across the saddle-bow. He came directly to our camp-fire, and, without uttering a word, slowly and with great effort swung himself out of his saddle and walked close to the flames, leaving his horse, who remained motionless, where he had reined him in. I saw that the man was nearly frozen to death, and immediately threw my blanket over his shoulders. The water in our camp kettle was still hot, and Cotter made haste to draw a pot of tea, while I broiled a slice of beef and pressed him to eat. He, however, shook his head and maintained a persistent silence, until at length, after turning round and round until I could have thought him done to a turn, in a very feeble, broken voice he ejaculated, " I was pretty near gone in, stranger!" Again I pressed him to drink a cup of tea, but he feebly answered, " Not yet." After roasting

for half an hour, in which I fully expected to see his
coat-tail smoke, he sat down and drank about two quarts
of tea. This had the effect of thawing him out, and he
remembered that his horse was still saddled and very
hungry. He told us that neither he nor the animal had
had anything to eat for three days, and that he was pushing hopelessly westward, expecting either the giving out
of his horse, or death by freezing. We took the saddle
from his tired little mustang, spread the saddle-blanket
over his back, and from the scanty supply of grain we
had brought for our own animals gave him a tolerable
supper. It is wonderful how in hours of danger and pri-
vation the horse clings to his human friend. Perfectly
tame, perfectly trusting, he throws the responsibility of
his care and life upon his rider; and it is not the least
pathetic among our mountain experiences to see this
patient confidence continue until death. Observing that
the logs were likely to burn freely all night, we divided
our blankets with the mountaineer, and Cotter and I
turned in together. In the morning our new friend had
entirely recovered from his numb, stupid condition.
Recognizing at a glance his whereabouts, and thanking
us feelingly for our rough hospitality, he headed toward
the Mariposa trail, with quite an affecting good-by.

After breakfast we ourselves mounted and rode up a long
forest-covered spur leading to the summit of a granite divide, which we crossed at a narrow pass between two abrupt
cliffs, and descended its eastern slope in full view of the
whole Merced group. This long abrupt descent in front
of us led to the Illilluette Creek, and directly opposite on
the other side of the trough-like valley rose the high
sharp summit of Mount Clark. We were all day in
crossing and riding up the crest of a sharply curved
medial moraine which traced itself from the mountain

south of Mount Clark in a long parabolic curve, dying
out at last in the bottom of the Illilluette basin. The
moraine was one of the most perfect I have ever seen;
its smooth graded summit rose as regularly as a railway
embankment, and seemed to be formed altogether of
irregular boulders piled securely together and cemented
by a thick deposit of granitic glacier-dust. Late in the
afternoon we had reached its head, where the two converging glaciers of Mount Clark and Mount Kyle had
joined, clasping a rugged promontory of granite. To our
left, in a depression of the forest-covered basin, lay a little
patch of meadow wholly surrounded by dense groups of
alpine trees, which grew in clusters of five and six, apparently from one root. A little stream from the Obelisk
snows fell in a series of shallow cascades by the meadow's
margin. We jumped across the brook and went into
camp, tethering the mules close by us. One of the great
charms of high mountain camps is their very domestic
nature. Your animals are picketed close by the kitchen,
your beds are between the two, and the water and the
wood are always in most comfortable apposition.

For the first time in many months a mild moist wind
sprang up from the south, and with it came slowly creeping over the sky a dull, leaden bank of ominous-looking
cloud. Since April we had had no storm. The perpetually cloudless sky had banished all thought, almost
memory, of foul weather; but winter tempests had already
held off remarkably, and we knew that at any moment
they might set in, and in twenty-four hours render the
plateaus impassable. It was with some anxiety that I
closed my eyes that night, and, sleeping lightly, often
woke as a freshening wind moved the pines. At dawn we
were up, and observed that a dark heavy mass of storm-
cloud covered the whole sky, and had settled down over

the Obelisk, wrapping even the snow-fields at its base in gray folds. The entire peak was lost, except now and then, when the torn vapors parted for a few moments and disclosed its sharp summit, whitened by new-fallen snow. A strange moan filled the air. The winds howled piti- lessly over the rocks, and swept in deafening blasts through the pines. It was my duty to saddle up directly and flee for the Yosemite, but I am naturally an opti- mist, a sort of geological Micawber, so I dodged my duty, and determined to give the weather every opportunity for a clear-off. Accordingly we remained in camp all day, studying the minerals of the granite as the thickly strewn boulders gave us material. At nightfall I climbed a little rise back of our meadow, and looked out over the basin of Illilluette, and up in the direction of the Obelisk. Now and then the parting clouds opened a glimpse of the mountain, and occasionally an unusual blast of wind blew away the deeply settled vapors from the cañon to westward; but each time they closed in more threaten- ingly, and before I descended to camp the whole land was obscured in the cloud which settled densely down.

The mules had made themselves comfortable with a re- past of rich mountain grasses, which, though slightly frost- ed, still retained much of their original juice and nutriment. We ourselves made a deep inroad on the supply of pro- visions, and, after chatting awhile by the firelight, went to bed, taking the precaution to pile our effects carefully to- gether, covering them with an india-rubber blanket. Our bivouac was in the middle of a cluster of firs, quite well protected overhead, but open to the sudden gusts which blew roughly hither and thither. By nine o'clock wind died away altogether, and in a few moments a thick cloud of snow was falling. We had gone to bed together, pulled the blankets as a cover over our heads, and in a few

moments fell into a heavy sleep. Once or twice in the
night I woke with a slight sense of suffocation, and cautiously lifted the blanket over my head, but each time
found it growing heavier and heavier with a freight of
snow.   In the morning we awoke quite early, and, pushing back the blanket, found that we had been covered by
about a foot and a half of snow.   The poor mules had
approached us to the limit of their rope, and stood within
a few feet of our beds, anxiously waiting our first signs
of life.

We hurried to breakfast, and hastily putting on the
saddles, and wrapping ourselves from head to foot in
our blankets, mounted, and started for the crest of the
moraine.   I had taken the precaution to make a little
sketch-map in my note-book, with the compass directions
of our march from the Yosemite, and we had now the difficult task of retracing our steps in a storm so blinding and
fierce that we could never see more than a rod in advance.
But for the regular form of the moraine, with whose
curve we were already familiar, I fear we must have lost
our way in the real labyrinth of glaciated rocks which
covered the whole Illilluette basin.   Snow blew in every
direction, filling our eyes and blinding the poor mules, who
often turned quickly from some sudden gust, and refused
to go on.   It was a cruel necessity, but we spurred them
inexorably forward, guiding them to the right and left to
avoid rocks and trees which, in their blindness, they were
constantly threatening to strike.   Warmly rolled in our
blankets, we suffered little from cold, but the driving sleet
and hail very soon bruised our cheeks and eyelids most
painfully.   It required real effort of will to face the
storm, and we very soon learned to take turns in breaking
trail. The snow constantly balled upon our animals' feet,
and they slid in every direction. Now and then, in de-

scending a sharp slope of granite, the poor creatures would get sliding, and rush to the bottom, their legs stiffened out, and their heads thrust forward in fear. After crossing the Illilluette, which we did at our old ford, we found it very difficult to climb the long steep hillside ; for the mules were quite unable to carry us, obliging us to lead them, and to throw ourselves upon the snow-drifts to break a pathway.

This slope almost wore us out, and when at last we reached its summit we threw ourselves upon the snow for a rest, but were in such a profuse perspiration that I deemed it unsafe to lie there for a moment, and, getting up again, we mounted the mules and rode slowly on toward open plateaus near great meadows. The snow gradually decreased in depth as we descended upon the plain directly south of the Yosemite. The wind abated somewhat, and there were only occasional slow flurries between half-hours of tolerable comfort. Constant use of the compass and reference to my little map at length brought us to the Mariposa trail, but not until after eight hours of anxious, exhaustive labor, — anxious from the constant dread of losing our way in the blinding confusion of storm ; exhausting, for we had more than half of the way acted as trail-breakers, dragging our frightened and tired brutes after us. The poor creatures instantly recognized the trail, and started in a brisk trot toward Inspiration Point. Suddenly an icy wind swept up the valley, carrying with it a storm of snow and hail. The wind blew with such violence that the whole freight of sleet and ice was carried horizontally with fearful swiftness, cutting the bruised faces of the mules, and giving our own eyelids exquisite torture. The brutes refused to carry us farther. We were obliged to dismount and drive them before us, beating them constantly with clubs.

Fighting our way against this bitter blast, half blinded by hard, wind-driven snow-crystals, we at last gave up and took refuge in a dense clump of firs which crown the spur by Inspiration Point. Our poor mules cowered under shelter with us, and turned tail to the storm. The fir-trees were solid cones of snow, which now and then unloaded themselves when severely bent by a sudden gust, half burying us in dry white powder. Wind roared below us in the Yosemite gorge; it blew from the west, rolling up in waves which smote the cliffs, and surged on up the valley. While we sat still the drifts began to pile up at our backs; the mules were belly-deep, and our situation began to be serious.

Looking over the cliff-brink we saw but the hurrying snow, and only heard a confused tumult of wind. A steady increase in the severity of the gale made us fear that the trees might crash down over us; so we left the mules and crept cautiously over the edge of the cliff, and ensconced ourselves in a sheltered nook, protected by walls of rock which rose at our back.

We were on the brink of the Yosemite, and but for snow might have looked down three thousand feet. The storm eddied below us, sucking down whirlwinds of snow, and sometimes opening deep rifts, — never enough, however, to disclose more than a few hundred feet of cliffs.

We had been in this position about an hour, half frozen and soaked through, when I at length gathered conscience enough to climb back and take a look at our brutes. The forlorn pair were frosted over with a thick coating, their pitiful eyes staring eagerly at me. I had half a mind to turn them loose, but, considering that their obstinate nature might lead them back to our Obelisk camp, I patted their noses, and climbed back to the shelf by Cotter, determined to try it for a quarter of an

K

hour more, when, if the tempest did not lull, I thought
we must press on and face the snow for an hour more,
while we tramped down to the valley.

Suddenly there came a lull in the storm ; its blinding
fury of snow and wind ceased. Overhead, still hurrying
eastward, the white bank drove on, unveiling, as it fled,
the Yosemite walls, plateau, and every object to the eastward as far as Mount Clark. As yet the valley bottom
was obscured by a layer of mist and cloud, which rose to
the height of about a thousand feet, submerging cliff-foot
and *débris* pile. Between these strata, the cloud above
and the cloud below, every object was in clear, distinct
view ; the sharp terrible fronts of precipices, capped with
a fresh cover of white, plunged down into the still, gray
river of cloud below, their stony surfaces clouded with
purple, salmon-color, and bandings of brown, — all hues
unnoticeable in every-day lights. Forest, and crag, and
plateau, and distant mountain were snow-covered to a
uniform whiteness ; only the dark gorge beneath us
showed the least traces of color. There all was rich,
deep, gloomy. Even over the snowy surfaces above there
prevailed an almost ashen grey, which reflected itself
from the dull, drifting sky. A few torn locks of vapor
poured over the cliff-edge at intervals, and crawled down
like wreaths of smoke, floating gracefully and losing themselves at last in the bank of cloud which lay upon the
bottom of the valley. ·

On a sudden the whole gray roof rolled away like a
scroll, leaving the heavens from west to far east one
expanse of pure, warm blue. Setting sunlight smote full
upon the stony walls below, and shot over the plateau
country, gilding here a snowy forest group, and there a
wave-crest of whitened ridge. The whole air sparkled
with diamond particles ; red light streamed in through

the open Yosemite gateway, brightening those vast, solemn faces of stone, and intensifying the deep neutral blue of shadowed alcoves.

The luminous cloud-bank in the east rolled from the last Sierra crest, leaving the whole chain of peaks in broad light, each rocky crest strongly red, the newly fallen snow marbling them over with a soft, deep rose; and, wherever a cañon carved itself down their rocky fronts, its course was traceable by a shadowy band of blue. The middle distance glowed with a tint of golden yellow; the broken heights along the cañon-brinks and edges of the cliff in front were of an intense spotless white. Far below us the cloud stratum melted away, revealing the floor of the valley, whose russet and emerald and brown and red burned in the broad evening sun. It was a marvellous piece of contrasted lights, — the distance so pure, so soft in its rosy warmth, so cool in the depth of its shadowy blue; the foreground strong in fiery orange, or sparkling in absolute whiteness. I enjoyed, too, looking up at the pure unclouded sky, which now wore an aspect of intense serenity. For half an hour nature seemed in entire repose; not a breath of wind stirred the white snow-laden shafts of the trees; not a sound of animate creature, or the most distant reverberation of waterfall reached us; no film of vapor moved across the tranquil sapphire sky; absolute quiet reigned until a loud roar proceeding from Capitan turned our eyes in that direction. From the round, dome-like cap of its summit there moved down an avalanche, gathering volume and swiftness as it rushed to the brink, and then, leaping out two or three hundred feet into space, fell, slowly filtering down through the lighted air, like a silver cloud, until within a thousand feet of the earth it floated into the shadow of the cliff and sank to the ground as a faint blue mist. Next the Cathedral snow poured from its lighted summit in resounding avalanches; then the Three Brothers shot off their loads, and afar from the east a deep roar reached us as the whole snow-cover thundered down the flank of Cloud's Rest.

We were warned by the hour to make all haste, and, driving the poor brutes before us, made our way down the trail as fast as possible. The light, already pale, left the distant heights in still more glorious contrast. A zone of amber sky rose behind the glowing peaks, and a cold, steel-blue plain of snow skirted their bases. Mist slowly gathered again in the gorge below us and over-spread the valley floor, shutting it out from our view.

We ran down the zigzag trail until we came to that shelf of bare granite immediately below the final descent into the valley. Here we paused just above the surface of the clouds, which, swept by fitful breezes, rose in swells, floating up and sinking again like waves of the sea. Intense light, more glowing than ever, streamed in upon the upper half of the cliffs, their bases sunken in the purple mist. As the cloud-waves crawled upward in the breeze, they here and there touched a red-purple light and fell back again into the shadow.

We watched these effects with greatest interest, and, just as we were about moving on again, a loud burst as of heavy thunder arrested us, sounding as if the very walls were crashing in. We looked, and from the whole brow of Capitan rushed over, one huge avalanche, breaking into the finest powder and floating down through orange light, disappearing in the sea of purple cloud beneath us.

We soon mounted and pressed up the valley to our camp, where our anxious friends greeted us with enthu-siastic welcome and never-to-be-forgotten beans. We fed our exhausted animals a full ration of barley, and turned

them out to shelter themselves as best they might under
friendly oaks or among young pines. In anticipation
of our return the party had gotten up a capital supper, to which we first administered justice, then punishment, and finally annihilation. Brief starvation and
a healthy combat for life with the elements lent a most
marvellous zest to the appetite. Under the subtle in-
fluences of a free circulation and a stinging cold night,
I perceived a region of the taste which answers to
those most refined blue waves of the spectrum. Clouds
which had infolded the heavens rolled off to the east in
torn fillets of gold. The stars came out full and flashing
in the darkling sky of evening. We left our cabins and
grouped ourselves around a loquacious camp-fire, which
prattled incessantly and distilled volumes of that mild
stimulant, pyroligneous acid, — an ill-savored gas which
seems to have inspired much domestic poetry, however
it may have affected the New England olfactory nerves.

The vast valley walls, light in contrast with the deep
nocturnal violet heavens, rose far into the night, apparently holding up a roof of stars whose brilliancy faded
quite rapidly, until finally the last blinking points of
light died out, and cold, hard gray stretched from cliff to
cliff. Far up cañons and in the heart of the mountains
we could hear terrible tempest gusts crashing among the
trees, and breaking in deep, long surges against faces of
granite; coming nearer and nearer, they swept down the
gorges, with volume increasing every moment, until they
poured into the upper end of the valley and fell upon its
groves with terrible fury. The wind shrieked wild and
high among the summit crags, it tore through the pine-
belts, and now and then a sudden sharp crash resounded
through the valley as, one after another, old infirm pines
were hurled down before its blast. The very walls seemed

to tremble; the air was thick with flying leaves and dead branches; the snow of the summits, hard frozen by a sudden chill, was blown from the walls and filled the air with its keen cutting crystals. At last the very clouds, torn into wild flocks, were swept down into the valley, filling it with opaque hurrying vapors. Rocks loosening themselves from the plateau came thundering down precipice-faces, crashing upon *débris* piles and forest groups below. Sleet and snow and rain fell fast, and the boom of falling trees and crashing avalanches followed one another in an almost uninterrupted roar. In the Sentinel gorge, back of our camp, an avalanche of rock suddenly let loose and came down with a harsh rattle, the boulders bounding over *débris* piles and crashing through the trees by our camp. A vivid belt of blue lightning flashed down through the blackness, and •for a moment every outline of cliff and forest forms, and the rushing clouds of snow and sleet, were lighted up with a cold pallid gleam. The burst of thunder which followed rolled but for a moment, and was silenced by the furious storm. In the moment of lightning I saw that the Yosemite Fall, which had been dry for a month, had suddenly sprung into life again. Vast volumes of water and ice were pouring over and beating like sea-waves upon the granite below. Our mules came up to the cabin, and stood on its lee side trembling, and uttering suppressed moans. After hours the fitfulness of the tempest passed away, leaving a grand monotonous roar. It had torn off all the rotten branches of the year, and prostrated every decrepit tree, and at last settled down to a continuous gale, laden with torrents of rain. We lay down upon our bunks in our clothes, watching and listening through all the first hours of the night. Sleep was impossible; angry winds and the fury of drifting rain shook our little shelters, and kept us wide awake. Toward morning a second thunder-storm burst, and by the light of its flashes I saw that the river had risen nearly to our cabin door, covering the broad valley in front of us with a sheet of flood. Gradually the sound of Yosemite Fall grew louder and stronger, the throbs, as it beat upon the rocks, rising higher and higher till the whole valley rung with its pulsations. By dawn the storm had spent its fury, rain ceased, and around us the air was perfectly still; but aloft, among cliffs and walls, it might still be heard sweeping across the forest and tearing itself among granite needles. Fearing that so continuous a storm might block up our mountain trails, Hyde and Cotter and Wilmer, with instruments and pack-animals, started early and went out to Clark's Ranch.

So dense and impenetrable a fog overhung us, that day-light came with extreme slowness; and it was nine o'clock before we rose for breakfast, and at ten a gloomy sea of mist still hung over the valley. The Merced had over-flowed its banks and ran wild. Toward noon the mist began to draw down the valley, and finally all drifted away, leaving us shut in by a gray canopy of cloud which stretched from wall to wall, hanging down here and there in deep blue sags. In this stratum of gray were lost many higher summits, but the whole form of valley and cliff could be seen with terrible distinctness, the walls apparently drawn together, their bases at one or two points pushed into yellow floods of water which lay like lakes upon the level expanse. The whole lip of Yosemite was filled to the brim, and through it there poured a broad full torrent of white. Shortly after noon a few rifts opened overhead, showing a far sky, from which poured gushes of strong yellow sunlight, touching here and there upon sombre faces of cliff, and occasionally gilding the falling torrent. A wind still blew, smiting

the Yosemite precipice, and playing strangest games with
the fall itself. At one time a gust rushed upon the lip
of the fall with such violence as to dam back all its
waters. We could see its white pile in the lip mounting
higher and higher, still held back by the wind, until there
must have been a front of from a hundred and fifty to two
hundred feet of boiling white water. For a whole minute
not a drop poured down the wall; but, gathering strength,
the torrent overcame the wind, rushed out with tremendous violence, leaped one hundred and fifty feet straight
out into air, and fell clear to the rocks below, dashing
high and white again, and breaking into a cloud of spray
that filled the lower air of the valley for a mile.

While the water was held back in the gorge there was
a moment of complete silence, but when it finally burst
out again a crash as of sudden thunder shook the air.
At times gusts of wind would drive upon the Three
Brothers cliff, and be deflected toward the Yosemite,
swinging the whole mighty cataract like a pendulum;
and again, pouring upon the rocks at the bottom of the
valley, it would gather up the whole fall in mid-air, whirl
it in a festoon, and carry it back over the very summit
of the walls. I got out the theodolite to measure the
angle of its deflection, and, while watching, it swung over
an entire semicircle, now carried from the cliffs to the
right, and then whirled back in a cloud of foam over the
head of the Three Brothers. A very frequent prank was
to loop the whole twenty-six hundred feet of cataract
into a single semicircular festoon, which fell in the form
of fine fringe.

Throughout the afternoon we did little else than watch
these ever-changing forms of falling water, until toward
evening, when we walked up to see the Merced. I never
beheld such a rapid rise in any river; from a mere brook

hiding itself away under overhanging banks and among shrubby islands, it sprang in one night to the size of a full large river, flowing with the rapidity of a torrent and whirling in its eddies huge trunks of storm-blown pines. As twilight gathered, the scene deepened into a most indescribable gloom; dark-blue shadows covered half the precipices, and sullen unvaried sky stretched over us its implacable gray. There was something positively fearful in this color; such an impenetrable sky might overarch the Inferno. As we looked, it slowly sank, creeping down precipices, filling the whole gorge; coming down, down, and fitting the cliffs like the piston of an air-pump, till within a thousand feet of us it became stationary, and then slowly lifted again, clearing the summit and rising to an almost infinite remoteness. Slowly a few hard sharp crystals of snow floated down.

Later the air became intensely chilly, and by dark was full of slowly falling snow, giving prospect of a great mountain storm which might close the Sierras. On the following morning we determined at all costs to pack our remaining instruments and escape. The ground was covered with snow to the depth of seven or eight inches, and through drifting fog-banks we could occasionally get glimpses and see that every cliff was deeply buried in snow. We had still a few barometrical observations along the Mariposa trail which were necessary to complete our series of altitudes; and I started in advance of Gardner and Clark to break the trail, expecting that when I stopped to make readings they would easily overtake me. Two hours' hard work was needed to reach the ascent. It was not until noon that I made Inspiration Point, snow having deepened to eighteen inches, entirely obliterating the trail, and had it not been for the extreme frequency of our journeys I should never have been able

8

to follow it; as it was, with occasional mistakes which
were soon remedied, I kept the way very well, and my
tracks made it easy for the party behind. Having reached
the plateau, I made my two barometrical stations, and
then started alone through forests for Westfall's cabin.
Every fir-tree was a solid cone of white, and often clusters of five and six were buried together in one common
pile. Now and then a little sunlight broke through the
clouds, and in these intervals the scene was one of
wonderful beauty. Tall shafts of fir, often one hundred
and eighty feet high, trimmed with white branches, cast
their blue shadows upon snowy ground.

At about four o'clock, after nine hours of hard tramping, I reached Westfall's cabin, built a fire, and sat down
to warm myself and wait for my friends. In half an hour
they made their appearance, looking haggard and weary,
declaring they would go no farther that night. They led
their mule into the cabin, and unpacked, and began to
make themselves comfortably at home.

About five the darkness of night had fairly settled
down, and with it came a gentle but dense snow-storm.
It seemed to me a terrible risk for us to remain in the
mountains, and I felt it to be absolutely necessary that
one, at least, should press on to Clark's, so that, if a really
great storm should come, he could bring up aid. Accordingly I volunteered to go on myself, Clark and Gardner
expressing their determination to remain where they were
at all costs.

At this juncture Cotter's well-known voice sounded
through the woods as he approached the cabin. He had
been all day climbing from Clark's, and had come to lend
a hand in getting the things down. He was of my opinion that it was absolutely necessary for one of us, at least,
to go back to Clark's, and offered, if I thought best, to try

to accompany me. I had come from Yosemite and he
from Clark's, having travelled all day, and it was no slight
task for us to face storm and darkness in the forest, and
among complicated spurs of the Sierra.

We ate our lunch by the cabin fire, bade our friends
good night, and walked out together into the darkness.
For the first mile there was no danger of missing our way,
— even in the darkness of night Cotter's tracks could be
seen,— but after about half an hour it began to be very
difficult to keep the trail. The storm increased to a tempest, and exhaustion compelled us to travel slower and
slower. It was with intense anxiety that we searched
for well-known blazed trees along the trail, often thrusting our arms down in the snow to feel for a blaze that
we knew of. If it was not there, we had for a moment an
overpowering sense of being lost; but we were ordinarily
rewarded after searching upon a few trees, and the blaze
once found reanimated us with new courage. Hour after
hour we travelled down the mountain, falling off high
banks now and then, for in the dark all ideas of slope
were lost. It must have been about midnight when we
reached what seemed to be the verge of a precipice. If
our calculations were right, we must have reached the
edge of the South Fork Cañon. Here Cotter sank with
exhaustion and declared that he must sleep. I rolled
him over and implored him to get up and struggle on for
a little while longer, when I felt sure that we must get
down to the South Fork Cañon. He utterly refused, and
lay there in a drowsy condition, fast giving up to the
effects of fatigue and cold. I unbound a long scarf which
was tied round his neck, put it under his arms like a
harness, and, tying it round my body, started on, dragging
him through the snow, to see if by that means I might
not exasperate him to rise and labor on. In a few min-

utes it had its effect, and he sprang to his feet and fell upon me in a burst of indignation. A few words were enough to bring him to himself, when the old calm courage was reasserted, and we started together to make our way down the cliff. Happily we at length found the right ridge, and rapidly descended through forest to the river side.

Believing that we must still be below the bridge, we walked rapidly up the bank until, at last, we found it, and came quickly to Clark's. We pounded upon the cabin door, and waked up our friends, who received us with joy, and set about cooking us a supper.

It was two o'clock when we arrived, and by three we all went off again to our bunks. My anxiety about Gardner and Clark prevented my sleeping. Every few minutes I went to the door.

Before dawn it had cleared again, and remained fair till the next noon, when the two made their appearance. No sooner were they quietly housed than the storm burst again with renewed strength, howling among the forest trees grandly. Snow drifted heavily all the afternoon, and through the night it still fell, reaching an average depth of about two feet by the following morning.

We were up early, and packed upon the animals our instruments, note-books, and personal effects, leaving all the blankets and heavy baggage to be gotten out in the following spring. We toiled slowly and heavily up Chowchilla trail. The branches of the great pines and firs were overloaded with snow, which now and then fell in small avalanches upon our heads. Here and there an old bough gave way under its weight, and fell with a soft thud into the snow. We took turns breaking trail, Napoleon, the one-eyed mule, distinguishing himself greatly by following its intricate crooks, while the bravest of us, by turns, held

to his tail. There is something deeply humiliating in
this process. All the domineering qualities of mankind
vanished before the quick subtle instinct of that noble
animal, the mule, and his superior strength came out in
magnificent style. With a sublime scorn of his former
master, he started ahead, dragging me proudly after him.
I had sometimes thrashed that mule with unsympa-
thetic violence, and I fancied it was something very
like poetic justice thus submissively to follow in his
wake.

Midday found us upon the Chowchilla summit, following a trail deeply buried and often obliterated, and undiscoverable but for our long-eared leader. As we descended
the west slope the snow grew more and more moist, less
deep, and gradually turned into rain. An hour's tramp
found us upon bare ground, under the fiercely driving rain,
which quickly soaked us to the bone. The streams, as
we descended, were found to be more and more swollen,
until at last it required some nerve to ford the little
brooklets, which the mule had drunk dry on our upward journey. The earth was thoroughly softened, and
here and there the trail was filled with brimming brooks,
which rapidly gullied it out.

A more drowned and bedraggled set of fellows never
walked out upon the wagon-road and turned toward
Mariposa. Streams of water flowed from every fold of
our garments, our soaked hats clung to our cheeks, the
baggage was a mass of pulp, and the mules smelled violently of wet hide. Fortunately our note-books, carefully strapped in oil-cloth, so far resisted wetting. It
was three o'clock in the afternoon when we reached
Dulong's house, and were surprised to see the water flowing over the top of the bridge. In ordinary times a dry
arroyo traverses this farm, and runs under a bridge in

front of the house. Clark, our only mounted man, rode
out, as he supposed, upon the bridge; but unfortunately it
was gone, and he and his horse plunged splendidly into
the stream. They came to the surface, Clark with a look
of intense astonishment on his face, and the mare sputter-
ing and striking out wildly for the other side. Being a
strong swimmer she reached the bank, climbed out, and
Clark politely invited us to follow. The one-eyed Napoleon was brought to the brink and induced to plunge in
by an application of fence-rails *a tergo*, his cyclopean
organ piloting him safely across, when he was quickly followed by the other mules. We watched the load of
instruments with some anxiety, and were not reassured
when their heavy weight bore the mule quite under; but
she climbed successfully out, and we ourselves, half swimming, half floundering, managed to cross.

A little way farther we came upon another stream
rushing violently across the road, sweeping down logs
and sections of fence. Here Clark dismounted, and we
drove the whole train in. Three animals got safely over,
but the instrument mule was swept down stream and
badly snagged, lying upon one side with his head under
the water.

Cotter and Gardner and Clark ran up stream and got
across upon a log. I made a dash for the snagged mule,
and by strong swimming managed to catch one of his feet,
and then his tail, and worked myself toward the shore.
It was something of a task to hold his head out of the
water, but I was quickly joined by the others, and we
managed to drag him out by the head and tail. There
he lay upon the bank on his side, tired of life, utterly
refusing to get upon his feet, the most abominable specimen
of inertia and indifference. While I was pricking him
vigorously with a tripod, the ground caved under my feet

and I quickly sank. Cotter, who was standing close by, seized me by the cape of my soldier's overcoat, and landed me as carefully as he would a fish. As we marched down the road, unconsciously keeping step, the sound of our boots had quite a symphonic effect; they were all full of water, and with soft melodious slushing acted as a calmer upon our spirits.

The road in some places was cut out many feet deep, and we were obliged to climb upon the wooded banks, and make laborious *détours*. At last we reached a branch of the Chowchilla which was pouring in a flood between a man's house and his barn. Here we formed a line, a mule between each two men. Our line was swept frightfully down stream, but the leader gained his feet, and we came out safe and dripping upon *terra firma* on the other side. A mile farther we came upon the main Chowchilla, which was running a perfect flood ; from being a mere brooklet, it had swollen to a considerable river, with waves five and six feet high sweeping down its centre. We formed our line and attempted the passage, but were thrown back. It would have been madness to try it again, and we turned sorrowfully back to the last ranch. Cotter and I piloted the animals over to the barn, and, upon returning, threw a rope to our friends upon the other side, and were drawn through the swift water.

In the ranch house we found two bachelors, typical California partners, who were quietly partaking of their supper of bacon, fried onions, Japanese tea, and biscuits, which, like "Harry York's," had too much saleratus. We stood upon their threshold awhile and dripped, quite a rill descending over the two steps, trickling down the door yard as a new fork of the Chowchilla.

We asked for supper and shelter, but were met with such a gruff, inhospitable reply that we lost all sense of

modesty, and walked in with all our moisture. We
stretched a rope across the middle of the sitting-room
before a huge fire in an open chimney, then, stripping
ourselves to the buff, we hung up our steaming clothes
upon the line, and turned solemnly round and round
before the fire, drying our persons.

In the mean while our inhospitable landlords made the
best of the situation, and proceeded to achieve more
onions and more saleratus biscuit for our entertainment.

Upon our departure in the morning the generous rancher
charged us first-class hotel prices.

The flood had utterly disappeared, and we passed over
the Chowchilla with surprise and dry shoes.

At Mariposa we parted from Clark, and devoted two
whole days to struggling through the mud of San Joaquin
Valley to San Francisco, where we arrived, wet and exhausted, just in time to get on board the New York
steamer.

On the morning of the twelfth day Gardner and I
seated ourselves under the grateful shadow of palm-trees,
a bewitching black-and-tan sister thrumming her guitar
while the chocolate for our breakfast boiled. The slumberous haze of the tropics hung over Lake Nicaragua, but
high above its indistinct pearly veil rose the smooth cone
of the volcano of Omatepec, robed in a cover of pale emerald green. Warmth, repose, the verdure of eternal spring,
the poetical whisper of palms, the heavy odor of the
tropical blooms, banished the grand cold fury of the Sierra,
which had left a permanent chill in our bones.

IX.

MERCED RAMBLINGS.

1866.

DELIGHTFUL oaks cast protecting shadows over our camp on the 1st of June, 1866. Just beyond a little cook-fire where Hoover was preparing his mind and pan for an omelet stood Mrs. Fremont's Mariposa cottage, with doors and windows wide open, still keeping up its air of hospitable invitation, though now deserted and fallen into decay. A little farther on, through an opening, a few clustered roofs and chimneys of the Bear Valley village showed their distant red-brown tint among heavy masses of green. Eastward swelled up a great ridge, upon whose grassy slopes were rough serpentine outcrops, — groups of pines, and oak-groves with pale green foliage and clean white bark. Under the roots of this famous Mount Bullion have been mined those gold veins whose treasure enriched so few, whose promise allured so many.

As I altogether distrust my ability to speak of this region without sooner or later alluding to a certain discovery of some scientific value which I once made here, I deem it wise frankly to tell the story and discharge my mind of it at once, and if possible forever.

In the winter of 1863 I came to Bear Valley as the sole occupant of a stage-coach. The Sierras were quite cloud-hidden, and desolation such as drought has never before or since been able to make reigned in dreary monotony over all the plains from Stockton to Hornitas.

8 *   L

Ordinarily solitude is with me only a happy synonyme
for content; but throughout that ride I was preyed upon
by self-reproach, and in an aggravated manner.   The paleontologist of our survey, my senior in rank and experience, had just said of me, rather in sorrow than in
unkindness, yet with unwonted severity, " I believe that
fellow had rather sit on a peak all day, and stare at those
snow-mountains, than find a fossil in the metamorphic
Sierra " ; and, in spite of me, all that weary ride his judgment rang in my ear.

Can it be ? I asked myself; has a student of geology
so far forgotten his devotion to science ?   Am I really
fallen to the level of a mere nature-lover ?   Later, when
evening approached, and our wheels began to rumble over
upturned edges of Sierra slate, every jolt seemed aimed
at me, every thin sharp outcrop appeared risen up to
preach a sermon on my friend's text.

I re-dedicated myself to geology, and was framing a
resolution to delve for that greatly important but missing
link of evidence, the fossil which should clear up an old
unsolved riddle of upheaval age, when over to eastward a fervid crimson light smote the vapor-bank and
cleared a bright pathway through to the peaks, and on to
a pale sea-green sky.   Through this gateway of rolling
gold and red cloud the summits seemed infinitely high
and far, their stone and snow hung in the sky with
lucent delicacy of hue, brilliant as gems yet soft as air, —
a mosaic of amethyst and opal transfigured with passionate light, as gloriously above words as beyond art.   Obsolete shell-fishes in the metamorphic were promptly
forgotten, and during those lingering moments, while peak
after peak flushed and faded back into recesses of the
heavens, I forgot what paleontological unworthiness was
loading me down, becoming finally quite jolly of heart.

But for many days thereafter I did search and hope, leaving no stone unturned, and usually going so far as to break them open. Indeed, my third hammer and I were losing temper together, when one noon I was tired and sat down to rest and lunch in the bottom of Hell's Hollow, a cañon whose profound uninterestingness is quite beyond portrayal. Shut in by great monotonous slopes and innumerable spurs, each the exact fac-simile of the other; with no distance, no faintest suggestion of a snow-peak, only a lofty chaparral ridge sweeping around, cutting off all eastern lookout; with a few disordered boulders tumbled pell-mell into the bed of a feeble brooklet of bitter water, — it seemed to me the place of places for a fossil. Here was nadir, the snow-capped zenith of my heart banished even from sight. A swallow of tepid alkaline water, with which I crowned the frugal and appropriate lunch, burned my throat, and completed the misery of the occasion.

Jagged outcrops of slate cut through vulgar gold-dirt at my feet. Picking up my hammer to turn homeward, I noticed in the rock an object about the size and shape of a small cigar. It was the fossil, the object for which science had searched and yearned and despaired! There he reclined comfortably upon his side, half bedded in luxuriously fine-grained argillaceous material, — a plump pampered belemnites (if it is belemnites), whom the terrible ordeal of metamorphism had spared. I knelt and observed the radiating structure as well as the characteristic central cavity, and assured myself it was beyond doubt he. The age of the gold-belt was discovered! I was at pains to chip my victim out whole, and when he chose to break in two was easily consoled, reflecting that he would do as well gummed together.

I knew this mollusk perfectly by sight, could remember

how he looked on half a dozen plates of fossils, but I failed exactly to recollect his name. It troubled me that I could come so near uttering without ever precisely hitting upon it. In ten or fifteen minutes I judged it full time for my joy to begin.

Down the perspective of years I could see before me spectacled wise men of some scientific society, and one who pronounced my obituary, ending thus: "In summing up the character and labors of this fallen follower of science, let it never be forgotten that he discovered the belemnites"; and perhaps, I mused, they will put over me a slab of fossil rain-drops, those eternally embalmed tears of nature.

But all this came and went without the longed-for elation. There was no doubt I was not so happy as I thought I should be.

Once in after years I met an aged German paleontologist, fresh from his fatherland, where through threescore years and ten his soul had fattened on Solenhofen limestone and effete shells from many and wide-spread strata.

We were introduced.

"Ach!" he said, with a kindle of enthusiasm, "I have pleasure you to meet, when it is you which the cephalopoda discovered has."

Then turning to one who enacted the part of Ganymede, he remarked, "Zwei lager."

Now, with freed mind, I should say something of the foot-hills about our camp as they looked in June. Once before, the reader may remember, I pictured their autumn garb.

It has become a fixed habit with me to climb Mount Bullion whenever I get a chance. My winter Sundays were many times spent there in a peace and repose which Bear Valley village did not afford; for that hamlet gave itself up, after the Saturday night's sleep, to a day of hellish jocularity. The town passed through a period of horse-racing, noisy quarrelsome drinking, and disorderly service of Satan; then an hour in which the Spaniard loved and "treated" the "Americano." Later the Americano kicked the "damned Greaser" out of town. Manly forms slept serenely under steps, and the few "gentlemen of the old school" steadied themselves against the bar-room door-posts, and in ingenious language told of the good old pandemonium of 1849.

Thus Mount Bullion came to mean for me a Sabbath retreat over which heaven arched pure and blue; silent hours (marked by the slow sun) passing sacredly by in presence of nature and of God.

So now in June I climbed on a Sunday morning to my old retreat, found the same stone seat with leaning oak-tree back and wide low canopy of boughs. A little down to the left, welling among tufts of grass and waving tulips, is the spring which Mrs. Fremont found for her camp-ground. North and south for miles extends our ridge in gently rising or falling outline, its top broadly round, and for the most part an open oak-grove with grass carpet and mountain flowers in wayward loveliness of growth. West, you overlook a wide panorama; oak and pine mottled foot-hills with rusty groundwork and cloudings of green wander down in rolling lines to the ripe plain; beyond are plains, then coast ranges, rising in peaks, or curved down in passes, through which gray banks of fog drift in and vanish before the hot air of the plains. East, the Sierra slope is rent and gashed in a wilderness of cañons, yawning deep and savage. Miles of chaparral tangle in dense growth over walls and spurs, covering with kindly olive-green the staring red of riven mountain-side and gashed earth. Beyond this swells up the more

refined plateau and hill country made of granite and
trimmed with pine, bold domes rising above the green
cover; and there the sharp terrible front of El Capitan,
guarding Yosemite and looking down into its purple gulf.
Beyond, again, are the peaks, and among them one looms
sharpest. It is that Obelisk from which the great storm
drove Cotter and me in 1864. We were now bound to
push there as soon as grass should grow among the upper
cañons.

The air around my Sunday mountain in June is dry,
bland, and fragrant; a full sunlight ripens it to a perfect
temperature, giving you at once stimulus and rest. You
sleep in it without fear of dew, and no excess of hot or
cold breaks up the even flow of balmy delight. You see
the wild tulips open, and watch wind-ripples course over
slopes of thick-standing grass-blades. Birds, so rare on
plains or pine-hills, here sing you their fullest, and enjoy
with you the soft white light, or come to see you in your
chosen shadow and bathe in your spring.

Mountain oaks, less wonderful than great straight pines,
but altogether domestic in their generous way of reaching
out low long boughs, roofing in spots of shade, are the
only trees on the Pacific slope which seem to me at all
allied to men; and these quiet foot-hill summits, these
islands of modest, lovely verdure floating in an ocean of
sunlight, lifted enough above San Joaquin plains to reach
pure high air and thrill your blood and brain with mountain oxygen, are yet far enough below the rugged wild-
ness of pine and ice and rock to leave you in peace, and
not forever challenge you to combat. They are almost the
only places in the Sierras impressing me as rightly fitted
for human company. I cannot find in wholesale vineyards and ranches dotted along the Sierra foot anything
which savors of the eternal indigenous perfume of home.

They are scenes of speculation and thrift, of immense enterprise and comfort, with no end of fences and square miles of grain, with here and there astounding specimens of modern upholstery, to say nothing of pianos with elaborate legs and always discordant keys ; but they never comfort the soul with that air of sacred household reserve, of simple human poetry, which elsewhere greets you under plainer roofs, and broods over your days and nights familiarly.

Here on these still summits the oaks lock their arms and gather in groves around open slopes of natural park, and you are at home. A cottage or a castle would seem in keeping, nor would the savage gorges and snow-capped Sierras overcome the sober kindliness of these affectionate trees. It is almost as hard now, as I write, to turn my back on Mount Bullion and descend to camp again, as it was that afternoon in 1866.

Evening and supper were at hand, Hoover having achieved a repast of rabbit-pie, with salad from the Italian garden near at hand. It added no little to my peace that two obese squaws from the neighboring rancheria had come and squatted in silence on either side of our camp-fire, adding their statuesque sobriety and fire-flushed bronze to the dusky druidical scene.

To be welcomed at White and Hatch's next evening was reward for our dusty ride, and over the next day's familiar trail we hurried to Clark's, there again finding friends who took us by the hand. Another day's end found us within the Yosemite, and there for a week we walked and rode, studied and looked, revisiting all our old points, lingering hours here and half-days there, to complete within our minds the conception of this place. My chief has written so fully in his charming Yosemite book of all main facts and details, that I would not, if I could, rehearse them here.

What sentiment, what idea, does this wonder-valley leave upon the earnest observer? what impression does it leave upon his heart?

From some up-surging crag upon its brink you look out over wide expanse of granite swells, upon whose solid surface the firs climb and cluster, and afar on the sky-line only darken together in one deep green cover. Upward heave the eastern ridges; above them looms a white rank of peaks. Into this plateau is rent a chasm; the fresh-splintered granite falls down, down, thousands of feet in sheer blank faces or giant crags broken in cleft and stair, gorge and bluff, down till they sink under that winding ribbon of park with its flash of river among sunlit grass, its darkness, where within shadows of jutting wall cloud-like gather the pine companies, or, in summer opening, stand oak and cottonwood, casting together their lengthening shadow over meadow and pool. The falls, like torrents of snow, pour in white lines over purpled precipice, or, as the wind wills, float and drift in vanishing film of airy lacework.

Two leading ideas are wrought here with a force hardly to be seen elsewhere. First, the titanic power, the awful stress, which has rent this solid table-land of granite in twain; secondly, the magical faculty displayed by vegetation in redeeming the aspect of wreck and masking a vast geological tragedy behind draperies of fresh and living green. I can never cease marvelling how all this terrible crush and sundering is made fair, even lovely, by meadow, by wandering groves, and by those climbing files of pine which thread every gorge and camp in armies over every brink; nor can I ever banish from memory another gorge and fall, that of the Shoshone in Idaho, a sketch of which may help the reader to see more vividly those peculiarities of color and sentiment that make Yosemite so unique.

The Snake or Lewis's Fork of the Columbia River drains an oval basin, the extent of whose longer axis measures about four hundred miles westward from the base of the Rocky Mountains across Idaho and into the middle of Oregon, and whose breadth, in the direction of the meridian, averages about seventy miles. Irregular chains of mountains bound it in every direction, piling up in a few places to an elevation of nine thousand feet. The surface of this basin is unbroken by any considerable peak. Here and there, knobs, belonging to the earlier geological formations, rise above its level; and, in a few instances, dome-like mounds of volcanic rock are lifted from the expanse. It has an inclination from east to west, and a quite perceptible sag along the middle line. In general outline, the geology of the region is simple. Its bounding ranges were chiefly blocked out at the period of Jurassic upheaval, when the Sierra Nevada and Wahsatch Mountains were folded. Masses of upheaved granite, with overlying slates and limestones, form the main materials of the cordon of surrounding hills. During the Cretaceous and Tertiary periods, the entire basin, from the Rocky Mountains to the Blue Mountains of Oregon, was a fresh-water lake, on whose bottom was deposited a curious succession of sand and clay-beds, including, near the surface, a layer of white, infusorial silica. At the exposures of these rocks in the cañon-walls of the present drainage system are found ample evidences of the kind of life which flourished in the lake itself and lived upon its borders. Savage fishes, of the garpike type, and vast numbers of cyprinoids, together with mollusks, are among the prominent water-fossils. Enough relics of the land vegetation remain to indicate a flora of a sub-tropical climate; and among the land-fossils are numerous bones of elephant, camel, horse, elk, and deer.

The *savant* to whose tender mercies these *disjecta membra* have been committed, finds in the molluscan life the most recent types yet discovered in the American Tertiaries, — forms closely allied to existing Asiatic species. How and wherefore this lake dried up, and gave place to the present barren wilderness of sand and sage, is one of those profound conundrums of nature yet unguessed by geologists. From being a wide and beautiful expanse of water, edged by winding mountain-shores, with forest-clad slopes containing a fauna whose remains are now charming those light-minded fellows, the paleontologists, the scene has entirely changed, and a monotonous, blank desert spreads itself as far as the eye can reach. Only here and there, near the snowy mountain-tops, a bit of cool green contrasts refreshingly with the sterile uniformity of the plain. During the period of desiccation, perhaps in a measure accounting for it, a general flood of lava poured down from the mountains and deluged nearly the whole Snake basin. The chief sources of this lava lay at the eastern edge, where subsequent erosion has failed to level several commanding groups of volcanic peaks. The three buttes and three tetons mark centres of flow. Remarkable features of the volcanic period were the sheets of basaltic lava which closed the eruptive era, and in thin, continuous layers overspread the plain for three hundred miles. The earlier flows extended farthest to the west. The ragged, broken terminations of the later sheets recede successively eastward, in a broad, gradual stairway; so that the present topography of the basin is a gently inclined field of basaltic lava, sinking to the west, and finally, by a series of terraced steps, descending to the level of lacustrine sand-rocks which mark the bottom of the ancient lake and cover the plain westward into Oregon.

The head-waters of the Snake River, gathering snow-drainage from a considerable portion of the Rocky Mountains, find their way through a series of upland valleys to the eastern margin of the Snake plain, and there gathering in one main stream flow westward, occupying a gradually deepening cañon ; a narrow, dark gorge, water-worn through the thin sheets of basalt, cutting down as it proceeds to the westward, until, in longitude 114° 20′, it has worn seven hundred feet into the lava. Several tributaries flowing through similar though less profound cañons join the Snake both north and south. From the days of Lewis, for whom this Snake or Shoshone River was originally named, up to the present day, rumors have been current of cataracts in the Snake cañon. It is curious to observe that all the earlier accounts estimate their height as six hundred feet, which is exactly the figure given by the first Jesuit observers of Niagara. That erratic amateur Indian, Catlin, actually visited these falls ; and his account of them, while it entirely fails to give an adequate idea of their formation and grandeur, is nevertheless, in the main, truthful. Since the mining development of Idaho, several parties have visited and examined the Shoshone.

In October, 1868, with a small detachment of the United States Geological Survey of the 40th Parallel, the writer crossed Goose Creek Mountains, in northern Utah, and descended by the old Fort Boise road to the level of the Snake plain. A gray, opaque haze hung close to the ground, and shut out all distance. The monotony of sage-desert was overpowering. We would have given anything for a good outlook ; but for three days the mists continued, and we were forced to amuse ourselves by chasing occasional antelopes.

The evening we camped on Rock Creek was signal-

ized by a fierce wind from the northeast. It was a dry
storm, which continued with tremendous fury through the
night, dying away at daybreak, leaving the heavens brilliantly clear. We were breakfasting when the sun rose,
and shortly afterward, mounting into the saddle, headed
toward the cañon of the Shoshone. The air was cold
and clear. The remotest mountain-peaks upon the
horizon could be distinctly seen, and the forlorn details of their brown slopes stared at us as through a
vacuum. A few miles in front the smooth surface of
the plain was broken by a ragged, zigzag line of black,
which marked the edge of the farther wall of the
Snake cañon. A dull throbbing sound greeted us. Its
pulsations were deep, and seemed to proceed from the
ground beneath our feet. Leaving the cavalry to bring
up the wagon, my two friends and I galloped on, and
were quickly upon the edge of the cañon-wall. We
looked down into a broad, circular excavation, three
quarters of a mile in diameter, and nearly seven hundred
feet deep. East and north, over the edges of the cañon,
we looked across miles and miles of the Snake plain, far
on to the blue boundary mountains. The wall of the
gorge opposite us, like the cliff at our feet, sank in perpendicular bluffs nearly to the level of the river, the
broad excavation being covered by rough piles of black
lava and rounded domes of trachyte rock. An horizon as
level as the sea; a circling wall, whose sharp edges were
here and there battlemented in huge, fortress-like masses;
a broad river, smooth and unruffled, flowing quietly into
the middle of the scene, and then plunging into a labyrinth of rocks, tumbling over a precipice two hundred
feet high, and moving westward in a still, deep current to
disappear behind a black promontory. It is a strange,
savage scene: a monotony of pale blue sky, olive and

gray stretches of desert, frowning walls of jetty lava, deep
beryl-green of river-stretches, reflecting, here and there,
the intense solemnity of the cliffs, and in the centre a
dazzling sheet of foam. In the early morning light, the
shadows of the cliffs were cast over half the basin, defining themselves in sharp outline here and there on the
river. Upon the foam of the cataract one point of the
rock cast a cobalt-blue shadow. Where the river flowed
around the western promontory, it was wholly in shadow,
and of a deep sea-green. A scanty growth of coniferous
trees fringed the brink of the lower cliffs, overhanging
the river. Dead barrenness is the whole sentiment of the
scene. The mere suggestion of trees clinging here and
there along the walls serves rather to heighten than to
relieve the forbidding gloom of the place. Nor does the
flashing whiteness, where the river tears itself among the
rocky islands, or rolls in spray down the cliff, brighten
the aspect. In contrast with its brilliancy, the rocks
seem darker and more wild. The descent of four hundred feet, from our stand-point to the level of the river
above the falls, has to be made by a narrow, winding
path, among rough ledges of lava. We were obliged to
leave our wagon at the summit, and pack down the camp
equipment and photographic apparatus upon carefully led
mules. By midday we were comfortably camped on the
margin of the left bank, just above the brink of the falls.
My tent was pitched upon the edge of a cliff, directly
overhanging the rapids. From my door I looked over
the cataract, and, whenever the veil of mist was blown
aside, could see for a mile down the river. The lower
half of the cañon is excavated in a gray, porphyritic trachyte. It is over this material that the Snake falls.
Above the brink, the whole breadth of the river is broken
by a dozen small, trachyte islands, which the water has

carved into fantastic forms: rounding some into low domes, sharpening others into mere pillars, and now and then wearing out deep caves. At the very brink of the fall a few twisted evergreens cling with their roots to the rock, and lean over the abyss of foam with something of that air of fatal fascination which is apt to take possession of men.

In plan the fall recurves up stream in a deep horseshoe, resembling the outline of Niagara. The total breadth is about seven hundred feet, and the greatest height of the single fall about one hundred and ninety. Among the islands above the brink are several beautiful cascades, where portions of the river pour over in lace-like forms. The whole mass of cataract is one ever-varying sheet of spray. In the early spring, when swollen by the rapidly melted snows, the river pours over with something like the grand volume of Niagara, but, at the time of my visit, it was wholly white foam. Here and there, along the brink, the underlying rock shows through, and among the islands shallow green pools disclose the form of the underlying trachyte. Numberless rough shelves break the fall, but the volume is so great that they are only discovered by the glancing outward of the foam. The river below the falls is very deep. The right bank sinks into the water in a clear, sharp precipice, but on the left side a narrow, pebbly beach extends along the foot of the cliff. From the top of the wall, at a point a quarter of a mile below the falls, a stream has gradually worn a little stairway: thick growths of evergreens have huddled together in this ravine. By careful climbing, we descended to the level of the river. The trachytes are very curiously worn in vertical forms. Here and there an obelisk, either wholly or half detached from the cañon-wall, juts out like a buttress. Farther down, these projecting masses stand like a row of columns upon the left bank. Above them, a solid capping of black lava reaches out to the edge, and overhangs the river in abrupt black precipices. Wherever large fields of basalt have overflowed an earlier rock, and erosion has afterward laid it bare, there is found a strong tendency to fracture in vertical lines. The immense expansion of the upper surface from heat seems to cause deep fissures in the mass.

Under the influence of the cool shadow of cliffs and pine, and constant percolating of surface-waters, a rare fertility is developed in the ravines opening upon the cañon shore. A luxuriance of ferns and mosses, an almost tropical wealth of green leaves and velvety carpeting, line the banks. There are no rocks at the base of the fall. The sheet of foam plunges almost vertically into a dark, beryl-green, lake-like expanse of the river. Immense volumes of foam roll up from the cataract-base, and, whirling about in the eddying winds, rise often a thousand feet in the air. When the wind blows down the cañon, a gray mist obscures the river for half a mile; and when, as is usually the case in the afternoon, the breezes blow eastward, the foam-cloud curls over the brink of the fall, and hangs like a veil over the upper river. On what conditions depends the height to which the foam-cloud rises from the base of the fall, it is apparently impossible to determine. Without the slightest wind, the cloud of spray often rises several hundred feet above the cañon-wall, and again, with apparently the same conditions of river and atmosphere, it hardly reaches the brink. Incessant roar, reinforced by a thousand echoes, fills the cañon. Out of this monotone, from time to time, rise strange, wild sounds, and now and then may be heard a slow, measured beat, not unlike the recurring fall of breakers. From the white front of the cataract the eye constantly wanders up to the black, frowning parapet of lava. Angular bastions rise sharply from the general level of the wall, and here and there isolated blocks, profiling upon their sky-line, strikingly recall barbette batteries. To goad one's imagination up to the point of perpetually seeing resemblances of everything else in the forms of rocks, is the most vulgar vice of travellers. To refuse to see the architectural suggestions upon the Snake cañon, however, is to administer a flat snub to one's fancy. The whole edge of the cañon is deeply cleft in vertical *crevasses*. The actual brink is usually formed of irregular blocks and prisms of lava, poised upon their ends in an unstable equilibrium, ready to be tumbled over at the first leverage of the frost. Hardly an hour passes without the sudden boom of one of those rock-masses falling upon the ragged *débris* piles below.

Night is the true time to appreciate the full force of the scene. I lay and watched it many hours. The broken rim of the basin profiled itself upon a mass of drifting clouds where torn openings revealed gleams of pale moonlight and bits of remote sky trembling with misty stars. Intervals of light and blank darkness hurriedly followed each other. For a moment the black gorge would be crowded with forms. Tall cliffs, ramparts of lava, the rugged outlines of islands huddled together on the cataract's brink, faintly luminous foam breaking over black rapids, the swift, white leap of the river, and a ghostly, formless mist through which the cañon-walls and far reach of the lower river were veiled and unveiled again and again. A moment of this strange picture, and then a rush of black shadow, when nothing could be seen but the breaks in the clouds, the basin-rim, and a vague, white centre in the general darkness.

After sleeping on the nightmarish brink of the falls, it

was no small satisfaction to climb out of this Dantean gulf and find myself once more upon a pleasantly prosaic foreground of sage. Nothing more effectually banishes a melotragic state of the mind than the obtrusive ugliness and abominable smell of this plant. From my feet a hundred miles of it stretched eastward. A half-hour's walk took me out of sight of the cañon, and as the wind blew westward, only occasional indistinct pulsations of the fall could be heard. The sky was bright and cloudless, and arched in cheerful vacancy over the meaningless disk of the desert.

I walked for an hour, following an old Indian trail which occasionally approached within seeing distance of the river, and then, apparently quite satisfied, diverged again into the desert. When about four miles from the Shoshone, it bent abruptly to the north, and led to the cañon edge. Here again the narrow gorge widened into a broad theatre, surrounded, as before, by black vertical walls, and crowded over its whole surface by rude piles and ridges of volcanic rock. The river entered it from the east through a magnificent gateway of basalt, and, having reached the middle, flowed on either side of a low, rocky island, and plunges in two falls into a deep green basin. A very singular ridge of the basalt projects like an arm almost across the river, enclosing within its semicircle a bowl three hundred feet in diameter and two hundred feet deep. Within this the water was of the same peculiar beryl-green, dappled here and there by masses of foam which swim around and around with a spiral tendency toward the centre. To the left of the island half the river plunges off an overhanging lip, and falls about one hundred and fifty feet, the whole volume reaching the surface of the basin many feet from the wall. The other half has worn away the edge, and de-

9   M

scends in a tumbling cascade at an angle of about forty-five degrees. The river at this point has not yet worn through the fields of basaltic lava which form the upper four hundred feet of the plain. Between the two falls it cuts through the remaining beds of basalt, and has eroded its channel a hundred feet into underlying porphyritic trachyte. The trachyte erodes far more easily than the basalt, and its resultant forms are quite unlike those of the black lava. The trachyte islands and walls are ex-cavated here and there in deep caves, leaving island masses in the forms of mounds and towers. In general, spherical outlines predominate, while the erosion of the• basalt results always in sharp, perpendicular cliffs, with a steeply inclined talus of ragged *débris*.

The cliffs around the upper cataract are inferior to those of the Shoshone. While the level of the upper plain remains nearly the same, the river constantly deep-ens the channel in its westward course. In returning from the upper fall, I attempted to climb along the very edge of the cliff, in order to study carefully the habits of the basalt; but I found myself in a labyrinth of side *cre-vasses* which were cut into the plain from a hundred to a thousand feet back from the main wall. These recesses were usually in the form of an amphitheatre, with black walls two hundred feet high, and a bottom filled with immense fragments of basalt rudely piled together.

By dint of hard climbing I reached the actual brink in a few places, and saw the same general features each time: the cañon successively widening and narrowing, its walls here and there approaching each other and standing like pillars of a gateway; the river alternately flowing along smooth, placid reaches of level, and rush-ing swiftly down rocky cascades. Here and there along the cliff are disclosed mouths of black caverns, where

the lava seems to have been blown up in the form
of a great blister, as if the original flow had poured over
some pool of water, and, converted into steam by contact
with the hot rock, had been blown up bubble-like by its
immense expansion. I continued my excursions along
the cañon west of the Shoshone. About a mile below
the fall a very fine promontory juts sharply out and projects nearly to the middle of the cañon. Climbing with
difficulty along its toppling crest, I reached a point
which I found composed of immense angular fragments
piled up in dangerous poise. Eastward, the battlemented
rocks around the falls limited the view; but westward I
could see down long reaches of river, where islands of
trachyte rose above white cascades. A peculiar and fine
effect is noticeable upon the river during all the midday.
The shadow of the southern cliff is cast down here and
there, completely darkening the river, but often defining
itself upon the water. The contrast between the rich,
gem-like green of the sunlit portions and the deep violet
shadow of the cliff is of extreme beauty. The Snake
River deriving its volume wholly from the melting of
the mountain snows, is a direct gauge of the annual
advance of the sun. In June and July it is a tremendous torrent, carrying a full half of the Columbia. From
the middle of July it constantly shrinks, reaching its
minimum in midwinter. At the lowest, it is a river
equal to the Sacramento or Connecticut.

After ten days devoted to walking around the neighborhood and studying the falls and rocks, we climbed to
our wagon, and rested for a farewell look at the gorge.
It was with great relief that we breathed the free air of
the plain, and turned from the rocky cañon where darkness, and roar, and perpetual cliffs had bounded our
senses, and headed southward, across the noiseless plain.

Far ahead rose a lofty, blue barrier, a mountain-wall, marbled upon its summit by flecks of perpetual snow. A deep notch in its profile opened a gateway. Toward this, for leagues ahead of us, a white thread in the gray desert marked the winding of our road. Those sensitively organized creatures, the mules, thrilled with relief at their escape from the cañons, pressed forward with a vigor that utterly silenced the customary poppings of the whip, and expurgated the language of the driver from his usual breaking of the Third Commandment.

The three great falls of America, — Niagara, Shoshone, and Yosemite, — all happily bearing Indian names, are as characteristically different as possible. There seems little left for a cataract to express. Niagara rolls forward with something like the inexorable sway of a natural law. It is force, power; forever banishing before its irresistible rush all ideas of restraint.

No sheltering pine or mountain distance of up-piled Sierras guards the approach to the Shoshone. You ride upon a waste, — the pale earth stretched in desolation. Suddenly you stand upon a brink, as if the earth had yawned. Black walls flank the abyss. Deep in the bed a great river fights its way through labyrinths of blackened ruins, and plunges in foaming whiteness over a cliff of lava. You turn from the brink as from a frightful glimpse of the Inferno, and when you have gone a mile the earth seems to have closed again; every trace of cañon has vanished, and the stillness of the desert reigns.

As you stand at the base of those cool walls of granite that rise to the clouds from the green floor of Yosemite, a beautiful park, carpeted with verdure, expands from your feet. Vast and stately pines band with their shadows the sunny reaches of the pure Merced. An arch of blue bridges over from cliff to cliff. From the far summit of a wall of pearly granite, over stains of purple and yellow, — leaping, as it were, from the very cloud, — falls a silver scarf, light, lace-like, graceful, luminous, swayed by the wind.

The cliffs' repose is undisturbed by the silvery fall whose endlessly varying forms of wind-tossed spray lend an element of life to what would otherwise be masses of inanimate stone. The Yosemite is a grace. It is an adornment. It is a ray of light on the solid front of the precipice.

From Yosemite our course was bent toward the Merced Obelisk. An afternoon in early July brought us to camp in the self-same spot where Cotter and I had bivouacked in the storm more than two years before.

I remembered the crash and wail of those two dreary nights, the thunderous fulness of tempest beating upon cliffs, and the stealthy, silent snow-burial; and perhaps to the memory of that bitter experience was added the contrasting force of to-day's beauty.

A warm afternoon sun poured through cloudless skies into one rocky amphitheatre. The little alpine meadow and full arrowy brook were flanked upon either side by broad rounded masses of granite, and margined by groups of vigorous upland trees; firs for the most part, but watched over here and there by towering pines and great aged junipers whose massive red trunks seemed welded to the very stone.

It was altogether exhilarating; even Little Billy, the gray horse, found it so, and devoted more time to practical jokes upon thick-headed mules than to the rich and tempting verdure; nor did the high, cool air banish from his tender heart a glowing Platonic affection for our brown mare Sally.

To the ripened charms of middle age Sally united something more than the memory of youth; she was remarkably plump and well-preserved; her figure firm and elastic, and she did not hesitate to display it with many little arts. In presence of her favored Billy she drew deep sighs, and had quite an irresistible fashion of turning sadly aside and moving away among trees alone, as if she had no one to love her, — a wile never failing to bring him to her side and elicit such attention as smoothing her mane or even a pressure of lips upon her brow. And woe to the emotional mule who ventured to cross our little meadow just to feel for a moment the soft comfort of her presence. With the bitterness of a rejected suit he always bore away shoe-prints of jealous Billy.

He led her quietly down to the brook, and never drank a drop until the mare was done; then they paid a call at camp, nosing about among the kettles with familiar freedom, nibbling playfully at dish-towel and coffee-pot, and when we threw sticks at them, trotted off as closely as if they had been harnessed together. In quiet moonlit hours, before I went to bed, I saw them still side by side, her head leaning over his withers; Billy at *qui vive* staring dramatically with pointed ears into forest depths, a true and watchful guardian.

A little reconnoitering had shown us the most direct way to the Obelisk, whose sharp summit looked from the moraine to west of us as grand and alluring as we had ever thought it.

There was in our hope of scaling this point something more than mere desire to master a difficult peak. It was a station of great topographical value, the apex of many triangles, and, more than all, would command a grander view of the Merced region than any other summit.

July 11th, about five P. M., Gardner and I strapped

packs upon our shoulders. My friend's load consisted of
the Temple transit, his blanket, and a great tin cup;
mine was made up of field-glass, compass, level, blanket,
and provisions for both, besides the barometer which, as
usual, I slung over one shoulder.

For the first time that year we found ourselves slowly
zigzagging to and fro, following a grade with that peculiarly deliberate gait to which mountaineering experience
very soon confines one. Black firs and thick-clustered
pines covered in clumps all the lower slope, but, ascending, we came more and more into open ground, walking
on glacial *débris* among trains of huge boulders and occasional thickets of slender, delicate young trees. Emer-
ging finally into open granite country, we came full in
sight of our goal, whose great western precipice rose sheer
and solid above us.

From the south base of the Obelisk a sharp mural
ridge curves east, surrounding an amphitheatre whose
sloping rugged sides were picturesquely mottled in snow
and stone. From the summit of this ridge we knew we
should look over into the upper Merced basin, a great
billowy granite depression lying between the Merced
group and Mount Lyell; the birthplace of all those ice
rivers and deep-cañoned torrents which join in the Little
Yosemite and form the river Merced. Toward this we
pressed, hurrying rapidly, as the sun declined, in hopes
of making our point before darkness should obscure the
terra incognita beyond.

It put us at our best to hasten over the rough, rudely
piled blocks and up cracks among solid bluffs of granite,
but with the sun fully half an hour high we reached
the Obelisk foot and looked from our ridge-top eastward
into the new land.

From our feet granite and ice in steep, roof-like curves

fell abruptly down to the Merced Cañon brink, and beyond, over the great gulf, rose terraces and ridges of
sculptured stone, dressed with snow-field, one above another, up to the eastern rank of peaks whose sharp solid
forms were still in full light.

From below, it is always a most interesting feature of
the mountaineer's daily life to watch fading sunlight upon
the summit-rocks and snow. There is something peculiarly charming in the deep carmine flush and in the pale
gradations of violet and cool blue-purple into which it
successively fades. We were now in the very midst of
this alpine glow. Our rocky amphitheatre opening directly
to the sun was crowded full of this pure red light; snow-
fields warmed to deepest rose, gnarled stems of dead pines
were dark vermilion, the rocks yellow, and the vast body
of the Obelisk at our left one spire of gold piercing the
sapphire zenith. Eastward, far below us, the Illilluette
basin lay in a peculiarly mild haze, its deep carpet of
forest warmed into faint bronze, and the bare domes and
rounded granite ridges which everywhere rise above the
trees were yellow, of a soft creamy tint. Farther down,
every foothill was perceptibly reddened under the level
beams. Sunlight reflecting from every object shot up to
us, enriching the brightness of our amphitheatre.

We drank and breathed the light, its mellow warmth
permeating every fibre. We spread our blankets under
the lee of an overhanging rock, sheltered from the keen
east-wind, and in full view of the broad western horizon.

After a short half-hour of this wonderful light the sun
rested for an instant upon the Coast ranges, and sank,
leaving our mountains suddenly dead, as if the very breath
of life had ebbed away; cold gray shadows covering their
rigid bodies, and pale sheets of snow half shrouding their
forms.

For a full hour after the sun went down we did little else than study the western sky, watching with greatest interest a wonderful permanence and singular gradation of lingering light. Over two hundred miles of horizon a low stratum of pure orange covered the sky for seven or eight degrees; above that another narrow band of beryl-green, and then the cool dark evening blue.

I always notice, whenever one gets. a very wide view of remote horizon from some lofty mountain-top, the sky loses its high domed appearance, the gradations reaching but a few degrees upward from the earth, creating the general form of an inverted saucer. The orange and beryl bands occupied only about fifteen degrees in altitude, but swept around nearly from north to south. It was as if a wonderfully transparent and brilliant rainbow had been stretched along the sky-line. At eleven the colors were still perceptible, and at midnight, when I rose to observe the thermometer, they were gone, but a low faint zone of light still lingered.

At gray dawn we were up and cooking our rasher of bacon, and soon had shouldered our instruments and started for the top.

The Obelisk is flattened, and expands its base into two sharp serrated ridges which form its north and south edges. The broad faces turned to the east and west are solid and utterly inaccessible; the latter being almost vertical, the former quite too steep to climb. We started, therefore, to work our way up the south edge, and, having crossed a little ravine from whose head we could look down eastward upon steep thousand-foot *névé*, and on the western along the forest-covered ridge up which we had clambered, began in good earnest to mount rough blocks of granite.

The edge here is made of immense broken rocks poised

9 *

on each other in delicate balance, vast masses threatening to topple over at a touch.   This blade has from a distance a considerably smooth and even appearance, but we
found it composed of pinnacles often a hundred feet high,
separated from the main top by a deep vertical cleft.
More than once, after struggling to the top of one of these
pinnacles, we were obliged to climb down the same way
in order to avoid the notches.   Finally, when we had
reached the brink of a vertical *cul-de-sac,* the edge no
longer afforded us even a foothold.   There were left but
the smooth impossible western face and the treacherous
cracked front of the eastern precipice.   We were driven
out upon the latter, and here forced to climb with the
very greatest care, one of us always in advance making
sure of his foothold, the other passing up instruments by
hand, and then cautiously following.

In this way we spent nearly a full hour going from
crack to crack, clinging by the least protruding masses of
stone, now and then looking over our shoulders at the
wreck of granite, the slopes of ice, and frozen lake thousands of feet below, and then upward to gather courage
from the bold red spike which still rose grandly above
us.

At last we struggled up to what we had all along believed the summit, and found ourselves only on a minor
turret, the great needle still a hundred feet above.   From
rock to rock and crevice to crevice we made our way up
a fractured edge until within fifty feet of the top, and
here its sharp angle rose smooth and vertical, the eastern
precipice carved in a flat face upon the one side, the
western broken by a smoothly curved recess like the
corner of a room.   No human being could scale the edge.
An arctic bluebird fluttered along the eastern slope in
vain quest of a foothold, and alighted panting at our

feet. One step more and we stood together on a little detached pinnacle, where, by steadying ourselves against the sharp, vertical Obelisk edge, we could rest, although the keen sense of steepness below was not altogether pleasing.

About seven feet across the open head of a *cul-de-sac* (a mere recess in the west face) was a vertical crack riven into the granite not more than three feet wide, but as much as eight feet deep; in it were wedged a few loose boulders; below, it opened out into space. At the head of this crack a rough crevice led up to the summit.

Summoning nerve, I knew I could make the leap, but the life and death question was whether the *débris* would give way under my weight, and leave me struggling in the smooth recess, sure to fall and be dashed to atoms.

Two years we had longed to climb that peak, and now within a few yards of the summit no weak-heartedness could stop us. I thought, should the *débris* give way, by a very quick turn and powerful spring I could regain our rock in safety.

There was no discussion, but, planting my foot on the brink, I sprang, my side brushing the rough projecting crag. While in the air I looked down, and a picture stamped itself on my brain never to be forgotten. The *débris* crumbled and moved. I clutched both sides of the cleft, relieving all possible weight from my feet. The rocks wedged themselves again, and I was safe.

It was a delicate feat of balancing for us to bridge that chasm with a transit and pass it across; the view it afforded down the abyss was calculated to make a man cool and steady.

Barometer and knapsack were next passed over. I

placed them all at the crevice head, and flattened myself
against the rock to make room for Gardner. I shall
never forget the look in his eye as he caught a glimpse
of the abyss in his leap. It gave me such a chill as no
amount of danger nor even death coming to myself could
ever give. The *débris* grated under his weight an instant
and wedged themselves again.

We sprang up on the rocks like chamois, and stood on
the top shouting for joy.

Our summit was four feet across, not large enough for
the transit instrument and both of us; so I, whose duties
were geological, descended to a niche a few feet lower and
sat down to my writing.

The sense of aerial isolation was thrilling. Away below, rocks, ridges, crags, and fields of ice swell up in jos-
tling confusion to make a base from which springs the
spire of stone 11,600 feet high. On all sides I could
look right down at the narrow pedestal. Eastward great
ranks of peaks culminating in Mount Lyell were in
full clear view; all streams and cañons tributary to the
Merced were beneath us in map-like distinctness. Afar
to the west lay the rolling plateau gashed with cañons; there the white line of Yosemite Fall; and beyond, half submerged in warm haze, my Sunday mountain.

The same little arctic bluebird came again and perched
close by me, pouring out his sweet simple song with a
gayety and freedom which wholly charmed me.

During our four hours' stay the thought that we must
make that leap again gradually intruded itself, and whether
writing or studying the country I could not altogether
free myself from its pressure.

It was a relief when we packed up and descended to
the horrible cleft to actually meet our danger. We had

now an unreliable footing to spring from, and a mere block of rock to balance us after the jump.

We sprang strongly, struck firmly, and were safe. We worked patiently down the east face, wound among blocks and pinnacles of the lower descent, and hurried through moraines to camp, well pleased that the Obelisk had not vanquished us.

X.

CUT–OFF COPPLES'S.

1870.

ONE October day, as Kaweah and I travelled by ourselves over a lonely foothill trail, I came to consider myself the friend of woodpeckers. With rather more reserve
as regards the bluejay, let me admit great interest in his
worldly wisdom. As an instance of co-operative living
the partnership of these two birds is rather more hopeful
than most mundane experiments. For many autumn and
winter months such food as their dainty taste chooses is
so rare throughout the Sierras that in default of any climatic temptation to migrate the birds get in harvests
with annual regularity and surprising labor. Oak and
pine mingle in open growth. Acorns from the one are
their grain ; the soft pine bark is granary ; and this the
process : —

Armies of woodpeckers drill small round holes in the
bark of standing pine-trees, sometimes perforating it
thickly up to twenty or thirty and even forty feet above
the ground ; then about equal numbers of woodpeckers
and jays gather acorns, rejecting always the little cup,
and insert the gland tightly in the pine bark with its
tender base outward and exposed to the air.

A woodpecker, having drilled a hole, has its exact
measure in mind, and after examining a number of
acorns makes his selection, and never fails of a perfect
fit. Not so the jolly, careless jay, who picks up any
sound acorn he finds, and if it is too large for a hole,

drops it in the most off-hand way, as if it were an affair of no consequence; utters one of his dry chuckling
squawks, and either tries another or loafs about lazily
watching the hard-working woodpeckers.

Thus they live, amicably harvesting, and with this
sequel: those acorns in which grubs form become the
sole property of woodpeckers, while all sound ones fall to
the jays. Ordinarily chances are in favor of woodpeckers,
and when there are absolutely no sound nuts the jays
sell short, so to speak, and go over to Nevada and specu-
late in juniper-berries.

The monotony of hill and glade failing to interest me,
and in default of other diversion, I all day long watched
the birds, recalling how many gay and successful jays I
knew who lived, as these, on the wit and industry of less
ostentatious woodpeckers; thinking, too, what naïvely
dogmatic and richly worded political economy Mr. Ruskin would phrase from my feathered friends. Thus I
came to Ruskin, wishing I might see the work of his
idol, and after that longing for some equal artist who
should arise and choose to paint our Sierras as they are,
with all their color-glory, power of innumerable pine and
countless pinnacle, gloom of tempest, or splendor, where
rushing light shatters itself upon granite crag, or burns in
dying rose upon far fields of snow.

Had I rubbed Aladdin's lamp? A turn in the trail
brought suddenly in view a man who sat under shadow
of oaks, painting upon a large canvas.

As I approached, the artist turned half round upon his
stool, rested pallette and brushes upon one knee, and in
familiar tone said, "Dern'd if you ain't just naturally
ketched me at it! Get off and set down. You ain't going
for no doctor, I know."

My artist was of short, good-natured, butcher-boy

make-up, dressed in what had formerly been black broad-cloth, with an enlivening show of red flannel shirt about the throat, wrists, and a considerable display of the same where his waistcoat might once have overlapped a strained but as yet coherent waistband. The cut of these garments, by length of coat-tail and voluminous leg, proudly asserted a "Bay" origin. His small feet were squeezed into tight, short boots, with high, raking heels.

A round face, with small full mouth, non-committal nose, and black protruding eyes, showed no more sign of the ideal temperament than did the broad daub upon his square yard of canvas.

"Going to Copples's?" inquired my friend.

That was my destination, and I answered, "Yes."

"That 's me," he ejaculated. "Right over there, down below those two oaks! Ever there?"

"No."

"My *studio* 's there now"; giving impressive accent to the word.

All the while these few words were passing he scrutinized me with unconcealed curiosity, puzzled, as well he might be, by my dress and equipment. Finally, after I had tied Kaweah to a tree and seated myself by the easel, and after he had absently rubbed some raw sienna into his little store of white, he softly ventured: "Was you looking out a ditch?"

"No," I replied.

He neatly rubbed up the white and sienna with his "blender," unconsciously adding a dash of Veronese green, gazed at my leggings, then at the barometer, and again meeting my eye with a look as if he feared I might be a disguised duke, said in slow tone, with hyphens of silence between each two syllables, giving to his language all the dignity of an unabridged Webster, "I would take pleasure in stating that my name is Hank G. Smith, artist"; and, seeing me smile, he relaxed a little, and giving the blender another vigorous twist, added, "I would request yours."

Mr. Smith having learned my name, occupation, and that my home was on the Hudson, near New York, quickly assumed a familiar me-and-you-old-fel' tone, and rattled on merrily about his winter in New York spent in "going through the Academy," — a period of deep moment to one who before that painted only wagons for his livelihood.

Storing away canvas, stool, and easel in a deserted cabin close by, he rejoined me, and, leading Kaweah by his lariat, I walked beside Smith down the trail toward Copples's.

He talked freely, and as if composing his own biography, beginning: —

"California-born and mountain-raised, his nature soon drove him into a painter's career." Then he reverted fondly to New York and his experience there.

"O no!" he mused in pleasant irony, "he never spread his napkin over his legs and partook French victuals up to old Delmonico's. 'T was n't H. G. which took *her* to the theatre."

In a sort of stage-aside to me, he added, "*She* was a *model!* Stood for them sculptors, you know; perfectly virtuous, and built from the ground up." Then, as if words failed him, made an expressive gesture with both hands over his shirt-bosom to indicate the topography of her figure, and, sliding them down sharply against his waistband, he added, "Anatomical torso!"

Mr. Smith found relief in meeting one so near himself, as he conceived me to be, in habit and experience. The long-pent-up emotions and ambitions of his life found ready utterance, and a willing listener.

N

I learned that his aim was to become a characteristically California painter, with special designs for making himself famous as the delineator of mule-trains and ox-wagons; to be, as he expressed it, "the Pacific Slope Bonheur."

"There," he said, "is old Eastman Johnson; he's made the riffle on barns, and that everlasting girl with the ears of corn; but it ain't *life*, it ain't got the real git-up.

"If you want to see *the* thing, just look at a Gerome; his Arab folks and Egyptian dancing-girls, they ain't assuming a pleasant expression and looking at spots while their likenesses is took.

"H. G. will discount Eastman yet."

He avowed his great admiration of Church, which, with a little leaning toward Mr. Gifford, seemed his only hearty approval.

"It's all Bierstadt and Bierstadt and Bierstadt nowadays! What has he done but twist and skew and distort and discolor and belittle and be-pretty this whole doggonned country? Why, his mountains are too high and too slim; they'd blow over in one of our fall winds.

"I've herded colts two summers in Yosemite, and honest now, when I stood right up in front of his picture, I did n't know it.

"He has n't what old Ruskin calls for."

By this time the station buildings were in sight, and far down the cañon, winding in even grade around spur after spur, outlined by a low clinging cloud of red dust, we could see the great Sierra mule-train, — that industrial gulf-stream flowing from California plains over into arid Nevada, carrying thither materials for life and luxury. In a vast perpetual caravan of heavy wagons, drawn by teams of from eight to fourteen mules, all the supplies of many cities and villages were hauled across the Sierra at an immense cost, and with such skill of driving and generalship of mules as the world has never seen before.

Our trail descended toward the grade, quickly bringing us to a high bank immediately overlooking the trains a few rods below the group of station buildings.

I had by this time learned that Copples, the former station-proprietor, had suffered amputation of the leg three times, receiving from the road men, in consequence, the name of "Cut-off," and that, while his doctors disagreed as to whether they better try a fourth, the kindly hand of death had spared him that pain, and Mrs. Copples an added extortion in the bill.

The dying "Cut-off" had made his wife promise she would stay by and carry on the station until all his debts, which were many and heavy, should be paid, and then do as she chose.

The poor woman, a New Englander of some refinement, lingered, sadly fulfilling her task, though longing for liberty.

When Smith came to speak of Sarah Jane, her niece, a new light kindled in my friend's eye.

"You never saw Sarah Jane?" he inquired.

I shook my head.

He went on to tell me that he was living in hope of making her Mrs. H. G., but that the bar-keeper also indulged a hope, and as this important functionary was a man of ready cash, and of derringers and few words, it became a delicate matter to avow open rivalry; but it was evident my friend's star was ascendant, and, learning that he considered himself to possess the "dead-wood," and to have "gaited" the bar-keeper, I was more than amused, even comforted.

It was pleasure to sit there leaning against a vigorous old oak while Smith opened his heart to me, in easy confidence, and, with quick eye watching the passing mules, pencilled in a little sketch-book a leg, a head, or such

212 MOUNTAINEERING IN THE SIERRA NEVADA.

portions of body and harness as seemed to him useful for future works.

"These are notes," he said, "and I 've pretty much made up my mind to paint my great picture on a *gee-pull*. I 'll scumble in a sunset effect, lighting up the dust, and striking across the backs of team and driver, and I 'll paint a come-up-there-d'n-you look on the old teamster's face, and the mules will be just a humping their little selves and laying down to work like they 'd expire. And the wagon! Don't you see what fine color-material there is in the heavy load and canvas-top with sunlight and shadow in the folds? And that 's what 's the matter with H. G. Smith.

"Orders, sir, orders; that 's what I 'll get then, and I 'll take my little old Sarah Jane and light out for New York, and you 'll see *Smith* on a studio doorplate, and folks 'll say, Fine feeling for nature, has Smith!"

I let this singular man speak for himself in his own vernacular, pruning nothing of its idiom or slang, as you shall choose to call it. In this faithful transcript there are words I could have wished to expunge, but they are his, not mine, and illustrate his mental construction.

The breath of most Californians is as unconsciously charged with slang as an Italian's of garlic, and the two, after all, have much the same function; you touch the bowl or your language, but should never let either be fairly recognized in salad or conversation. But Smith's English was the well undefiled when compared with what I every moment heard from the current of teamsters which set constantly by us in the direction of Copples's.

Close in front came a huge wagon piled high with cases of freight, and drawn along by a team of twelve mules, whose heavy breathing and drenched skins showed them hard-worked and well tired out. The driver looked anxiously ahead at a soft spot in the road, and on at the station, as if calculating whether his team had courage left to haul through.

He called kindly to them, cracked his black-snake whip, and all together they strained bravely on.

The great van rocked, settled a little on the near side, and stuck fast.

With a look of despair the driver got off and laid the lash freely among his team; they jumped and jerked, frantically tangled themselves up, and at last all sulked and became stubbornly immovable. Meanwhile, a mile of teams behind, unable to pass on the narrow grade, came to an unwilling halt.

About five wagons back I noticed a tall Pike, dressed in checked shirt, and pantaloons tucked into jack-boots. A soft felt hat, worn on the back of his head, displayed long locks of flaxen hair, which hung freely about a florid pink countenance, noticeable for its pair of violent little blue eyes, and facial angle rendered acute by a sharp, long nose.

This fellow watched the stoppage with impatience, and at last, when it was more than he could bear, walked up by the other teams with a look of wrath absolutely devilish. One would have expected him to blow up with rage; yet withal his gait and manner were cool and soft in the extreme. In a bland, almost tender voice, he said to the unfortunate driver, "My friend, perhaps I can help you"; and his gentle way of disentangling and patting the leaders as he headed them round in the right direction, would have given him a high office under Mr. Bergh. He leisurely examined the embedded wheel, and cast an eye along the road ahead. He then began in rather excited manner to swear, pouring it out louder and more profane, till he utterly eclipsed the most horrid blasphe-

mies I ever heard, piling them up thicker and more
fiendish till it seemed as if the very earth must open and
engulf him.

I noticed one mule after another give a little squat,
bringing their breasts hard against the collars, and straining traces, till only one old mule with ears back and dangling chain still held out. The Pike walked up and yelled
one gigantic oath; her ears sprang forward, she squatted
in terror, and the iron links grated under her strain. He
then stepped back and took the rein, every trembling mule
looking out of the corner of its eye and listening at *qui
vive.*

With a peculiar air of deliberation and of childlike
simplicity, he said in every-day tones, "Come up there,
mules!"

One quick strain, a slight rumble, and the wagon rolled
on to Copples's.

Smith and I followed, and as we neared the house he
punched me familiarly and said, as a brown petticoat disappeared in the station door, "There's Sarah Jane! When
I see that girl I feel like I'd reach out and gather her
in"; then clasping her imaginary form as if she was about
to dance with him, he executed a couple of waltz turns,
softly intimating, "That's what's the matter with H. G."

Kaweah being stabled, we betook ourselves to the office,
which was of course bar-room as well. As I entered, the
unfortunate teamster was about paying his liquid compliment to the florid Pike. Their glasses were filled. "My
respects," said the little driver. The whiskey became lost
to view, and went eroding its way through the dust these
poor fellows had swallowed. He added, "Well, Billy,
you *can* swear."

"Swear?" repeated the Pike in a tone of incredulous
questioning. "Me swear?" as if the compliment were

greater than his modest desert. "No, I can't blaspheme worth a cuss. You 'd jest orter hear Pete Green. *He can exhort the impenitent mule.* I 've known a ten-mule-team to renounce the flesh and haul thirty-one thousand through a foot of clay mud under one of his outpourings."

As a hotel, Copples's is on the Mongolian plan, which means that dining-room and kitchen are given over to the mercies — never very tender — of Chinamen; not such Chinamen as learned the art of pig-roasting that they might be served up by Elia, but the average John, and a sadly low average that John is. I grant him a certain general air of thrift, admitting, too, that his lack of sobriety never makes itself apparent in loud Celtic brawl. But he is, when all is said, and in spite of timid and fawning obedience, a very poor servant.

Now and then at one friend's house it has happened to me that I dined upon artistic Chinese cookery, and all they who come home from living in China smack their lips over the relishing *cuisine.* I wish they had sat down that day at Copples's. No; on second thought I would spare them.

John may go peacefully to North Adams and make shoes for us, but I shall not solve the awful domestic problem by bringing him into my kitchen; certainly so long as Howells's "Mrs. Johnson" lives, nor even while I can get an Irish lady to torment me, and offer the hospitality of my home to her cousins.

After the warning bell, fifty or sixty teamsters inserted their dusty heads in buckets of water, turned their once white neck-handkerchiefs inside out, producing a sudden effect of clean linen, and made use of the two mournful wrecks of combs which hung on strings at either side the Copples's mirror. Many went to the bar and partook of a "dust-cutter." There was then such clearing of throats, and such loud and prolonged blowing of noses as may not often be heard upon this globe.

In the calm which ensued, conversation sprung up on "lead harness," the "Stockton wagon that had went off the grade," with here and there a sentiment called out by two framed lithographic belles, who in great richness of color and scantiness of raiment flanked the bar-mirror; — a dazzling reflector, chiefly destined to portray the bar-keeper's back hair, which work of art involved much affectionate labor.

A second bell, and rolling away of doors revealed a long dining-room, with three parallel tables, cleanly set and watched over by Chinamen, whose fresh white clothes and bright olive-buff skin made a contrast of color which was always chief among my yearnings for the Nile.

While I loitered in the background every seat was taken, and I found myself with a few dilatory teamsters destined to await a second table.

The dining-room communicated with a kitchen beyond by means of two square apertures cut in the partition wall. Through these portholes a glare of red light poured, except when the square framed a Chinese cook's head, or discharged hundreds of little dishes.

The teamsters sat down in patience; a few of the more elegant sort cleaned their nails with the three-tine forks, others picked their teeth with them, and nearly all speared with this implement small specimens from the dishes before them, securing a pickle or a square inch of pie or even that luxury a dried apple; a few, on tilted-back chairs, drummed upon the bottom of their plates the latest tune of the road.

When fairly under way the scene became active and animated beyond belief. Waiters balancing upon their arms twenty or thirty plates, hurried along and shot them dexterously over the teamsters' heads with crash and spatter.

Beans swimming in fat, meats slimed with pale ropy gravy, and over everything a faint Mongol odor, — the flavor of moral degeneracy and of a disintegrating race.

Sharks and wolves may no longer be figured as types of prandial haste. My friends, the teamsters, stuffed and swallowed with a rapidity which was alarming but for the dexterity they showed, and which could only have come of long practice.

In fifteen minutes the room was empty, and those fellows who were not feeding grain to their mules lighted cigars and lingered around the bar.

Just then my artist rushed in, seized me by the arm, and said in my ear, "We 'll have *our* supper over to Mrs. Copples's. O no, I guess not — Sarah Jane — arms peeled — cooking up stuff — old woman gone into the milk-room with a skimmer." He then added that if I wanted to see what I had been spared, I might follow him.

We went round an angle of the building and came upon a high bank, where, through wide-open windows, I could look into the Chinese kitchen.

By this time the second table of teamsters were under way, and the waiters yelled their orders through to the three cooks.

This large unpainted kitchen was lighted up by kerosene lamps. Through clouds of smoke and steam dodged and sprang the cooks, dripping with perspiration and grease, grabbing a steak in the hand and slapping it down on the gridiron, slipping and sliding around on the damp floor, dropping a card of biscuits and picking them up again in their fists, which were garnished by the whole bill of fare. The red papers with Chinese inscriptions, and little joss-sticks here and there pasted upon each

10

wall, the spry devils themselves, and that faint sickening odor of China which pervaded the room, combined to produce a sense of deep sober gratitude that I had not risked their fare.

"Now," demanded Smith, "You see that there little white building yonder?"

I did.

He struck a contemplative position, leaned against the house, extending one hand after the manner of the minstrel sentimentalist, and softly chanted:—

"'T is, O 't is the cottage of me love";

and there 's where they 're getting up as nice a little supper as can be found on this road or any other. Let 's go over!"

So we strolled across an open space where were two giant pines towering sombre against the twilight, a little mountain brooklet, and a few quiet cows.

"Stop," said Smith, leaning his back against a pine, and encircling my neck affectionately with an arm; "I told you, as regards Sarah Jane, how my feelings stand. Well now, you just bet she 's on the reciprocate! When I told old woman Copples I 'd like to invite you over, — Sarah Jane she past me in the doorway, — and said she, ' Glad to see *your* friends.' "

Then *sotto voce*, for we were very near, he sang again:—

"'T is, O 't is the cottage of me love";

"and C. K.," he continued familiarly, "You 're a judge of wimmen," chucking his knuckles into my ribs, whereat I jumped; when he added, "There, I knew you was. Well, Sarah Jane is a derned magnificent female; number three boot, just the height for me. *Venus de* Copples, I call her, and would make the most touching artist's wife in this planet. If I design to paint a head, or a foot, or an arm, get my little old Sarah Jane to peel the particular charm, and just whack her in on the canvas."

We passed in through low doors, turned from a small dark entry into the family sitting-room, and were alone there in presence of a cheery log fire which good-naturedly bade us welcome, crackling freely and tossing its sparks out upon floor of pine and Coyote-skin rug. A few old framed prints hung upon dark walls, their faces looking serenely down upon the scanty old-fashioned furniture, and windows full of flowering plants. A low-cushioned chair, not long since vacated, was drawn close by the centre-table, whereon were a lamp, and a large open Bible with a pair of silver-bowed spectacles lying upon its lighted page.

Smith made a gesture of silence toward the door, touched the Bible, and whispered, "*Here 's* where old woman Copples lives, and it is a good thing; I read it aloud to her evenings, and I can just feel the high local lights of it. It 'll fetch H. G. yet!"

At this juncture the door opened; a pale, thin, elderly woman entered, and with tired smile greeted me. While her hard, labor-stiffened, needle-roughened hand was in mine, I looked into her face and felt something (it may be, it must be but little, yet something) of the sorrow of her life; that of a woman large in sympathy, deep in faith, eternal in constancy, thrown away on a rough worthless fellow. All things she hoped for had failed her; the tenderness which never came, the hopes years ago in ashes, the whole world of her yearnings long buried, leaving only the duty of living and the hope of Heaven. As she sat down, took up her spectacles and knitting, and closed the Bible, she began pleasantly to talk to us of the warm bright autumn nights, of Smith's work, and then of my own profession, and of her niece,

Sarah Jane. Her genuinely sweet spirit and natively gentle manner were very beautiful, and far overbalanced all traces of rustic birth and mountain life.

O that unquenchable Christian fire, how pure the gold of its result! It needs no practiced elegance, no social greatness, for its success; only the warm human heart, and out of it shall come a sacred calm and gentleness, such as no power, no wealth, no culture may ever hope to win.

No words of mine would outline the beauty of that plain weary old woman, the sad sweet patience of those gray eyes, nor the spirit of overflowing goodness which cheered and enlivened the half hour we spent there.

H. G. might perhaps be pardoned for showing an alacrity when the door again opened and Sarah Jane rolled, I might almost say trundled in, and was introduced to me.

Sarah Jane was an essentially Californian product, as much so as one of those vast potatoes or massive pears; she had a suggestion of State-Fair in the fulness of her physique, yet with all was pretty and modest.

If I could have rid myself of a fear that her buttons might sooner or later burst off and go singing by my ear, I think I might have felt as H. G. did, that she was a "magnificent female" with her smooth brilliant skin and ropes of soft brown hair.

H. G., in presence of the ladies, lost something of his original flavor, and rose into studied elegance, greatly to the comfort of Sarah, whose glow of pride as his talk ran on came without show of restraint.

The supper was delicious.

But Sarah was quiet, quiet to H. G. and to me, until after tea, when the old lady said: "You young folks will have to excuse me this evening," and withdrew to her chamber.

More logs were then piled on the sitting-room hearth, and we three gathered in semicircle.

Presently H. G. took the poker and twisted it about among coals and ashes, prying up the oak sticks, as he announced, in a measured, studied way, "An artist's wife, that is," he explained, "an Academician's wife orter, well she 'd orter *sabe* the beautiful, and take her regular æsthetics; and then again," he continued in explanatory tone, "she 'd orter know how to keep a hotel, derned if she had n't, for it 's rough like furst off, 'fore a feller gits his name up. But then when he does tho' she 's got a salubrious old time of it. It 's touch a little bell" (he pressed the andiron-top to show us how the thing was done), "and 'Brooks, the morning paper!' Open your regular Herald : —

"'ART NOTES. — Another of H. G. Smith's tender works entitled, "Off the Grade," so full of out-of-doors and subtle feeling of nature, is now on exhibition at Goupel's.'

"Look down a little further.

"'ITALIAN OPERA. — Between the acts all eyes turned to the *distingué*, Mrs. H. G. Smith, who looked,'" — then turning to me, and waving his hand at Sarah Jane, " I leave it to you if she don't."

Sarah Jane assumed the pleasing color of the sugar-beet without seeming inwardly unhappy.

"It 's only a question of time with H. G.," continued my friend. "Art is long you know, derned long, and it may be a year before I paint my great picture, but after that Smith works in lead harness."

He used the poker freely, and more and more his flow of hopes turned a shade of sentiment to Sarah Jane, who smiled broader and broader, showing teeth of healthy whiteness.

At last I withdrew and sought my room, which was

H. G.'s also, and his studio. I had gone with a candle around the walls whereon were tacked studies and sketches, finding here and there a bit of real merit among the profusion of trash, when the door burst open and my friend entered, kicked off his boots and trousers, and walked up and down at a sort of quadrille step singing : —

> "Yes, it's the cottage of me love ;
> You bet, it's the cottage of me love,"

and what 's more, H. G. has just had his genteel goodnight kiss; and when and where is the good old barkeep ? "

I checked his exuberance as best I might, knowing full well that the quiet and elegant dispenser of neat and mixed beverages hearing this inquiry would put in an appearance in person and offer a few remarks designed to provoke ill-feeling. So I at last got Smith in bed and the lamp out. All was quiet for a few moments, and when I had almost gotten asleep, I heard my room-mate in low tones say to himself : —

" Married, by the Rev. Gospel, our talented California artist, Mr. H. G. Smith, to Miss Sarah Jane Copples. No cards."

A pause, and then with more gentle utterance, " and that 's what 's the matter with H. G."

Slowly from this atmosphere of art I passed away into the tranquil land of dreams.

XI.

SHASTA.

1870.

WE escaped the harvesting season of 1870. I try to believe all its poetry is not forever immolated under the strong wheels of that pastoral Juggernaut of our day, the steam-reaper, and to be grateful that Ruths have not now to glean the fallen wheat-heads and loaf around at questionable hours setting their caps for susceptible ranchers. Whatever stirring rhythm may to-day measure time with the quick fire-breath of reaping-machines shall await a more poetic pen than this. Some modern Virgil coming along the boundless wheat plain may perhaps sing you bucolic phrases of the new iron age; but he will soon see his mistake, as will you. The harvest home, with its Longfellow mellowness of atmosphere, or even those ideally colored barns of Eastman Johnson's, with corn and girls and some of the lingering personal relationship between crops and human hands; all that is tradition here, not even memory.

It is quite as well. These people are more germane with enterprise and hurry, and with the winding-up drink at some vulgar tavern when the hired hands are paid off and gather to have "a real nice time with the boys."

This was over. The herds of men had poured back to their cities and wandered away among distant mines as far as their earnings would carry them.

A few stranded bummers who awoke from their "nice

time " penniless, still lingered in pathetic humiliation around the scene of their labor, rather heightening that air of sleep which now pervaded every ranch in the Sacramento valley.

We quitted the hotel at Chico with relief, gratefully turning our backs upon the Chinamen whose cookery had spoiled our two days' peace. Mr. Freeman Clark will have to make out a better case for Confucius or else these fellows were apostate. But they were soon behind us, a straight dusty avenue leading us past clusters of ranches into a quiet expanse of level land, and beneath the occasional shadow of roadside oaks. Miles of harvested plain lay close shaven in monotonous Naples yellow, stretching on, soft and vague, losing itself in a gray, half-luminous haze. Now and then, through more transparent intervals, we could see the brown Sierra feet walling us in to eastward, their oak-clad tops fainter and fainter as they rose into this sky. Directly overhead hung an arch of pale blue, but a few degrees down the hue melted into golden gray. Looming through the mist before us rose sombre forms of trees, growing in processions along the margins of snow-fed streams which flow from the Sierra across the Sacramento plain. Through these silent sleepy groves the seclusion is perfect. You come in from blinding sun-scorched plains to the great aged oaks, whose immense breadth of bough seems outstretched with effort to shade more and more ground.

Alders and cottonwoods line the stream banks ; native grapes in tropical profusion drape the shores, and hang in trailing curtains from tree to tree. Here and there glimpses open into dark thickets. The stream comes into view between walls of green. Evening sunlight, broken with shadow, falls over rippling shallows ; still expanses of deep pool reflect blue from the zenith, and

flow on into dark-shaded coves beneath overhanging verdure. Vineyards and orchards gather themselves pleasantly around ranch-houses.

Men and women are dull, unrelieved; they are all
alike. The eternal flatness of landscape, the monotony
of endlessly pleasant weather, the scarcely varying year,
the utter want of anything unforeseen, and absence of all
surprise in life, are legible upon their quiet uninteresting
faces. They loaf through eleven months to harvest one.
Individuality is wanting. The same kind of tiresome
ranch-gossip you hear at one table spreads itself over
listening acres to the next.

The great American poet, it may confidently be pre-
dicted, will not book his name from the Sacramento
Valley. The people, the acres, the industry seem to be
created solely to furnish vulgar fractions in the census.
It was not wholly fancy that detected in the grapes
something of the same flatness and sugary insipidity
which characterized the girls I chatted with on certain
piazzas.

What an antipode is the condition of sterile poverty in
the farm-life of the East. Frugality, energy, self-preserv-
ing mental activity contrast sharply with the contented
lethargy of this commonplace opulence. Mile after mile,
in recurring succession of wheatland and vineyard, oak-
grove and dusty shabbiness of graceless ranch-buildings,
stretches on, flanking our way on either side, until at last
the undulations of the foot-hills are reached, and the first
signs of vigorous life are observed in the trees. Attitude
and consciousness are displayed in the lordly oaks which
cluster upon brown hillsides. The Sacramento, which
through the slumberous plain had flowed in a still deep
current, reflecting only the hot haze and motionless forms
of the trees upon its banks, here courses along with the

10 *   o

ripple of life, displaying through its clear waters boulders and pebbles freighted from the higher mountains.

Our road, ascending through sunny valleys and among rolling oak-clad hills, at length reaches the level of the pines, and climbing to a considerable crest descends among a fine coniferous forest into the deeply-wooded valley of the Pitt. Lifted high against the sky, ragged hills of granite and limestone limit the view. The river, through a sharp rocky cañon, has descended from the volcanic plains of northeastern California, cutting its way across the sea of hills which represents the Sierra Nevada, and falling toward the west in a series of white rapids.

Our camp in the cool mountain air banished the fatigues of weary miles; night, under the mountain stars, gave us refreshing sleep; and, from the morning we crossed Pitt Ferry, we dated a new life.

In a deep gorge between lofty pine-clad walls we came upon the McCloud, a brilliantly pure stream, wearing its way through lava rocks, and still bearing the ice-chill of Shasta. Dark feathery firs stand in files along the swift river. Oaks, with lustrous leaves, rise above hill-slopes of red and brown. Numbers of Indian camps are posted here. I find them picturesque: low conical huts, opening upon small smoking fires attended by squaws. Numberless salmon, split and drying in rows upon light scaffoldings, make their light-red conspicuous amid the generally dingy surroundings.

These Indian faces are fairly good-natured, especially when young. I visited one camp, upon the left river bank, finding Madam at home seated by her fireside engaged in maternal duties. I am almost afraid to describe the squallor and grotesque hideousness of her person. She was emaciated and scantily clad in a sort of short petticoat; shaggy, unkempt hair overhanging a pair of wild wolf's eyes. The ribs and collar-bone stood out as upon an anatomical specimen; hard black flesh clinging in formless masses upon her body and arms. Altogether she had the appearance of an animated mummy. Her child, a mere amorphous roll, clung to her, and emphasized, with cubbish fatness, the wan, shrunken form of its mother, looking like some ravenous leech which was draining the woman's very blood. Shuddering, I hurried away to observe the husband.

The "buck" was spearing salmon a short distance down stream, his naked form poised upon a beam which projected over the river, his eyes riveted, and spear uplifted waiting for the prey; sunlight, streaming down in broken masses through trees, fell brilliantly upon his muscular shoulder and tense compact thigh, glancing now and then across rigid arms and the polished point of his spear. The swift dark water rushed beneath him, flashing upon its surface a shimmering reflection of his red figure. Cast in bronze he would have made a companion for Quincy Ward's Indian hunter; and better than a companion, for in his wolfish sinew and panther muscle there was not, so far as I could observe, that free Greek suppleness which is so fine a feature in Mr. Ward's statue; though Ajax, disguised as an American Indian, might be a better name for that great and powerful piece of sculpture.

A day's march brought us from McCloud to the Sacramento here a small stream, with banks fringed by a pleasing variety of trees and margins graceful with water-plants.

Northward for two days we followed closely the line of the Sacramento River, now descending along slopes to its bed, where the stream played among picturesque rocks and boulders, and again climbing by toilsome as-

cents into the forest a thousand feet up on the cañon
wall, catching glimpses of towering ridges of pine-clad
Sierra above, and curves of the foaming river deep in the
blue shadow beneath us.

More and more the woods became darkened with mountain pine, the air freshened by northern life gave us the
inspiration of altitude.

At last, through a notch to the northward, rose the
conical summit of Shasta, its pale, rosy lavas enamelled
with ice.   Body and base of the great peak were hidden
by intervening hills, over whose smooth rolls of forest
green the bright, blue sky and the brilliant Shasta summit were sharp and strong.   From that moment the peak
became the centre of our life.   From every crest we
strained our eyes forward, as now and then, either through
forest vistas the incandescent snow greeted us, or from
some high summit the opening cañon walls displayed
grander and grander views of the great volcano.   It was
sometimes, after all, a pleasure to descend from these cool
heights, with the *impression* of the mountain upon our
minds, to the cañon bottom, where, among the endlessly
varying bits of beautiful detail, the mental strain wore
off.

When our tents were pitched at Sisson's, while a picturesque haze floated up from southward, we enjoyed the
grand uncertain form of Shasta with its heaven-piercing
crest of white, and wide placid sweep of base ; full of lines
as deeply reposeful as a Greek temple.   Its dark head
lifted among the fading stars of dawn, and strongly set
upon the arch of coming rose, appealed to our emotions ;
but best we liked to sit at evening near Munger's easel,
watching the great lava cone glow with light almost as
wild and lurid as if its crater still streamed.

Watkins thought it " photographic luck " that the mountain should so have draped itself with mist as to defy his camera. Palmer stayed at camp to make observations in the coloring of meerschaums at fixed altitudes, and to watch now and then the station barometer.

Shasta from Sisson's is a broad triple mountain, the central summit being flanked on the west by a large and quite perfect crater whose rim reaches about twelve thousand feet altitude. On the west a broad shoulder-like spur juts from the general slope. The cone rises from its base eleven thousand feet in one sweep.

A forest of tall, rich pines surrounds Strawberry Valley, and the little group of ranches near Sisson's. Under this high sky, and a pure quality of light, the whole varied foreground of green and gold stretches out toward the rocky mountain base in charming contrast. Brooks from the snow thread their way through open meadow, waving overhead a tent-work of willows, silvery and cool.

Shasta, as a whole, is the single cone of an immense extinct volcano. It occupies almost precisely the axial line of the Sierra Nevada, but the range, instead of carrying its great wave-like ridge through this region, breaks down in the neighborhood of Lassen's Butte, and for eighty miles northward is only represented by low confused masses of mountain cut through and through by the cañons of the McCloud, Pitt, and Sacramento.

A broad volcanic plain, interrupted here and there by inconsiderable chains, occupies the country east of Scott's Mountain. From this general plain, whose altitude is from twenty-five hundred to thirty-five hundred feet, rises Mount Shasta. About its base cluster hillocks of a hundred little volcanoes, but they are utterly inconspicuous under the shadow of the great peak. The volcanic plain-land is partly overgrown by forest, and in part covers itself with fields of grass or sage. Riding

over it in almost any part the one great point in the
landscape is the cone of Shasta; its crest of solid white,.
its vast altitude, the pale-gray or rosy tints of its lavas,
and the dark girdle of forest which swells up over cañon-
carved foothills give it a grandeur equalled by hardly
any American mountain.

September 11th found the climbers of our party, —
S. F. Emmons, Frederick A. Clark, Albert B. Clark, Mr.
Sisson, the pioneer guide of the region, and myself,—
mounted upon our mules, heading for the crater cone over
rough rocks and among the stunted firs and pines which
mark the upper limit of forest growth. The morning
was cool and clear with a fresh north wind sweeping
around the volcano and bringing in its descent invigora-
ting cold of the snow region. When we had gone as far
as our mules could carry us, threading their difficult
way among piles of lava, we dismounted and made up
our packs of beds, instruments, food, and fuel for a three
days' trip, turned the animals over to George and John,
our two muleteers, bade them good day, and with Sisson,
who was to accompany us up the first descent, struck out
on foot. Already above vegetation, we looked out over
all the valley south and west, observing its arabesque of
forest, meadow, and chaparral, the files of pines' which
struggled up almost to our feet, and just below us the
volcano slope strewn with red and brown wreck and
patches of shrunken snow-drift.

Our climb up the steep western crater slope was slow
and tiresome, quite without risk or excitement. The
footing, altogether of lodged *débris*, at times gave way
provokingly, and threw us out of balance. Once upon
the spiry pinnacles which crown the crater rim, a scene
of wild power broke upon us. The round crater-bowl,
about a mile in diameter and nearly a thousand feet

deep, lay beneath us, its steep, shelving sides of shattered lava mantled in places to the very bottom by fields
of snow.

We clambered along the edge toward Shasta, and came
to a place where for a thousand feet it was a mere blade
of ice, sharpened by the snow into a thin, frail edge,
upon which we walked in cautious balance, a misstep
likely to hurl us down into the chaos of lava blocks
within the crater.

Passing this, we reached the north edge of the rim,
and from a rugged mound of shattered rock looked down
into a gorge between us and the main Shasta. There,
winding its huge body along, lay a glacier, riven with
sharp, deep crevasses yawning fifty or sixty feet wide,
the blue hollows of their shadowed depth contrasting
with the brilliant surfaces of ice.

We studied its whole length from the far, high Shasta
crest down in winding course, deepening its cañon more
and more as it extends, crowding past our crater cone,
and at last terminating in bold ice-billows and a wide
belt of hilly moraine. The surface over half of its length
was quite clean, but directly opposite us occurs a fine ice
cascade; there its entire surface is cut with transverse
crevasses, which have a general tendency to curve downward; and all this dislocation is accompanied by a freight
of lava blocks which shoot down the cañon walls on
either side, bounding out all over the glacier.

In a later trip, while Watkins was making his photographic views, I climbed about, going to the edges of
some crevasses and looking over into their blue vaults,
where icicles overhang and a whispered sound of water-
flow comes up faintly from beneath.

From a point about midway across where I had climbed
and rested upon the brink of an ice-cliff, the glacier below

me breaking off into its wild pile of cascade blocks and
sérac, I looked down over all the lower flow, broken with
billowy upheavals, and bright with bristling spires
of sunlit ice. Upon the right rose the great cone of
Shasta, formed of chocolate-colored lavas, its skyline a
single curved sweep of snow cut sharply against a deep
blue sky. To the left the precipices of the lesser cone
rose to the altitude of twelve thousand feet, their surfaces
half jagged ledges of lava and half irregular sheets of ice.
From my feet the glacier sank rapidly between volcanic
walls, and the shadow of the lesser cone fell in a dark
band across the brilliantly lighted surface. Looking
down its course, my eye ranged over sunny and shadowed
zones of ice, over the gray, boulder region of the terminal
moraine; still lower, along the former track of ancient and
grander glaciers, and down upon undulating pine-clad foot-
hills descending in green steps, reaching out like promontories into the sea of plain which lay outspread nine thousand feet below, basking in the half-tropical sunshine, its
checkered green fields and orchards ripening their wheat
and figs.

Our little party separated, each going about his labor.
The Clarks, with theodolite and barometer, were engaged
on a pinnacle over on the western crater-edge. Mr.
Sisson, who had helped us thus far with a huge pack-load
of wood, now said good by, and was soon out of sight
on his homeward tramp. Emmons and I geologized
about the rim and interior slope, getting at last out of
sight of one another.

In mid-crater sprang up a sharp cone several hundred
feet high, composed of much shattered lava, and indicating doubtless the very latest volcanic activity. At its
base lay a small lakelet, frozen over with rough black
ice. Far below us, cold, gray banks and floating flocks

of vapor began to drift and circle about the lava slopes, rising higher at sunset, till they quite enveloped us, and at times shut out the view.

Later we met for bivouac, spread our beds upon small *débris* under lee of a mass of rock on the rim, and built a little camp-fire, around which we sat closely. Clouds still eddied about us, opening now wide rifts of deep-blue sky, and then glimpses of the Shasta summit glowing with evening light, and again views down upon the far earth, where sunlight had long faded, leaving forest and field and village sunken in purple gloom. Through the old broken crater lip, over foreground of pallid ice and sharp black lava rocks, the clouds whirled away, and, yawning wide, revealed an objectless expanse, out of which emerged dim mountain tops, for a moment seen, then veiled. Thus, in the midst of clouds, I found it extremely interesting to watch them and their habits. Drifting slowly across the crater-bowl I saw them float over and among the points of cindery lava, whose savage forms contrasted wonderfully with the infinite softness of their texture.

I found it strange and suggestive that fields of perpetual snow should mantle the slopes of an old lava caldron, that the very volcano's throat should be choked with a pure little lakelet, and sealed with unmelting ice. That power of extremes, which held sway over lifeless nature before there were human hearts to experience its crush, expressed itself with poetic eloquence. Had Lowell been in our bivouac, I know he must have felt again the power of his own perfect figure of

" Burned-out craters healed with snow."

It was a wild moment. Wind smiting in shocks against the rock beside us, flaring up our little fire, and whirling

on with its cloud-freight into the darkening crater
gulf.

We turned in ; the Clarks together, Emmons and I in
our fur bags. Upon cold stone our bed was anything but
comfortable, angular fragments of trachyte finding their
way with great directness among our ribs and under
shoulder-blades, keeping us almost awake in that despairing semi-consciousness where dreams and thoughts
tangle in tiresome confusion.

Just after midnight, from sheer weariness, I arose, finding the sky cloudless, its whole black dome crowded with
stars. A silver dawn over the slope of Shasta brightened
till the moon sailed clear. Under its light all the rugged
topography came out with unnatural distinctness, every
impression of height and depth greatly exaggerated. The
empty crater lifted its rampart into the light. I could
not tell which seemed most desolate, that dim moonlit
rim with pallid snow-mantle and gaunt crags, or the solid
black shadow which was cast downward from southern
walls, darkening half the bowl. From the silent air
every breath of wind or whisper of sound seemed frozen.
Naked lava slopes and walls, the high gray body of
Shasta with ridge and gorge, glacier and snow-field, all
cold and still under the icy brightness of the moon, produced a scene of Arctic terribleness such as I had never
imagined. I looked down, eagerly straining my eyes,
through the solemn crater's lip, hoping to catch a glimpse
of the lower world ; but far below, hiding the earth,
stretched out a level plain of cloud, upon which the
light fell cold and gray as upon a frozen ocean.

I scrambled back to bed, and happily to sleep, a real,
sound, dreamless repose.

We breakfasted some time after sunrise, and were soon
under way with packs on our shoulders.

The day was brilliant and cloudless, the cold, still air full of life and inspiration. Through its clear blue the Shasta peak seemed illusively near, and we hurried down to the saddle which connects our cone with the peak, and across the head of a small tributary glacier, and up over the first *débris* slopes. It was a slow, tedious three hours' climb over stones which lay as steeply as loose material possibly can, up to the base of a red trachyte spur; then on up a gorge, and out upon a level mountain shoulder, where are considerable flats covered with deep ice. To the north it overflows in a much crevassed tributary of the glacier we had studied below.

Here we rested, and hung the barometer from Clark's tripod.

The further ascent lies up a long scoria ridge of loose, red, pumiceous rock for seven or eight hundred feet, then across another level step curved with rugged ice, and up into a sort of corridor between two steep, much broken, and stained ridges. Here in the hollow are boiling sulphurous springs and hot earth. We sat down by them, eating our lunch in the lee of some stones.

A short, rapid climb brought us to the top; four hours and thirty minutes working time from our crater bivouac.

There is no reason why any one of sound wind and limb should not, after a little mountaineering practice, be able to make the Shasta climb. There is nowhere the shadow of danger and never a real piece of mountain climbing, — climbing, I mean, with hands and feet, — no scaling of walls or labor involving other qualities than simple muscular endurance. The fact that two young girls have made the ascent proves it a comparatively easy one. Indeed, I have never reached a corresponding altitude with so little labor and difficulty. Whoever visits California, and wishes to depart from the beaten track of

Yosemite scenes, could not do better than come to Strawberry Valley and get Mr. Sisson to pilot him up Shasta.

When I ask myself to-day what were the sensations on Shasta, they render themselves into three, — geography, shadows, and uplifted isolation.

After we had walked along a short curved ridge which forms the summit, representing, as I believe, all that remains of the original crater, it became my occupation to study the view.

A singularly transparent air revealed every plain and peak on till the earth's curve rolled them under remote horizons. The whole great disc of world outspread beneath wore an aspect of glorious cheerfulness. The cascade range, a roll of blue forest land, stretched northward, surmounted at intervals by volcanoes; the lower, like symmetrical Mount Pitt, bare and warm with rosy lava colors; those farther north lifting against the pale, horizon-blue solid white cones upon which strong light rested with brilliance. It seemed incredible that we could see so far toward the Columbia River, almost across the State of Oregon, but there stood Pitt, Jefferson, and the Three Sisters in unmistakable plainness. Northeast and east spread those great plains out of which rise low lava chains, and a few small, burned-out volcanoes, and there, too, were the group of Klamath and Goose Lakes lying in mid plain glassing the deep upper violet. Farther and farther from our mountain base in that direction the greenness of forest and meadow fades out into rich mellow brown, with warm cloudings of sienna over bare lava hills, and shades, as you reach the eastern limit, in pale ash and lavender and buff, where stretches of level land slope down over Madelin plains into Nevada deserts. An unmistakable purity and delicacy of tint, with transparent air and paleness of tone, give all desert scenes the aspect of water-color drawings. Even at this immense distance I could see the gradual change from rich, warm hues of rocky slope, or plain overspread with ripened vegetation, out to the high pale key of the desert.

Southeast the mountain spurs are smoothed into a broad glacis, densely overgrown with chaparral, and ending in open groves around plains of yellow grass.

A little farther begin the wild, cañon-curved piles of green mountains which represent the Sierras, and afar, towering over them, eighty miles away, the lava dome of Lassen's Peak standing up bold and fine. South, the Sacramento cañon cuts down to unseen depths, its deep trough opening a view of the California plain, a brown, sunny expanse, over which loom in vanishing perspective the coast range peaks. West of us, and quite around the semicircle of view, stretches a vast sea of ridges, chains, peaks, and sharp walls of cañons, as wild and tumultuous as an ocean storm. Here and there above the blue billows rise snow-crests and shaggy rock-chains, but the topography is indistinguishable. With difficulty I could trace for a short distance the Klamath cañon course, recognizing Siskiyou peaks, where Professor Brewer and I had been years before; but in that broad area no further unravelling was possible. So high is Shasta, so dominant above the field of view, we looked over it all as upon a great shield which rose gently in all directions to the sky.

Whichever way we turned the great cone fell off from our feet in dizzying abruptness. We looked down steep slopes of *névé*, on over shattered ice-wreck, where glaciers roll over cliffs, and around the whole broad massive base curved deeply through its lava crusts in straight cañons.

These flutings of ancient and grander glaciers are

flanked by straight, long moraines, for the most part bare, but reaching down part way into the forest. It is interesting to observe that those on the north and east, by greater massiveness and length, indicate that in former days the glacier distribution was related to the points of compass about as it is now. What volumes of geographical history lay in view! Old mountain uplift; volcanoes built upon the plain of fiery lava; the chill of ice and wearing force of torrent, written in glacier-gorge and water-curved cañon!

I think such vastness of prospect now and then extremely valuable in itself; it forcibly widens one's conception of country, driving away such false notion of extent or narrowing idea of limitation as we get in living on lower plains.

I never tire of overlooking these great wide fields, studying their rich variety, and giving myself up to the expansion which is the instant and lasting reward. In presence of these vast spaces and all but unbounded outlook, the hours hurry by with singular swiftness. Minutes or miles are nothing; days and degrees seem best fitted for one's thoughts. So it came sooner than I could have believed that the sun neared its setting, sinking into a warm, bright stratum of air. The light stretched from north to south, reflecting itself with an equal depth all along the east, until a perfect ring of soft, glowing rose edged the whole horizon. Over us the ever dark heaven hung near and flat. Light swept eastward across the earth, every uplift of hill-ridge or solitary cone warm and bright with its reflections, and from each object upon the plains, far and near, streamed out dense, sharp shadows, slowly lengthening their intense images. We were far enough lifted above it all to lose the ordinary landscape impression, and reach that extraordinary effect of black-

and-bright topography seen upon the moon through a telescope.

Afar in the north, bars of blue shadow streamed out from the peaks, tracing themselves upon rosy air. All the eastern slope of Shasta was of course in dark shade, the gray glacier forms, broken ridges of stone, and forest all dim and fading. A long cone of cobalt-blue, the shadow of Shasta fell strongly defined over the bright plain, its apex darkening the earth a hundred miles away. As the sun sank, this gigantic spectral volcano rose on the warm sky till its darker form stood huge and terrible over the whole east. It was intensely distinct at the summit, just as far-away peaks seen against the east in evening always are, and faded at base as it entered the stratum of earth mist.

Grand and impressive we had thought Shasta when studying in similar light from the plain. Infinitely more impressive was this phantom volcano as it stood overshadowing the land and slowly fading into night.

Before quitting the ridge, Fred Clark and I climbed together out upon the highest pinnacle, a trachyte needle rising a few feet above the rest, and so small we could barely balance there together, but we stood a moment and waved the American flag, looking down over our shoulders eleven thousand feet.

A fierce wind blew from the southwest, coming in gusts of great force. Below, we could hear it beat surflike upon the crags. We hurried down to the hot-spring flat, and just over the curve of its southern descent made our bivouac. Even here the wind howled merciless and cold.

We turned to and built of lava blocks a square pen about two and a half feet high, filled the chinks with pebbles, and banked it with sand. I have seen other

brown-stone fronts more imposing than our Shasta home,
but I have rarely felt more grateful to four walls than to
that little six-by-six pen. I have not forgotten that
through its chinks the sand and pebbles pelted us all
night, nor was I oblivious when sudden gusts toppled
over here and there a good-sized rock upon our feet.
When we sat up for our cup of coffee, which Clark artis-
tically concocted over the scanty and economical fire, the
walls sheltered our backs ; and for that we were thankful,
even if the wind had full sweep at our heads and stole
the very draught from our lips, whirling it about north
forty east by compass, in the form of an infinitesimal
spray. The zephyr, as we courteously called it, had a
fashion of dropping vertically out of the sky upon our
fire and leaving a clean hearth. For the space of a few
moments after these meteorological jokes there was a
lively gathering of burning knots from among our legs
and coats and blankets.

There are times when the extreme of discomfort so
overdoes itself as to extort a laugh and put one in the
best of humor. This tempest descended to so many
absurd personal tricks altogether beneath the dignity of
a reputable hurricane, that at last it seemed to us a sort
of furious burlesque.

Not so the cold ; that commanded entire respect,
whether carefully abstracting our animal heat through
the bed of gravel on which we lay, or brooding over us
hungry for those pleasant little waves of motion which,
taking Tyndall for granted, radiated all night long, in
spite of wildcat bags, from our unwilling particles. I
abominate thermometers at such times. Not one of my set
ever owned up the real state of things. Whenever I am
nearly frozen and conscious of every indurated bone, that
bland little instrument is sure to read twenty or thirty

degrees above any unprejudiced estimate. Lying there
and listening to the whispering sands that kindly drifted,
ever adding to our cover, and speculating as to any further possible meteorological affliction was but indifferent
amusement, from which I escaped to a slumber of great
industry. We lay like sardines hoping to encourage animal heat, but with small success.

The sunrise effect, with all its splendor, I find it convenient to leave to some future traveller. I shall be
generous with him, and say nothing of that hour of gold.
It had occurred long before we awoke, and many precious
minutes were consumed in united appeals to one another
to get up and make coffee. It was horridly cold and uncomfortable where we were, but no one stirred. How
natural it is under such circumstances to

> " Rather bear those ills we have
> Than fly to others that we know not of."

I lay musing on this, finding it singular that I should
rather be there stiff and cold while my like-minded com-
rades appealed to me, than to get up and comfort myself
with camp-fire and breakfast. We severally awaited
developments.

At last Clark gave up and made the fire, and he has
left me in doubt whether he loved cold less or coffee
more.

Digging out our breakfast from drifted sand was pleasant enough, nor did we object to excavating the frozen
shoes, but the mixture of disintegrated trachyte discovered among the sugar, and the manner in which our
brown-stone front had blown over and flattened out the
family provisions was received by us as calamity.

However, we did justice to Clark's coffee, and socially
toasted our bits of meat, while we chatted and ate zest-

11   P

fully portions not too freely brecciated with lava sand.   I
have been at times all but morbidly aware of the power
of local attachment, finding it absurdly hard to turn the
key on doors I have entered often and with pleasure.
My own early home, though in other hands, holds its
own against greater comfort, larger cheer; and a hundred
times, when our little train moved away from grand old
trees or willow-shaded springs by mountain camps, I
have felt all the pathos of nomadism, from the Aryan
migration down.

As we shouldered our loads and took to the ice-field I
looked back on our modest edifice, and for the first time
left my camp with gay relief.

Elation of success and the vital mountain air lent us
their quickening impulse. We tramped rapidly across
the ice-field and down a long spur of red trachyte, which
extended in a southerly course around the head of a
glacier. It was our purpose to descend the southern
slope of the mountain, to a camp which had been left
there awaiting us. The declivity in that direction is
more gentle than by our former trail, and had besides the
merit of lying open to our view almost from the very
start. It was interesting, as we followed the red trachyte
spur, to look down to our left upon *névé* of the McCloud
glacier. From its very head, dislocation and crevasses
had begun, the whole mass moving away from the wall,
leaving a deep gap between ice and rock. In its further
descent this glacier pours over such steep cascades, and
is so tortuous among the lava crags that we could only
see its beginning. To avoid those great pyramidal masses
which sprung fully a thousand feet from the general flank
of the mountain, we turned to the right and entered the
head of one of those long, eroded glacier cañons which
are scored down the slope. The ridges from both sides

had poured in their freight of *débris* until the cañon was one mass of rock fragments of every conceivable size and shape. Here and there considerable masses of ice and relics of former glaciers lay up and down the shaded sides, and, as we descended, occupied the whole broad bottom of the gorge. We congratulated ourselves when the steep, upper *débris* slope was passed and we found ourselves upon the wavy ice of the old glacier. Numerous streams flowed over its irregular face, losing themselves in the cracks and reappearing among the accumulation of boulders upon its surface. Here and there glacier tables of considerable size rose above the general level, supported on slender ice-columns. As the angle here was very steep, we amused ourselves by prying these off their pedestals with our alpine stocks, and watching them slide down before us.

More and more the ice became burdened with rocks, until at last it wholly disappeared under accumulation of moraine. Over this, for a half mile, we tramped, thinking the glacier ended; but in one or two depressions I again caught sight of the ice, which led me to believe that a very large portion of this rocky gorge may be underlaid by old glacial remains.

Tramping over this unstable moraine, where melting ice had left the boulders in every state of uncertain equilibrium, we were greatly fatigued, and at last, the strain telling seriously on our legs, we climbed over a ridge to the left of our amphitheatre into the next cañon, which was very broad and open, with gentle, undulating surface diversified by rock plateaus and fields of glacier sand. Here, by the margin of a little snow-brook, and among piles of immense *débris*, Emmons and I sat down to lunch, and rested until our friends came up.

A few scanty bunches of alpine plants began to deck

the gray earth and gradually to gather themselves in bits
of open sward, here and there decorated with delicate
flowers. Near one little spring meadow we came upon
gardens of a pale yellow flower with an agreeable aroma-
tic perfume, and after another mile of straining on among
erratic boulders and over the thick-strewn rock of the old
moraines, we came to the advanced guard of the forest.
Battle-twisted and gnarled old specimens of trees, of
rugged, muscular trunk, and scanty, irregular branch,
they showed in every line and color a life-long struggle
against their enemies, the avalanche and cold.   Gathering closer they grew in groves separated by long, open,
grassy glades, the clumps of trees twisting their roots
among the glacier blocks.   For a long time we followed
the pathway of an avalanche.   To the right and left of
us, upon considerable heights, the trees were sound and
whole, and preserved, even at their ripe age, the health
of youth.   But down the straight pathway of the valley
every tree had been swept away, the prostrate trunks
lying here and there, half buried in drifts of sand and
rock.   Here, over the whole surface, a fresh young
growth of not more than six or seven years old has
sprung up, and begun a hopeless struggle for ground
which the snow claims for its own.   Before us opened
winding avenues through forest; green meadows spread
their pale, fresh herbage in sunny beauty.   Along the
little stream which, after a mile's musical cascades, we
knew flowed past camp, tender green plants and frail
mountain flowers edged our pathway.   All was still and
peaceful with the soft brooding spirit of life.   The groves
were absolutely alive like ourselves, and drinking in the
broad, affluent light in their silent, beautiful way.   Back
over sunny tree-tops, the great cone of rock and icé
loomed in the cold blue; but we gladly turned away and

let our hearts open to the gentle influence of our new world.

There, at last; as we tramped over a knoll, were the mules dozing in sunshine or idling about among trees, and there that dear blue wreath floating up from our camp-fire and drifting softly among boughs of overhanging fir.

I always feel a strange renewal of life when I come down from one of these climbs ; they are with me points of departure more marked and powerful than I can account for upon any reasonable ground. In spite of any scientific labor or presence of fatigue, the lifeless region, with its savage elements of sky, ice and rock, grasps one's nature, and, whether he will or no, compels it into a stern, strong accord. Then, as you come again into softer air, and enter the comforting presence of trees, and feel the grass under your feet, one fetter after another seems to unbind from your soul, leaving it free, joyous, grateful !

XII.

SHASTA FLANKS.

1870.

THERE are certain women, I am informed, who place men under their spell without leaving them the melancholy satisfaction of understanding how the thing was done. They may have absolutely repulsive features, and a pretty permanent absence of mind; without that charm of cheerful grace before which we are said to succumb. Yet they manage to assume command of certain. It is thus with mules. I have heard them called awkward and personally plain, nor is it denied that their disposition, though rich in individuality, lacks some measure of qualities which should endear them to humanity. Despite all this, and even more, they have a way of tenderly getting the better of us, and, in the long run, absolutely enthroning themselves in our affections. Mystery as it is I confess to its potent sway, long ago owning it beyond solution.

Live on the intimate terms of brother-explorer with your mule, be thoughtful for his welfare, and you by-and-by take an emotional start toward him which will surprise you. You look into that reserved face, the embodiment of self-contained drollery, and begin to detect soft thought and tender feeling; and sometimes, as you cinch your saddle a little severely, the calm, reproachful visage will swing round and melt you with a single look. Nothing is left but to rub the velvet nose and loosen up the girth. When the mere brightness and gayety of mountain life carries one away with their hilarious current, there is something in the meek and humble air of a lot of pack animals altogether chastening in its prompt effect.

My " '69 " was one of these insidious beings who within a week of our first meeting asserted supremacy over my life, and formed a silent partnership with my conscience. She was a chubby, black mule, so sleek and rotund as distantly to suggest a pig on stilts. Upon the eye which still remained, a cataract had begun to spread its dimming film. Her make-up was also defective in a weak pair of hind legs, which gave way suddenly in going up steep places. She was clumsy, and in rugged pathways would squander much time in the selection of her foothold. At these moments, when she deliberated, as I fancied, needlessly long, I have very gently suggested with Spanish spur that it might be as well to start; the serious face then turned upon me, its mild eye looking into mine one long, earnest gaze, as much as to say, " I love and would spare you; remember Balaam!" I yielded.

These animals are always of the opposition party; they reverse your wishes, and from one year's end to another defy your best judgment. Yet I love them, and only in extreme moments " go for" them with a fence-rail or theodolite-tripod. Nothing can be pleasanter than to ride them through forest roads, chatting in a bright company, and catching glimpses of far quiet scenery framed by the long, furry ears.

So we thought on that sunny morning when we left Sisson's, starting ahead of wagons and pack animals, and riding out into the woodland on our trip around Shasta; a march of a hundred miles, with many proposed side-excursions into the mountain.

The California haze had again enveloped Shasta, this

time nearly obscuring it.   In forest along the southeast
base, we came upon the stream flowing from McCloud
glacier, its cold waters milky white with fine sandy sediment.   Such dense, impenetrable fields of chaparral cover
the south foothills that we were only able to fight our
way through limited parts, getting, however, a clear idea
of lava flows and topography.   Farther east, the plains
rise to seven thousand feet, and fine wooded ridges sweep
down from Shasta, inviting approach.

While Munger and Watkins camped to make studies
and negatives of the peak, Fred Clark and I packed one
mule with a week's provisions, and mounting our saddle-
animals, struck off into dark, silent forest.

It was a steep climb of eight or ten miles up tree-
covered ridges and among outcrops of gray trachyte;
nearly every foot showing more or less evidence of
glacial action; long trains of morainal rocks upon which
large forest-trees seemed satisfied to grow; great rough
regions of terminal rubbish, with enclosed patches of
level earth commonly grass-grown and picturesque.   It
was sunset before we came upon water, and then it flowed
a thousand feet below us in the bottom of a sharp, narrow
cañon, cut abruptly down in what seemed glacial *débris*.
I thought it unwise to take our mules down its steep
wall if there were any camp-spot high up in the opener
head of the cañon, and went off on foot to climb the
wooded moraines still farther, hoping to come upon a bit
of alpine sward with icy pool, or even upon a spring.
When up between two and three hundred feet the trees
became less and less frequent, rugged trains of stone and
glacier-scored rock in places covering the spurs.   I could
now overlook the snow amphitheatre which opened vast
and shadowy above.   Not a sign of vegetation enlivened
its stony bed.   The icy brook flowed between slopes of

débris. At my feet, a trachyte ridge narrowed the stream with a tortuous bed, and led it to the edge of a five hundred-feet cliff, over which poured a graceful cascade. Finding no camp-spot there, I turned northward and made a detour through deep woods, by-and-by coming back to Clark. We faced the necessity, and by dark were snugly camped in the wild cañon bottom. It was one of the loneliest bivouacs of my life. Shut in by high, dark walls, a few clustered trees growing here and there, others which floods had undermined lying prostrate, rough boulders thrown about, an icy stream hurrying by, and chilly winds coming down from the height, against which our blankets only half defended us.

Our excursion next day was south and west, across high, scantily wooded moraines, till we came to the deep cañon of the McCloud glacier.

I describe this gorge as it is one of several similar, all peculiar to Shasta. We had climbed to a point about ten thousand feet above the sea, and were upon the eastern edge of a cañon of eleven or twelve hundred feet depth. From the very crest of the Shasta, with here and there a few patches of snow, a long and remarkably even *débris* slope swept down. It seemed as if these small pieces of trachyte formed a great part of the region, for to the very bottom our cañon walls were worked out of it. A half mile below us the left bank was curiously eroded by side streams, resulting in a family of pillars from one to seven hundred feet high, each capped with some hard lava boulder which had protected the soft *débris* beneath from weathering. From its lofty *névé* the McCloud glacier descended over rugged slopes in one long cascade to a little above our station, where it impinged against a great rock buttress and turned sharply from the south wall towards us, rounding over in a great solid

11 *

ice-dome eight or nine hundred feet high. For a mile farther, a huge accumulation looking like a river of *débris* cumbered the bottom. Here and there, on close scrutiny, we found it to be pierced with caverns whose ice-walls showed that the glacier underlaid all this vast amount of stone. Boulders rattled continually from the upper glacier and down both cañon walls, increasing the already great burden. Along both sides were evidences of motion in the lateral moraine embankments, and a very perceptible rounding up of terminal ramparts, from which in white torrent poured the sub-glacial brook.

It is instructive to consider what an amount of freighting labor this shrunken ice-stream has to perform besides dragging its own vast weight along. In descending Shasta we had found glacial ice which evidently for a mile or more deeply underlaid a mass of rock similar to this. It is one of the curiosities of Mount Shasta that such great bulk of ice should be buried, and in large part preserved, by loads of rock fragments. Fine contrasts of color were afforded high up among the *sérac* by a combination of blue ice and red lavas. We hammered and surveyed here for half the day, then descended to our mules, who bore us eagerly back to their home, our wierd little cañon camp.

A pleasant day's march, altogether in woods and over glacial ridges, during which not a half hour passed without opening views of the cone, brought us high on the northern slope, at the upper forest limit, in a region of barren avalanche tracks and immense moraines.

Between those great straight ridges which jut almost parallel from the volcano's base, are wide, shelving valleys, the pathways of extinct glaciers; and here the forest, although it must once have obtained foothold, has been uprooted and swept away before powerful ava-

lanches, crushed and up-piled trunks in sad wreck marking spots where the snow-rush stopped.

Two brooks, separated by a wide, gently rounding zone
of drift, flowed down through the glacier valley which
opened directly in front of our camp.

Early next morning Clark and I made up a bag of
lunch, shouldered our instruments, and set out for a day
on the glacier. Our slow, laborious ascent of the valley
was not altogether uninteresting. Constant views obtained of moraines on either side gave us much pleasure
and study. It was instructive to observe that the bases
of their structure were solid floors of lava, upon which,
in rude though secure masonry, were piled embankments
not less than half a mile wide and four hundred feet
high. Among the huge rocks which formed the upper
structure, the tree-forms were peculiar. Apparently every
tree had made an effort to fill some gap and round out
the smooth general surface. No matter how deeply twisted
between high boulders, the branches spread themselves
out in a continuous, dense mat, stretching from stone to
stone. It was only rarely, and in the less elevated parts
of the moraine, that we could see a trunk. The whole
effect was of a causeway of rock overgrown by some
dense green vine.

Similar patches of stunted trees grew here and there
over the bottom of our broad amphitheatre. Oftentimes
we threaded our way among dense thickets of pines,
never over six or eight feet in height, having trunks
often two and three feet in diameter, and more than once
we walked over their tops, our feet sinking but two or
three inches into the dense mat of foliage. Here and
there, half buried in the drift, we came across the tall,
noble trunks of avalanche-killed trees. In comparing
their straight, symmetrical growth with the singularly

matted condition of the living dwarfed trees, I find the
indication of a great climatic change. Not only are the
present avalanches too great to permit their growth, but the
violent cold winds which drift over this region bend down
the young trees to such an extent that there are no longer
tall, normal specimens. Around the upper limits of
arborescent vegetation we passed some most enchanting
spots ; groves, not over eight feet in height, of large trees
whose white trunks and interwoven boughs formed a
colonnade, over which stretched thick living thatch.
Under these strange galleries we walked upon soft,
velvety turf and an elastic cushion of pine-needles ; nor
could we resist the temptation of lying down here to
rest beneath the dense roof. As we looked back, charming little vistas opened between the old and dwarfed
stems. In one direction we could see the moraine with
its long, graded slope and variegated green and brown
surface ; in another, the open pathway of the old glacier
worn deeper and deeper between lofty forest-clad spurs ;
and up to the great snow mass above us, with its slender
peak in the heavens looking down upon magnificent
sweep of *névé*.

Only the strong desire for glaciers led us away from
these delightful groves. A short tramp over sand and
boulders brought us to the foot of a broad, irregular, terminal moraine. Two or three milky cascades poured out
from under the great boulder region and united to form
two important streams. We followed one of these in our
climb up the moraine, and after an hour's hard work,
found ourselves upon an immense pile of lava blocks,
from which we could overlook the whole.

In irregular curve it continues not less than three
miles around the end of the glacier, and in no place that
I saw was less than a half mile in width. Where we had

attacked it the width cannot be less than a mile, and the portion over which we had climbed must reach a thickness of five or six hundred feet.

About a half mile above us, though but little lifted from our level, undulating hillocks of ice marked the division between glacier and moraine; above that, it stretched in uninterrupted white fields. The moraine in every direction extended in singularly abrupt hills, separated by deep, irregular pits and basins of a hundred and more feet deep.

As we climbed on the footing became more and more insecure, piles of rock giving way under our weight. Before long we came to a region of circular, funnel-shaped craters, where evidently the underlying glacier had melted out and a whole freight of boulders fallen in with a rush. Around the edges of these horrible traps we threaded our way with extreme caution, now and then a boulder, dislodging under our feet, rolled down into these pits, and many tons would settle out of sight. Altogether it was the most dangerous kind of climbing I have ever seen. You were never sure of your foothold. More than once, when crossing a comparatively smooth, level boulder-field, they began to sink under us, and we sprang on from stone to stone while the great mass caved and sank slowly behind us. At times, while making our way over solid seeming stretches, the sound of a deep, sub-glacial stream flowing far beneath us came up faint and muffled through the chinks of the rock. This sort of music is not encouraging to the nerves. To the siren babble of mountain brook is added all the tragic nearness of death.

We looked far and wide in hope of some solid region which should lead us up to the ice, but it was all alike, and we hurried on, the rocks settling and sinking beneath our tread, until we made our way to its edge, and climbed with relief upon its hard, white surface. After we had gained the height of an hundred feet, climbing up a comparatively smooth slope between brooks which flowed over it, a look back gave a more correct idea of the general billowy character of our moraine; and here and there in its deeper indentations we could detect the underlying ice.

It is, then, here as upon the McCloud glacier. For at least a mile's width the whole lower zone is buried under accumulation of morainal matter. Instead of ending like most Swiss glaciers, this ice wastes chiefly in contact with the ground, and when considerable caverns are formed the overlying moraine crushes its way through the rotten roof, making the funnels we had seen.

Thankful that we had not assisted at one of these engulfments, we scrambled on up the smooth, roof-like slope, steadying our ascent by the tripod legs used as alpine stock. When we had climbed perhaps a thousand feet the surface angle became somewhat gentler, and we were able to overlook before us the whole broad incline up to the very peak. For a mile or a mile and a half, the sharp blue edges of crevasses were apparent here and there yawning widely for the length of a thousand feet, and at other places intersecting each other confusedly, resulting in piled-up masses of shattered ice.

We were charmed to enter this wild region, and hurried to the edge of an immense chasm. It could hardly have been less than a thousand or twelve hundred feet in length. The solid white wall of the opposite side — sixty feet over — fell smooth and vertical for a hundred feet or more, where rough wedged blocks and bridges of clear blue ice stretched from wall to wall. From these

and from numerous overhanging shelves hung the long
crystal threads of icicles, and beyond, dark and impenetrable, opened ice-caverns of unknown limit. We cautiously walked along this brink, examining with deep
interest all the lines of stratification and veining, and the
strange succession of views down into the fractured
regions below.

I had the greatest desire to be let down with a line
and make my way among these pillars and bridges of ice,
but our little twenty feet of slender rope forbade the
attempt. Farther up, the crevasses walled us about more
and more. At last we got into a region where they cut
into one another, breaking the whole glacier body into a
confused pile of ice blocks. Here we had great difficulty
in seeing our way for more than a very few feet, and
were constantly obliged to climb to the top of some
dangerous block to get an outlook, and before long,
instead of a plain with here and there a crevasse, we
were in a mass of crevasses separated only by thin and
dangerous blades of ice.

We still pushed on, tied together with our short line,
jumping over pits and chasms, holding our breath over
slender snow-ridges, and beginning to think the work
serious. We climbed an ice-crag together; all around
rose strange, sharp forms; below, in every direction,
yawned narrow cuts, caves trimmed with long stalactites
of ice, walls ornamented with crystal pilasters, and dark-
blue grottoes opening down into deeper and more gloomy
chambers, as silent and cold as graves.

Far above the summit rose white and symmetrical, its
sky-line sweeping down sharp against the blue. Below,
over ice-wreck and frozen waves, opened the deep valley
of camp, leading our vision down to distant forest slopes.

We were in the middle of a vast convex glacier surface

which embraced the curve of Shasta for four miles around, and at least five on the slope line, ice stretching in every direction and actually bounding the view on all sides except where we looked down.

The idea of a mountain glacier formed from Swiss or Indian views is always of a stream of ice walled in by more or less lofty ridges. Here a great curved cover of ice flows down the conical surface of a volcano without lateral walls, a few lava pinnacles and inconspicuous piles of *débris* separating it from the next glacier, but they were unseen from our point. Sharp white profiles met the sky. It became evident we could go no farther in the old direction, and we at once set about retracing our steps, but in the labyrinth soon lost the barely discernible tracks and never refound them. Whichever way we turned impassable gulfs opened before us, but just a little way to the right or left it seemed safe and traversable. At last I got provoked at the ill-luck, and suggested to Clark that we might with advantage take a brief intermission for lunch, feeling that a lately quieted stomach is the best defence for nerves. So when we got into a pleasant, open spot where the glacier became for a little way smooth and level, we sat down, leisurely enjoying our repast. We saw a possible way out of our difficulty, and sat some time chatting pleasantly. When there was no more lunch we started again, and only three steps away came upon a narrow crack edged by sharp ice-jaws. There was something noticeable in the hollow, bottomless darkness seen through it which arrested us, and when we had jumped across to the other side, both knelt and looked into its depths. We saw a large domed grotto walled in with shattered ice and arched over by a roof of frozen snow so thin that the light came through quite easily. The middle of this dome overhung a terrible abyss. A block of ice thrown in fell from ledge to ledge, echoing back its stroke fainter and fainter. We had unconsciously sat for twenty minutes lunching and laughing on the thin roof, with only a few inches of frozen snow to hold us up over that still, deep grave. A noonday sun rapidly melting its surface, the warmth of our persons slowly thawing it, and both of us playfully drumming the frail crest with our tripod legs. We looked at one another, and agreed that we lost confidence in glaciers.

Splendid rifts now opened to north of us, with slant sunshine lighting up one· side in vivid contrast with the cold, shadowed wall. We greatly enjoyed a tall precipice with a gaping crevasse at its base, and found real pleasure in the north edge of the great ice-field, whither we now turned. A low moraine, with here and there a mass of rock which might be solid, flanked the glacier, but was separated from it by a deeply melted crevasse, opening irregular caverns along the wall down under the very glacier body. We were some time searching a point where this gulf might be safely crossed. A thin tongue of ice, sharpened by melting to a mere blade, jutted from the solid glacier over to the moraine, offering us a passage of some danger and much interest. We edged our way along astride its crest, until a good spring carried us over a final crevasse and up upon the moraine, which we found to be dangerously built up of honeycombed ice and boulders. The same perilous sinks and holes surrounded us, and alternated with hollow archways over subterranean streams. It was a relief, after an hour's labor, to find ourselves on solid lava, although the ridge, which proved to be a chain of old craters, was one of the most dreary reaches I have ever seen.

In the evidence of glacier motion there had seemed a
form of life, but here among silent, rigid crater rims and
stark fields of volcanic sand, we walked upon ground
lifeless and lonely beyond description : a frozen desert at
nine thousand feet altitude. Among the huge rude forms
of lava we tramped along, happy when the tracks of
mountain sheep suggested former explorers, and pleased
if a snowbank under rock shadow gave birth to spring
or pool. But the severe impression of arctic dreariness
passed off when, reaching a rim, we looked over and
down upon the volcano's north foot, a superb sweep of
forest country waved with ridgy flow of lava and gracefully curved moraines.

Afar off, the wide sunny Shasta Valley, dotted with
miniature volcanoes, and checked with the yellow and
green of grain and garden, spread pleasantly away to the
north, bounded by Klamath hills and horizoned by the
blue rank of Siskiyou Mountains. To our left the cone
slope stretched away to Sisson's, the sharp form of the
Black Cone rising in the gap between Shasta and Scott
Mountain.

Here again the tremendous contrast between lava and
ice about us, and that lovely expanse of ranches and verdure impressed anew its peculiar force.

We tramped on along the glacier edge, over rough
ridges and slopes of old moraine, rounding at last the ice
terminus, and crossing the valley to camp, where our
three mules welcomed us with friendly discord.

A day's march over forest-covered moraines and through
open glades brought us to the main camp at Sheep Rock,
uniting us with our friends. The heavier air of this lower
level soothed us into a pleasant laziness which lasted over
Sunday, resting our strained muscles and opening the
heart anew to human and sacred influence. If we are

sometimes at pain when realizing within what narrow range of latitude mankind reaches finer development, how short a step it is from tropical absence of spiritual life to dull boreal stupidity, it is added humiliation to experience our marked limitation in altitude. At fourteen thousand feet, little is left me but bodily appetite and impression of sense. The habit of scientific observation, which in time becomes one of the involuntary processes, goes on as do heart-beat and breathing; a certain general awe overshadows the mind; but on descending again to lowlands, one after another the whole riches of the human organization come back with delicious freshness. Something of this must account for my delight in finding the family of Preuxtemps (a half-Cherokee mountaineer known hereabouts as Pro-tem) camped near us. Protem was a barbarian by choice, and united all the wilder instincts with a domestic passion worthy his Caucasian ancestor, and quite charming in its childlike manifestation.

Protem *mère*, an obese Digger squaw, so evidently avoided us that I respected her feelings and never once visited their bivouac, although the flutter of gaudy rags and that picturesque squalor of which she and the camp-fire were centre and soul, sorely tempted me.

The old man and his four little barefoot girls, if not actually familiar were more than sociable, and spent much time with us. The elder three, ranging from eight to twelve, were shy and timid as little quails, dodging about and scampering off to some hiding-place when I strove to introduce myself through the medium of such massive sweet-cakes as our William produced. Not so the little six-year old Clarissa, who in all frankness met my advances and repaid me for the cookies she silently devoured by gentlest and most fascinating smiles.

A stained and earth-hued flour-sack rudely gathered into a band was her skirt, and confined the little, long-sleeved, pink calico sack. From out a voluminous sun-bonnet with long cape shone the chubby face of my little friend. For all she was so young and charmingly small, Clarissa was woman rather than child. She took entire care of herself, and prowled about in a self-contained way, making studies and observations with ludicrous gravity. Early mornings she came with slow matronly gait down to the horse-trough, and rolling up her sleeves, laid aside the huge sun-bonnet, washed her face and hands, wiping them on her petticoat, and arranged her jetty Indian hair with the quiet unconsciousness of fifty years.

Her good-morning nod, with the reserved yet affectionate smile, put me in happiness for the day, and when as I strolled about she overtook me and placed her little hand in mine, looking up with fearless, quiet confidence, I measured step with her, and we held sweet chats about squirrels and field-mice. But I thought her most charming when she brought her father down to our camp-fire after supper, and, alternately on his knee or mine, listened to our stories and wound a soft little arm about my neck. The twilight passed agreeably thus, Clarissa gradually paying less and less attention to our yarns, till she pulled the skirts of my cavalry coat over her, and curling up on my lap laid her dear little head on my breast, smiled, gaped, rubbed with plump knuckles the blinking eyes, dozed, and at last sank into a deep sleep.

I can even now see old Protem draw an explanatory map on the ground his moccasin had smoothed, and go on with his story of bear fight or wolf trap, illustrating by singularly apt gesture every trait and motion of the

animal he described, while firelight warmed the brown
skin and ruddy cheek of my little charge and flickered on
her soft black hair.

The last bear story of an evening being ended, Protem
took from me Clarissa, whose single yawn and pretty
bewilderment subsided in a second, leaving her sound
asleep on the buckskin shoulder of her father.

About half way between Sheep Rock and the snow-
line extensive eruptions of basalt have occurred, deluging
the lower slopes, and flowing in gently inclined fields and
streams down through Shasta Valley for many miles.
The surface of this basalt country is singularly diversified. Rising above its general level are numerous domes,
some of them smoothly arched over with rock, others
perforated at the top, and more broken in circular para-
pets. The origin of these singular blisters is probably
simple. Overflowing former trachyte fields the basalt
swept down, covering a series of pools and brooks. The
water converted into steam blew up the viscous rock in
such forms as we find. Here and there the basalt surface opens in circular orifices, into which you may look
a hundred feet or more.

In 1863, in company with Professor Brewer, I visited
this very region, and we were then shown an interesting
tubular cavern lying directly under the surface of a lava
plain.

Mr. Palmer and I revisited the spot, and, having tied our
mules, descended through a circular hole to the cavern's
mouth. An archway of black lava sixty feet wide by
eighty high, with a floor of lava sand and rough boulders,
led under the basalt in a northerly direction, preserving
an incline not more than the gentle slope of the country.
Our roof overhead could hardly have been more than
twenty or thirty feet thick. We followed the cavern,

which was a comparatively regular tube, for half or three-quarters of a mile. Now and then the roof would open up in larger chambers, and the floor be cumbered with huge piles of lava, over which we scrambled, sometimes nearly reaching the ceiling. Fresh lava-froth and smooth blister-holes lined the sides. Innumerable bats and owls on silent wing floated by our candles, fanning an air singularly still and dense.

After a cautious scramble over a long pile of immense basalt blocks, we came to the end of the cave, and sat down upon piles of *débris*. We then repeated an experiment, formerly made by Brewer and myself, of blowing out our candle to observe the intense darkness, then firing a pistol that we might hear its dull, muffled explosion.

The formation of this cave, as explained in Professor Whitney's Geological Report, is this : A basalt stream, flowing down from Shasta, cooled and hardened upon the surface, while within the mass remained molten and fluid. From simple pressure the lava burst out at the lower end, and flowing forth left an empty tube. Wonderfully fresh and recent the whole confused rock-walls appeared, and we felt, as we walked and climbed back to the opening and to daylight, as if we had been allowed to travel back into the volcano agè.

One more view of Shasta, obtained a few days later from Well's ranch on the Yreka road, seems worthy of mention. From here the cone and side crater are in line, making a single symmetrical form with broad broken summit singularly like Cotopaxi.

You look over green meadows and cultivated fields ; beyond is a chain of little volcanoes girdling Shasta's foot, for the most part bare and yellow, but clouded in places with dark forest, which a little farther up mantles

the broad grand cone, and sweeps up over ridge and
cañon to alpine heights of rock and ice.

Strange and splendid is the evening effect from here,
when shadow over base and light upon summit divide
the vast pile into two zones of blue-purple and red-gold.
We watched the colors fade and the peak recede farther
and dimmer among darkness and stars.

XIII.

MOUNT WHITNEY.

1871.

THERE lay between Carson and Mount Whitney a ride of two hundred and eighty miles along the east base of the Sierra. Stage-driving, like other exact professions, gathers among its followers certain types of men and manners, either by some mode of natural selection or else after a Darwinian way developing one set of traits to the exclusion of others. However interesting it might be to investigate the moulding power of whip and reins, or to discover what measure of coachman there is latent in every one of us, it cannot be questioned that the characters of drivers do resemble one another in surprising degree. That ostentatious silence and self-contained way of ignoring one's presence on the box for the first half hour, the tragi-comic, just audible undertone in which they remonstrate with the swing team, and such single refrain of obsolete song as they drone and drone a hundred times, may be observed on every coach from San Diego to Montana.

So I found it natural enough that the driver, my sole companion from Carson to Aurora, should sit for the first hour in a silence, etiquette forbade me to violate. His team, by strict attention to their duties, must have left his mind quite free, and I saw symptoms of suppressed sociability within forty minutes of our departure.

The nine-mile house, if my memory serves, was his landmark for taciturnity, for soon after passing it he be-

gan to skirmish along a sort of picket line of conversation.
To the wheel mares he remarked, " hot, gals ; ain't it tho' ? "
and to his off leader, who strained wild eyes in every direction for something to become excited about, " look at
him Dixie, would n't you like a rabbit to shy at ? "

With a true driver's pride in reading men, he scanned
me from boots to barometer, and at last, to my immense
delight, said, with the air of throwing his hat into a ring,
" What mountain was you going down to measure ? "
Had he inquired after my grandfather by his first name,
I could not have been more surprised. At once I told
him the plain truth, and waited for further developments ;
but like an indifferent shot who drives centre on a first
trial he proposed not to endanger his reputation for infallibility by other ventures, and withdrew again to that
conspicuous stupidity which coachmen and Buddhists
alike delight in.

Left to myself, I spent hours in looking out over the
desert and up along that bold front of Sierra which rose
on our right from the sage plains of Carson Valley up
through ramparts of pine land to summits of rock and
ravines with sunken snow-banks.

So far as Aurora, I remember little worth describing.
Sierras, or outlying volcanic foot hills, bound the west.
About our road are desert plains and rolling sage-clad
hills, fresh light olive at this June season, and softly sloping in long *glacis* down to wide impressive levels.

Green valleys and cultivated farms margin the Carson
and Walker rivers. Sierras are not lofty enough to be
grand, desert too gentle and overspread with sage to be
terrible ; yet the pale high key of all its colors, and singular aerial brilliancy lend an otherwise dreary enough
picture the charm, — as I once before said, — of water-
color drawings. There is no perspective under this fierce

12

white light; in midday, intensely sharp reflections glare
from hill and valley, except where the shadow of passing
cloud spreads cool and blue over olive slopes.

Alas for Aurora once so active and bustling with silver
mines and its almost daily murder. Twenty-six whiskey
hells and two Vigilance Committees graced those days of
prosperity and mirthful gallows, of stock-board and the
gay delirium of speculation. Now her sad streets are
lined with closed doors ; a painful silence broods over
quartz mills, and through the whole deserted town one
perceives that melancholy security of human life which
is hereabouts one of the pathetic symptoms of bankruptcy.
The " boys " have gone off to merrily shoot one another
somewhere else, leaving poor Aurora in the hands of a
sort of coroner's jury who gather nightly at the one saloon
and hold dreary inquests over departed enterprise.

My landlord's tread echoed through a large empty hotel,
and when I responded to his call for lunch the silentest
of girls became medium between me and a Chinaman
who gazed sad-eyed through his kitchen door as in pity for
one who must choose between starving and his own cookery. But I have always felt it unpardonable egotism for
a traveller to force the reader into sharing with him the
inevitable miseries of roadside food. Whatever merit
there may be in locking this prandial grief fast from
public view, I feel myself entitled to in a high degree,
for I hold it in my power to describe the most revolting
cuisine on the planet, yet refrain.

From Aurora my road, still parallel with the mountains though now hidden from them by banks of volcanic
hills, climbed a long wearisome slope from whose summit
a glorious panorama of snowy Sierras lay before us.
From our feet, steep declivities sloped two thousand feet
to the level of a wide desert basin, bounded upon the west

by long ranks of high white peaks, and otherwise walled
in by chains of volcanic hills, smooth with dull sage flanks,
and yet varied here and there by out-cropping formations
of eruptive rocks and dusky cedar forests.

Just at the Sierra foot, surrounded by bare gray volcanoes and reaches of ashen plain, lies Mono lake, a broad
oval darkened along its farther shore by reflecting the
shadowed mountains, and pale tranquil blue where among
light desert levels it mirrors the silken softness of sky
and cloud. Flocks of pelicans, high against the sky,
floated in slow wheeling flight, reflecting the sun from
white wings, and turning, were lost in the blue to gleam
out again like flakes of snow.

The eye ranges over strange forbidding hill-forms and
leagues of desert, from which no familiarity can ever
banish suggestions of death. Traced along boundary hills,
straight terraces of an ancient beach indicate former
water-levels, and afar in the Sierra, great empty gorges,
glacier-burnished and moraine-flanked, lead up to amphitheatres of rock once white with *névé*.

I recognized the old familiar summits: Mount Ritter,
Lyell, Dana, and that firm peak with titan strength and
brow so square and solid, it seems altogether natural we
should have named it for California's statesman, John
Conness.

We rumbled down hill and out upon the desert, plodding until evening through sand, and over rocky, cedar-
wooded spurs, at last crossing adobe meadows, where
were settlements and a herd of Spanish cattle which had
escaped the drought of California, and now marched,
northward bound, for Montana.

Frowning volcanic hills flanked our road as evening
wore on, lifting dark forms against a sky singularly pale
and luminous. Afar, we caught glimpses of the dark

swelling Sierra wave thrusting up "star-neighboring peaks," and then descending into hollows among lava mounds, found ourselves shut completely in. A night at the Hot Springs of Partzwick was notably free from anything which may be recounted.

Morning found me waiting alone on the hotel veranda, and I suppose the luxuries of the establishment must have left a stamp of melancholy upon my face, for the little solemn driver who drew up his vehicle at the door said in a tone of condolence, " the hearse is ready."

Stages, drivers and teams had been successively worse as I journeyed southward. This little old specimen, by whose side I sat from Partzwick to Independence, ought to be excepted, and I should neglect a duty were I not to portray one, at least, of his traits. He was a musical old fellow, and given to chanting in low tones songs, sometimes pathetic, often sentimental, but in every case preserved by him in most fragmentary recollection. Such singing suffered, too, from the necessary and frequent interruption of driving; the same breath quavering in cracked melody, and tossing some neatly rounded oath or horse-phrase at off or near wheeler, catching up an end of the refrain again in time to satisfy his musical requirements.

All the morning he had warned me most impressively to count myself favored if a certain bridge over Bishop's Creek should not sink under us and cast me upon wild waters. Rightly estimating my friend, I was not surprised when we reached the spot to find a good solid structure bridging a narrow creek not more than four feet deep.

As we rolled on down Owen's Valley, he sang, chatted, and drove in a manner which showed him capable of three distinct, yet simultaneous mental processes. I follow his words as nearly as memory serves.

" That creek, sir, was six feet deep.

'Oh Lillie, sweet Lillie, dear Lillie Dale.'

What the devil are you shying at ? You cursed mustang, come up out of that ;

. . . . . 'little green grave.'

Yes, seven feet, and if we'd have fell in, swimming would n't saved us.

You, Balley, what are you a doin' on ;

''Neath the hill in the flowing vale.'

and what's more, we could n't have crawled up that bank, no how.

'My own dear Lillie Dale.'

You'd like to kick over them traces, would you ? Keep your doggoned neck up snug against that collar, and take that.

We'd drowned, sir; drowned sure as thunder.

'In the place where the violets grow.'"

Desert hills, and low, mountain gateways opening views of vast sterile plains, no longer form our eastern outlook. The White Mountains, a lofty barren chain vieing with the Sierras in altitude, rose in splendid rank and stretched southeast parallel with the great range. Down the broad intermediate trough flows Owen's river, alternately through expanses of natural meadow and desolate reaches of sage.

The Sierra, as we travelled southward, grew bolder and bolder, strong granite spurs plunging steeply down into the desert ; above, the mountain sculpture grew grander and grander, until forms wild and rugged as the Alps stretched on in dense ranks as far as the eye could reach. More and more the granite came out in all its strength. Less and less soil covered the slopes : groves of pine became rarer, and sharp, rugged buttresses advanced boldly to the

plain.   Here and there a cañon-gate between rough granite pyramids, and flanked by huge moraines, opened its
savage gallery back among peaks.   Even around the summits there was but little snow, and the streams which at
short intervals flowed from the mountain foot, traversing
the plains, were sunken far below their ordinary volume.
The mountain forms and mode of sculpture of the opposite ranges are altogether different.   The White and Inyo
chains, formed chiefly of uplifted sedimentary beds, are
largely covered with soil, and wherever the solid rock is
exposed, its easily traced strata plains and soft wooded
surface combined in producing a general aspect of breadth
and smoothness ; while the Sierra, here more than anywhere else, hold up a front of solid stone, carved into
most intricate and highly ornamental forms.   Vast
aiguilles, trimmed from summit to base with line of slender minarets, huge broad domes, deeply fluted and surmounted with tall obelisks, and everywhere the greatest
profusion of bristling points.

From the base of each range a long sloping talus descends gently to the river, and here and there, bursting up
through Sierra foot-hills, rise the red and black forms of
recent volcanoes as regular and barren as if cooled but
yesterday.

I had reason for not regretting my departure from the
Inyo House at Independence next morning before sunrise ; and when a young woman in an elaborate brown
calico, copied evidently from some imperial evening
toilet, pertly demanded my place by the driver, adding
that she was not one of the " inside kind," I willingly
yielded, and made myself contented on the back seat
alone.   Presently, however, a companion came to me in
the person of a middle-aged Spanish donna, clad altogether in black, with a shawl worn over her head after

the manner of a mantilla. When it began to rain violently and beat upon that brown calico, I made bold to offer the young woman my sheltered place, but she ga'yly declined, averring herself not made of sugar. So the donna and I shared my great coat across our laps and established relations of civility, though she spoke no English, and I only that little Spanish so much more embarassing than none.

In her smile, in the large soft eyes, and that tinge of Castilian blood which shone red-warm through olive cheek, I saw the signs of a race blessed with sturdier health than ours. With snowy hair growing low on a massive forehead, and just a glimpse now and then of large gold beads, through a white handkerchief about her throat, she seemed to me a charming picture : though, perhaps, her fine looks gained something by contrasting with the sickly girl in front, whose pallor and cough could not have meant less than the pretubercular state.

Clouds covered the mountains on either hand, leaving me only ranches and people to observe. May I be forgiven if I am wrong in accounting for the late improvement of political tone in Tuolumne by the presence here of so large a share of her most degraded citizens ; people whose faces and dress and life and manners are sadder than any possibilities held up to us by Darwin.

My long ride ended in a few hours at Lone Pine, where, from the hotel window, I watched a dark-blue mass of storm which covered and veiled the region where I knew my goal, the Whitney summit, must stand.

For two days storm-curtains hung low about Sierra base, their vapor banks, dark with fringes of shower, at times drifted out over Lone Pine and quenched a thirsty earth. On the third afternoon blue sky shone through rifts overhead, and now and then a single peak, dashed with broken sunshine, rose for a moment over rolling clouds which swelled above it again like huge billows.

About an hour before sunset the storm began rapidly to sink into level fold, over which, in clear yellow light, emerged " cloud-compelling " peaks. The liberated sun poured down shafts of light, piercing the mist which now in locks of gold and gray blew about the mountain heads in wonderful splendor.

How deep and solemn a blue filled the cañon depths! what passion of light glowed around the summits! With delight I watched them one after another fading till only the sharp terrible crest of Whitney, still red with reflected light from the long sunken sun, showed bright and glorious above the whole Sierra.

Upon observing the topography, I saw that one bold spur advanced from Mount Whitney to the plain; on either side of it profound cañons opened back to the summit. I remembered the impossibility of making a climb up those northern precipices, and at once chose the more southern gorge.

Next morning we set out on horseback for the mountain base, twelve miles across plains and through an outlying range of hills. My companion for the trip was Paul Pinson, as tough and plucky a mountaineer as France ever sent us, who consented readily to follow me. José, the mild-mannered and grinning Mexican boy who rode with us, was to remain in care of our animals at the foot-hills while we made the climb.

I left a Green barometer to be observed at Lone Pine, and carried my short high-mountain instrument, by the same excellent maker.

Gauzy mists again enveloped the Sierra, leaving us free minds to enjoy a ride, of which the very first mile supplied me food for days of thought.

The American residents of Lone Pine outskirts live in a homeless fashion; sullen, almost arrogant neglect stares out from the open doors. There is no attempt at grace, no memory of comfort, no suggested hope for improvement.

Not so the Spanish homes; their low, adobe, wide-roofed cabins neatly enclosed with even basket-work fence, and lining hedge of blooming hollyhock.

We stopped to bow good morning to my friend and stage companion, the donna. She sat in the threshold of her open door, sewing; beyond her stretched a bare floor, clean and white: the few chairs, the table spread with snowy linen, everything, shone with an air of religious spotlessness. Symmetry reigned in the precise, well-kept garden, arranged in rows of pepper-plants and crisp heads of vernal lettuce.

I longed for a painter to catch her brilliant smile, and surround her on canvas as she was here, with order and dignity. The same plain, black dress clad her heavy ample figure, and about the neck heavy barbaric gold beads served again as collar.

Under low eaves above her, and quite around the house, hung, in triple row, festoons of flaming red peppers, in delicious contrast with the rich adobe gray.

It was a study of order and true womanly repose, fitted to cheer us, and a grouping of such splendid color as might tempt a painter to cross the world.

A little farther on we passed an Indian ranchero where several willow wickyups were built upon the bank of a cold brook. Half naked children played about here and there, a few old squaws bustled at household work; but nearly all lay outstretched, dozing. A sort of tattered brilliancy characterized the place. Gay, high-colored squalor reigned. There seemed hardly more lack of thrift or sense of decorum than in the American ranches,

12 *   B

yet somehow the latter send a stab of horror through one, while this quaint indolence and picturesque neglect seem aptly contrived to set off the Indian genius for loafing, and leave you with a sort of æsthetic satisfaction, rather than the sorrow their half development should properly evoke.

Leaving all this behind us, our road led westward across a long sage slope entering a narrow tortuous pass through a low range of outlying granite hills. Strangely weathered forms towered on either side, their bare brown surface contrasting pleasantly with the vivid ribbon of willows which wove a green and silver cover over swift water.

The granite was riven with innumerable cracks, showing here and there a strong tendency to concentric forms, and I judged the immense spheroidal boulders which lay on all sides, piled one upon another, to be the kernels or nuclei of larger masses.

Quickly crossing this ridge we came out upon the true Sierra foot-slope, a broad inclined plain stretching north and south as far as we could see. Directly in front of us rose the rugged form of Mount Whitney spur, a single mass of granite, rough-hewn, and darkened with coniferous groves. The summits were lost in a cloud of almost indigo hue.

Putting our horses at a trot we quickly ascended the *glacis*, and at the very foot of the rocks dismounted, and made up our packs. José, with the horses, left us and went back half a mile to a mountain ranch where he was to await our return; and presently Pinson and I, with heavy burdens upon our backs, began slowly to work our way up the granite spur and toward the great cañon.

An hour's climb brought us around upon the south wall of our spur, and about a thousand feet above a stream which dashed and leaped along the cañon bottom, through wild ravines and over granite bluffs. Our slope was a rugged rock-face, giving foothold here and there to pine and juniper trees, but for the greater part bare and bold.

Far above, at an elevation of ten thousand feet, a dark grove of alpine pines gathered in the cañon bed. Thither we bent our steps, edging from cleft to cleft, making constant, though insignificant, progress. At length our wall became so wild and deeply cut with side cañons, we found it impossible to follow it longer, and descended carefully to the bottom.

Almost immediately, with heavy wind gusts and sound as of torrents, a storm broke upon us, darkening the air and drenching us to the skin. The three hours we toiled up over rocks, through dripping willow-brooks and among trains of *débris*, were not noticeable for their cheerfulness.

The storm had ceased, but it was evening when, wet and exhausted, we at length reached the alpine grove, and threw ourselves down for rest under a huge overhanging rock which offered its shelter for our bivouac.

Logs, soon brought in by Pinson, were kindled. The hot blaze seemed pleasant to us, though I cannot claim to have enjoyed those two hours spent in turning round and round before it while steaming and drying. But the broiled beef, the toast, and those generous cups of tea to which we devoted the hour between ten and eleven were quite satisfactory. So, too, was the pleasant chat till midnight warned us to roll up in overcoats and close our eyes to the fire, to the dark sombre grove, and far stars crowding the now cloudless heavens.

The sun arose and shone on us while we breakfasted. Through all the visible sky not a cloud could be seen, and, thanks to yesterday's rain, the air was of crystal purity. Into it the granite summits above us projected forms of sunlit gray.

Up the glacier valley above camp we slowly tramped through a forest of noble Pinus Flexilis, the trunks of bright sienna contrasting richly with deep bronze foliage.

Minor flutings of a medial moraine offered gentle grade and agreeable footing for a mile and more, after which, by degrees, the woods gave way to a wide, open amphitheatre surrounded with cliffs.

I can never enter one of these great hollow mountain chambers without a pause. There is a grandeur and spaciousness which expand and fit the mind for yet larger sensations when you shall stand on the height above.

Velvet of alpine sward edging an icy brooklet by whose margin we sat down, reached to the right and left far enough to spread a narrow foreground, over which we saw a chain of peaks swelling from either side toward our amphitheatre's head, where, springing splendidly over them all, stood the sharp form of Whitney.

Precipices white with light and snow fields of incandescent brilliance grouped themselves along walls and slopes. All around us, in wild, huge heaps, lay wreck of glacier and avalanche.

We started again, passing the last tree and began to climb painfully up loose *débris* and lodged blocks of the north wall. From here to the very foot of that granite pyramid which crowns the mountain, we found neither difficulty nor danger, only a long, tedious climb over footing which, from time to time, gave way provokingly.

By this time mist floated around the brow of Mount Whitney, forming a gray helmet, from which, now and then, the wind blew out long waving plumes. After a brief rest we began to scale the southeast ridge, climbing from rock to rock, and making our way up steep fields of soft snow. Precipices, sharp and severe, fell away to east and west of us, but the rough pile above still afforded a way. We had to use extreme caution, for many blocks hung ready to fall at a touch, and the snow, where we were forced to work up it, often gave way, threatening to hurl us down into cavernous hollows.

When within a hundred feet of the top I suddenly fell through, but, supporting myself by my arms, looked down into a grotto of rock and ice, and out through a sort of window, over the western bluffs, and down thousands of feet to the far away valley of the Kern.

I carefully and slowly worked my body out, and crept on hands and knees up over steep and treacherous ice-crests, where a slide would have swept me over a brink of the southern precipice.

We kept to the granite as much as possible, Pinson taking one train of blocks and I another. Above us but thirty feet rose a crest, beyond which we saw nothing. I dared not think it the summit till we stood there, and Mount Whitney was under our feet.

Close beside us a small mound of rock was piled upon the peak, and solidly built into it an Indian arrow-shaft, pointing due west.

I climbed out to the southwest brink, and, looking down, could see that fatal precipice which had prevented me seven years before. I strained my eyes beyond, but already dense, impenetrable clouds had closed us in.

On the whole, this climb was far less dangerous than I had reason to hope. Only at the very crest, where ice and rock are thrown together insecurely, did we encounter any very trying work. The utter unreliableness of that honeycomb and cavernous cliff was rather uncomfortable, and might, at any moment, give the death-fall to one who had not coolness and muscular power at instant command.

I hung my barometer from the mound of our Indian

predecessor, nor did I grudge his hunter pride the honor
of first finding that one pathway to the summit of the
United States, fifteen thousand feet above two oceans.

While we lunched I engraved Pinson's and my name
upon a half dollar, and placed it in a hollow of the crest.
Clouds still hung motionless over us, but in half an hour
a west wind drew across, drifting the heavy vapors along
with it. Light poured in, reddening the clouds, which
soon rolled away, opening a grand view of the western
Sierra ridge, and of the whole system of the Kern.

Only here and there could blue sky be seen, but fortunately the sun streamed through one of these windows in
the storm, lighting up splendidly the snowy rank from
Kaweah to Mount Brewer.

There they rose as of old, firm and solid; even the
great snow-fields, though somewhat shrunken, lay as they
had seven years before. I saw the peaks and passes and
amphitheatres, dear old Cotter and I had climbed: even
that Mount Brewer pass where we looked back over the
pathway of our dangers, and up with regretful hearts to
the very rock on which I sat.

Deep below flowed the Kern, its hundred snow-fed
branches gleaming out amid rock and ice, or traced far
away in the great glacier trough by dark lines of pine.
There, only twelve miles northwest, stretched that ragged
divide where Cotter and I came down the precipice with
our rope. Beyond, into the vague blue of King's cañon,
sloped the ice and rock of Mount Brewer wall.

Sombre storm-clouds and their even gloomier shadows
darkened the northern sea of peaks. Only a few slant
bars of sudden light flashed in upon purple granite and
fields of ice. The rocky tower of Mount Tyndall, thrust
up through rolling billows, caught for a moment the full
light, and then sank into darkness and mist.

When all else was buried in cloud we watched the great west range. Weird and strange, it seemed shaded by some dark eclipse. Here and there through its gaps and passes, serpent-like streams of mist floated in and crept slowly down the cañons of the hither slope, then all along the crest, torn and rushing spray of clouds whirled about the peaks, and in a moment a vast gray wave reared high, and broke, overwhelming all.

Just for a moment every trace of vapor cleared away from the east, unveiling for the first time spurs and gorges and plains. I crept to a brink and looked down into the Whitney cañon, which was crowded with light. Great scarred and ice-hewn precipices reached down four thousand feet, curving together like a ship, and holding in their granite bed a thread of brook, the small sapphire gems of alpine lake, bronze dots of pine, and here and there a fine enamelling of snow.

Beyond and below lay Owen's Valley, walled in by the barren Inyo chain, and afar, under a pale sad sky, lengthened leagues and leagues of lifeless desert.

The storm had even swept across Kern cañon, and dashed high against the peaks north and south of us. A few sharp needles and spikes struggled above it for a moment, but it rolled over them and rushed in torrents down the desert slope, burying everything in a dark swift cloud.

We hastened to pack up our barometer and descend. A little way down the ice crust gave way under Pinson, but he saved himself, and we hurried on, reaching safely the cliff-base, leaving all dangerous ground above us.

So dense was the cloud we could not see a hundred feet, but tramped gayly down over rocks and sand, feeling quite assured of our direction, until suddenly we came upon the brink of a precipice and strained our eyes off into the mist. I threw a stone over and listened in vain for the sound of its fall. Pinson and I both thought we had deviated too far to the north, and were on the brink of Whitney cañon, so we turned in the opposite direction, thinking to cross the ridge entering our old amphitheatre, but in a few moments we again found ourselves upon the verge. This time a stone we threw over, answered with a faint dull crash from five hundred feet below. We were evidently upon a narrow blade. I remembered no such place, and sat down to carefully recall every detail of topography. At last I concluded that we had either strayed down upon the Kern side, or were on one of the cliffs overhanging the head of our true amphitheatre.

Feeling the necessity of keeping cool, I determined to ascend to the foot of the snow and search for our tracks. So we slowly climbed there again and took a new start.

By this time the wind howled fiercely, bearing a chill from snow-crystals and sleet. We hurried on before it, and after one or two vain attempts, succeeded in finding our old trail down the amphitheatre slope, descending very rapidly to its floor.

From here, an exhausting tramp of five hours through the pine forest to our camp, and on down the rough wearying slopes of the lower cañon, brought us to the plain where José and the horses awaited us.

From Lone Pine that evening, and from the open carriage in which I rode northward to Independence, I constantly looked back and up into the storm, hoping to catch one more glimpse of Mount Whitney; but all the range lay submerged in dark rolling cloud, from which now and then a sullen mutter of thunder reverberated.

For years our chief, Professor Whitney, has made brave campaigns into the unknown realm of Nature. Against low prejudice and dull indifference he has led the survey

of California onward to success. There stand for him
two monuments, — one a great report made by his own
hand; another the loftiest peak in the Union, begun for
him in the planet's youth and sculptured of enduring
granite by the slow hand of Time.

1873.

THE preceding pages were written immediately after
my return from Mount Whitney, and without a shadow
of suspicion that among the sea of peaks half seen, half
storm-hidden, I could have missed the true summit.

Professor Whitney alone possessed sufficiently studied
data to apply the annual corrections for barometric oscillation in the high Sierra, and to his office I at once for-
warded my observations noted upon the Mount Whitney
summit, together with the record of simultaneous readings
at Lone Pine, the station upon which I relied for a base.
As I was about mailing the chapter to our printer, from
my camp in the Rocky Mountains, I received from Professor Pettee, who had kindly made a computation, the
puzzling despatch that Mount Whitney only reached
fourteen thousand six hundred and ten feet in altitude.
Realizing at once that this must be an error, I attributed
it to some great abnormal oscillation of pressure due to
storm, and decided not to publish the measurement.

Then for a moment a sense of doubt came over me lest
I had been mistaken; but on carefully studying the map
it was reassuring to establish beyond doubt the identity of the peak designated on the Map of the Geological Survey of California as Mount Whitney with
the one I had climbed. The reader will perhaps appreciate, then, my surprise and disappointment, when, travel-

ling in the overland car to California in September, 1873, I read and re-read a communication by Mr. W. A. Goodyear, former Assistant of the Geological Survey, made to the California Academy of Sciences, in which he points out with great clearness that I had missed the real peak.

To explain most simply why Mr. Goodyear saw the true Mount Whitney when he reached the summit of my peak of 1871, it is only necessary to state that he had a clear day, and the evident fact stared him in the face. If the reader kindly refers to the preceding part of the chapter, descriptive of my 1871 climb, he will note that my visit was unfortunately during a great storm, through whose billows of cloud and eddying mists the landscape disclosed itself in fragmentary glimpses, — to repeat the expression of my note-book, " as through windows in the storm."

My little granite island was incessantly beaten by breakers of vague impenetrable cloud, and never once did the true Mount Whitney unveil its crest to my eager eyes. Only one glimpse and I should have bent my steps northward, restless till the peak was climbed. But then that would have left nothing for Goodyear, whose paper shows such evident relish in my mistake, that I accept my '71 ill-luck as providential. One has in this dark world so few chances of conferring innocent, pure delight.

It must always remain a bond between Goodyear and myself that in the only paper he has written on the high Sierras, it was his happy thought to point both pleasantry and argument with that most grotesque and sober of beasts, the mule ; and while my regard for all mules rises wellnigh into the realm of sentiment, I cherish no less a feeling than profound indebtedness toward the particular one who succeeded, with how great effort only a fellow-climber can know, in getting Mr. Goodyear on the now

nameless peak, whence, like Moses from Pisgah, he beheld
the promised land.

My gratitude is not all directed to the mule either;
from that just channel a stream is directed toward the
clear good judgment of my friend, who resolutely turned
his back on the alluring summit, and promptly quitted
the head of mule navigation to descend and hold me up
in my proper light. Pleasantry aside, and method being
largely a matter of taste, Mr. Goodyear deserves credit for
having so clearly pointed out my mistake, — credit which
I desire to bear honest tribute to, since his discovery has
already led several of us to climb the true peak, a labor
requiring little effort and rewarded by the most striking
view in the Sierra Nevada.

Of course I lost no time in directing my steps toward
Mount Whitney, animated with a lively delight which
was quite unclouded by the fact that two parties, who
had three thousand miles the start of me, were already
en route and certain to reach the goal before me.

Perhaps there is no element in the varied life of an
explorer so full of contemplative pleasure as the frequent
and rapid passages he makes between city life and home;
by that I mean his true home, where the flames of his
bivouac fire light up trunks of sheltering pine and make
an island of light in the silent darkness of the primeval
forest. The crushing juggernaut-car of modern life and
the smothering struggle of civilization are so far off that
the wail of suffering comes not, nor the din and dust of
it all; and out of your very memory for a time — alas!
only for a time — fade those too indelible examples of the
shallowness of society, those terrible pictures of sorrow
and wrong, and that perennial artifice which wellnigh
always chokes with its weedy growth the rare, fine flowers of art.

All is forgotten; those murky clouds which in town life dispute the serenity of one's spiritual air drift beyond view, and over you broods only the quiet sky of night, her white stars moving beyond fragrant pine-tops or lost in the dim tangle of their feathery foliage. Such is the mountaineer's evening spent contemplatively before his fire; the profound sense of nature's tranquillity filling his mind with its repose till the flames give way to embers, and guardian pines spread dusky arms over his sleep. Not less a contrast greets him when from simple field life the doors of a city suddenly open, and the huddled complexity of everything jostles him. Either way, and as often as one makes this transit between civilization and the wilds, one prizes most the pure, simple, strengthening joy of nature.

Thus, when from the heat and pressure of town in September, 1873, I suddenly plunged into the heart of the Sierra forest, a cool mountain sky of holy blue and my well-beloved trees, calm and vigorous as ever, communicated thrills of pleasure well worth my brief separation from them. Day after day through the green forest I rode on, leaving the mustang to choose his own gait, scarcely talking to my two campaign companions, who with the plodding pack-animals followed noiselessly behind. It was only when we ascended the east wall of the Kern Cañon on the Hockett trail, and reached the nebulous plateau where pine and granite and cloud form the three elements of a severe picture, that I felt myself filled to the brim with my long draught of nature and turned to my followers for society. I was accompanied by Seaman and Knowles, two settlers of Tule River, who had been good enough to take a thorough interest in my proposed trip. One less used than I to the strong originality and remarkable histories of frontiersmen might have marvelled at the

rich chat of these two men; for myself, however, I long
ago learned to expect under the rough garb and simple
manners of Western plainsmen and mountaineers a wealth
of experience, with its resultant harvest of philosophy.
Untrammelled by the schools, these men strike out boldly
and arrange the universe to suit themselves. Not alone
is this noticeable in matter of general interest; in the most
special subjects it will not do to assume an ignorance
at all in keeping with the primitive cut of their trousers
or their idiom, which shows strong affinities with the flint
period. As an instance, volcanic action has of late years
occupied much of my thoughts, and so dry a subject, one
would think, could not have fixed the interest of many
non-professional travellers. Judge of my feelings, therefore, on the night we reached the Kern Plateau and
camped with a solitary shepherd, to hear, without giving
direction to it myself, the conversation turn on volcanoes,
and to realize, as the group renewed our fire and hours
passed by, that my two companions had been in Iceland,
Hawaii, Java, and Ecuador, and that as for the sheep-
herder, he had rolled stones down nearly every prominent
approachable crater on the planet. I was reminded of
a certain vaquero who astounded Professor Brewer by
launching out boldly in the Latin names of Mexican
plants.

The Kern Plateau, so green and lovely on my former
visit in 1864, was now a gray sea of rolling granite
ridges, darkened at intervals by forest, but no longer vel-
veted with meadows and upland grasses. The indefati-
gable shepherds have camped everywhere, leaving hardly
a spear of grass behind them.

To the sad annoyance of our hungry horses we found
this true until we entered the rough, rocky cañon which
leads down from the false Mount Whitney, in whose

depths, among glacier erratics and dark pines, we se-
lected a spot where a vocal brook and patches of carex
meadow seemed to welcome us. During a three days'
painful illness which overtook me here, I felt that I
should never lose an opportunity to warn my fellow-
men against watermelon; which, after all, is only an
ingenious contrivance of nature to converge the waves
of motion from the midsummer sun, and, by the well-rec-
ognized principles of force conservation, transmute them
into so much potential colic.

Across from wall to wall of our deep glacier cañon the
morning sky stretched pure and blue, but without a trace
of that infinite depth, so dark and vacant, so alluringly
profound, when the sun nears its culmination. We arose
early, and were all three marching up the gentle acclivity
of the valley bottom, when from among the peaks darkly
profiled against the east, bold lances of light shot down
through gloom and shadow, touching with sudden brightness here a clump of feathery fir, there a heap of glacier
blocks, pencilling yellow lines across meadow-patch or
alpine tarn, and working out along the whole rocky amphitheatre above us those splendid contrasts of gold and
blue which are the delight of mountaineers and the despair of painters.

Knowles, with the keen eye of an accomplished hunter,
became conscious, as we marched along, just how lately
a mountain sheep had crossed our way, and occasionally
the whispered sound of light footfalls along the crags
overhead riveted his attention upon some gray mote on
the granite, and with the huntsman's habitual quiet he
would only ejaculate "two-year-old buck," or "too thin
for venison," or some similar phrase, indicating the marvellous acuteness of his senses.

Among the many serious losses man has suffered in

passing from a life of nature to one artificial, is to be numbered the fatal blunting of all his senses.

Step after step the cañon ascended, with great vacant corridors opening among the rocky buttresses on either side, till at last there were no more firs, the alpine meadows became mere patches, and a chilly wind drew down from among snow-drifts.

Here savage rock-grandeur and splendid sunlight forever struggle for mastery of effect. A cloud drifts over us, and the dark headlands of granite loom up with impending mightiness and seem to advance toward each other from opposite ranks; about their feet the wreck of centuries of avalanche, and above leaden vapors hurrying and whirling. All is dimness and gloom. Then overhead the clouds are furled away, and there is light, — light joyous, pure, gloom-dispelling, before whose intense, searching vividness shadows unfold and mystery vanishes.

Through such alternating sensations we wound our way around the débris-cumbered margin of two lakes of deep, transparent, beryl-colored water, and up to the very head of our amphitheatre, reaching an elevation of about thirteen thousand feet. We had thus far encountered very little snow and absolutely no climbing. All along it had seemed to us that from the cañon head we might easily climb to the dividing summit of the Sierras, and follow along it to Mount Whitney. I had taken pains to diverge from my unsuccessful route of 1864, which lay now to the east, and separated from us by a high wall, terminating in fantastic spires.

Upon mounting the ridge-top we found it impossible to reach the true summit of the range without first descending into a deep cañon, the ancient bed of a tributary glacier of the Kern; the ice now replaced by imposing slopes of granite débris, partly masked by snow, and plunging down into a lake of startling vitriol color.

We toiled cautiously down over insecure wreck of granite whose huge blocks threatened constantly to top-ple over us or to rush out from underfoot and gather into an avalanche.   A draught from the icy lake water, a brief rest on the sunny side of a huge erratic, and we began the slow, laborious ascent of the summit ridge. Unfortunately the footing was bad, being composed chiefly of granite gravel.   Of every stone in place and each snow spot we took advantage, making pauses for breath now and then, till at last we reached the crest, here a thin ridge, and hurriedly turned our eyes in the direction of Mount Whitney.

The sharp, dominating blade of granite rising a couple of miles northwest of us, over a group of spiry pinnacles, was unmistakable.   The same severe, beautiful crest I had struggled for in 1864 rose proudly into the blue, and, though near, seemed as inaccessible as ever.

In the opposite direction, about three miles away, in clear, uncolored plainness, stood the peak, where, in 1871, I had been led by the map, and my error perpetuated by the clouds.

In full view of both peaks it seemed strange I could have mistaken one for the other.

Infallibility in retrospect is one of the easiest condi-tions imaginable; yet when the ever-fresh memory of those seething cloud-forms comes back to me, when I see again the gloom made even wilder and darker by bolts of sunlight and illumined gauzes of mist, when I realize that the cloud-compelling peak itself never shone forth, I am free to confess that I should make the mistake again.

In charging this error upon the map, I do not in any

sense intend to reflect on Mr. C. F. Hoffmann, the accomplished chief topographer of the Survey, from whose skilful hand we owe the forthcoming map of Central California. His location of Mount Whitney depended upon two compass bearings only, — his own from Mount Brewer, which proves to have been unvitiated by local magnetic attraction; and mine from Mount Tyndall, which evidently is in error.

It is most curious to discover that my bearings made from a station on the northwest edge of Mount Tyndall, where I placed myself to observe on the peaks lying in that direction, are, when corrected for variation, true, while those taken from a block on the south edge of the summit not sixty feet from the first station are abnormal. This reminds me of the observations made by Professor Brewer during our hours of rest on the top of Lassen's Peak, where he found the summit block a local magnet.

Thus the map location on which Mr. Hoffmann relied, and of which, in 1871, I took copy, to identify the peak, was vitiated in a way neither of us could have foreseen, and a serious error might have crept into current geography but for the timely visit of Mr. Goodyear.

Mr. Hoffmann stands clear of blame in the matter. Upon my shoulders and those of my *participes criminis*, the storm and the local magnetic attraction, it all rests.

We sat for some time in that silence which even the rudest natures pay as an unconscious tribute to the august presence of a great mountain, and then began again the march toward Mount Whitney. Seaman, who had started ill, here felt so painfully the effect of altitude that we urged him to struggle no further against dizziness and nausea, but to return, which he did with reluctance. We parted at the very crown of the ridge, on the verge of a gulf which plunges down from Mount Whitney

13　　　　　　　　　　s

to Owen's Valley. Knowles, who is a sort of chamois, kept his head splendidly, and together we clambered around and up to the crest of a·bold needle about 14,400 feet high, from which the discouraging truth dawned upon us that it was impossible to surmount the three sharp pinnacles which lay between us and the delicately sculptured crest beyond.

To the right and below, three thousand feet down from our tower, I could trace the line of my attempted climb of 1864 to where it disappeared around a projecting buttress at the foot of the great precipice, which forms the eastern face of Mount Whitney and the subordinate pinnacles to the south.

To the left, through crags and splintered monoliths, we could catch a glimpse of a deep glacier basin lying west of Mount Whitney, enclosing great sweeps of débris and numerous vivid blue tarns.

Between the minarets we could also see portions of the southwest slope of Mount Whitney, which was evidently a smooth accessible face, and the one of all others to attempt. But the day was already too far advanced to leave us the remotest hope of even reaching the glacier basin west of Mount Whitney, and we decided to return to camp.

Before beginning our wearisome march I sketched the outline of the Mount Whitney group, which, so far as I know, differs from any other cluster of peaks. The Sierra here is a bold wall with an almost perpendicular front of about three thousand feet, which is crowned by sharp turrets, having a tendency to lean out over the eastern gulf; these are properly the crests of great rib-like buttresses which jut from the general surface of the granite front.

Mount Whitney itself springs up and out like the

prow of a sharp ocean steamer. Southward along the summit, my sketch is of a confused region òf rough-hewn granite obelisks and towers, all remarkable for the deep shattering to which the rock has- been subjected. It is a region which may even yet suffer considerable perceptible change, since a single winter's frost and snow must dislodge numberless blocks from the crests and flanks of the whole group. Indeed, at the time of my visit, notably the period of least snow and frost, we often heard the sharp rattle of falling débris.

We varied our course homeward by climbing along a lateral ridge, whence we could look into the Mount Whitney basin, and here we were favored by a fine view, chiefly pleasing to us because the whole accessible slope of the peak came out unobscured by intervening ridges.

It was evident that we must find a mule-pass through the granite waves, from our present camp around into the great glacier basin, or else plan our next attempt with provision and blankets on our backs and an uncertain number of days' clambering over the intervening cañons to the foot of our peak.

The shades of twilight were darkening the amphitheatre as we plodded homeward; ghostly cliffs and dim towers were hardly recognizable as defined against the evening sky, in which already a few pale stars shone tremulously.

I spare the reader the days of snow and sleet we spent under a temporary shelter constructed of blankets. I pass over the elaborate system of rivulets, which forever burrowed new channels and originated future geography under our tent. These were quickly forgotten the morning of the clear-up, as we quitted our camp under the shadow of the 1871 peak, and marched southwestward down the bowlder-strewn valley of our brook.

A fine series of lateral moraines flank this cañon on the left, moraines rising one above another in defined terraces, for the most part composed of granite blocks, but here and there of solid rock *in situ,* where the ridge throws out prominent spurs.

We ascended the north wall, zigzagging to and fro among pines, till, having climbed a thousand feet, we found ourselves upon a plateau of granite sand, among groves of *pinus flexilis,* which seemed (as to me the *sequoyas* always have) the relics of a past climatic condition, the well-preserved octogenarians of the forest. Through open groves of these giant trees, whose red gnarled trunks and dark green foliage stood out with artistic definition upon bare granite sand, we saw the deep cañon of the Kern a few miles to our left, and beyond it, swelling up in splendid rank against the west, my old friends, the Kaweah peaks, their dark pyramidal summits here and there touched with flashing ice-banks.

The deep bottom of Kern Cañon was hidden from us; its craggy edges broken and rounded by glacial action, and in part built upon by the fragments of great moraines, were especially powerful; and as a master's sketch emphasizes the leading lines, so here each sharply carved ravine or rock-rift is given force by lines of almost black pines. Startled bands of deer looked timidly at us for a moment and then bounded wildly away through the woods; all else was silent and motionless.

At evening we entered the long-hoped-for cañon and threaded our way up among moraines and forest, close to the foot of Mount Whitney, the peak itself rising grandly across the amphitheatre's head, every spire and rocky crevice brought sharply out in the warm evening sunlight. With my field-glass I could see that it was a simple brief walk of a few hours to the summit; and, all anxiety at rest, I lay down on my blankets to watch the effects of light.

As often as one camps at twelve thousand feet in the Sierra, the charm of crystally pure air, these cold, sparkling, gem-like tints of rock and alpine lake, the fiery bronze of foliage, and luminous though deep-toned sky, combine to produce an intellectual and even a spiritual elevation. Deep and stirring feelings come naturally, the present falls back into its true relation, one's own wearying identity shrinks from the broad, open foreground of the vision, and a calmness born of reverent reflections encompasses the soul.

At eleven o'clock next morning Knowles and I stood together on the topmost rock of Mount Whitney; we found there a monument of stones, and records of the two parties who had preceded us, the first Messrs. Hunter and Crapo, and afterward that of Rabe of the Geological Survey. The former were save Indian hunters; the first, so far as we know, who achieved this dominating summit. Mr. Rabe has the honor of the first measurement by barometer. Our three visits were all within a month.

The day was cloudless and the sky, milder than is common over these extreme heights, warmed to a mellow glow and rested in softening beauty over minaret and dome. Air and light seemed melted together; even the wild rocks springing up all about us wore an aspect of aerial delicacy. Round the wide panorama, half low desert, half rugged granite mountains, each detail was observable, but a uniform luminous medium toned, without obscuring, the field of vision. That fearful sense of wreck and desolation, of a world crushed into fragments, of the ice chisel which, unseen, has wrought this strange mountain sculpture, all the sensations of power and tragedy I had invariably felt before on high peaks, were totally

forgotten. It was the absolute reverse of the effect on
Mount Tyndall, where an unrelenting clearness discovered every object in all its power and reality. Then we
saw only unburied wreck of geologic struggles, black
with sudden shadow or white under searching focus, as if
the sun were a great burning-glass, gathering light from
all space, and hurling its fierce shafts upon spire and
wall.

Now it was like an opal world, submerged in a sea of
dreamy light, down through whose motionless, transparent depths I became conscious of sunken ranges, great
hollows of undiscernible depth, reefs of pearly granite as
clear and delicate as the coral banks in a tropical ocean.
It was not like a haze in the lower world which veils
away distance in softly vanishing perspective ; there
was no mist, no vagueness, no loss of form nor fading
of outline, only a strange harmonizing of earth and air.
Shadows were faint, yet defined, lights visible, but most
exquisitely modulated. The hollow blue which over
Tyndall led the eye up into vacant solitudes was here
replaced by a sense of sheltering nearness, a certain dove-
colored obscurity in the atmosphere which seemed to
filter the sunlight of all its harsher properties. I do not
permit myself to describe details, for they have left no
enduring impression, nor am I insensible of how vain
any attempt must be to reproduce the harmony of such
subtile aspects of nature, — aspects most rare and indescribable because producing their charm by negative
means.

I suppose such an atmospheric effect is to be accounted for by supposing a lower stratum of pure transparent air overlaid by an upper one so charged with
moisture (or perhaps one of those thus far unexplained
dry mists occasionally seen in the high Sierra) as to

intercept the blue rays of sunlight, and admit only softened yellow ones.

This is the true Mount Whitney, the one we named in
1864, and upon which the name of our chief is forever to
rest. It stands, not like white Shasta, in a grandeur of
solitude, but about it gather companies of crag and spire,
piercing the blue, or wrapped in monkish raiment of
snow-storm and mist. Far below, laid out in ashen death,
slumbers the desert.

Silence reigns on these icy heights, save when scream
of Sierra eagle or loud crescendo of avalanche inter-
rupts the frozen stillness, or when in symphonic fulness
a storm rolls through vacant cañons with its stern minor.
It is hard not to invest these great dominating peaks
with consciousness, difficult to realize that, sitting thus
for ages in presence of all nature can work, of light-
magic and color-beauty, no inner spirit has kindled, nor
throb of granite heart once responded, no Buddhistic
nirvana-life even has brooded in eternal calm within
these sphinx-like breasts of stone.

A week after my climb I lay on the desert sand at the
foot of the Inyo range and looked up at Mount Whitney,
realizing all its grand individuality, and saw the drifting clouds interrupt a sun-brightened serenity by frown
after frown of moving shadow; and I entered for a moment deeply and intimately into that strange realm
where admiration blends with superstition, that condition
in which the savage feels within him the greatness of a
natural object, and forever after endows it with consciousness and power. For a moment I was back in the
Aryan myth days, when they saw afar that snowy peak,
and called it Dhavalagiri (white elephant), and invested
it with mystic power.

These peculiar moments, rare enough in the life of a

scientific man, when one trembles on the edge of myth-making, are of interest, as unfolding the origin and manner of savage beliefs, and as awakening the unperishing germ of primitive manhood which is buried within us all under so much culture and science.

How generally the myth-maker has been extinguished in modern students of mountains may be realized by examining the tone of Alpine literature, which, once lifted above the fatiguing repetition of gymnastics, is almost invariably scientific.

Ruskin alone, among prose writers on the Alps, re-echoes the dim past, in ever-recurring myth-making, over cloud and peak and glacier; his is the Rigveda's idea of nature. The varying hues which mood and emotion forever pass before his own mental vision mask with their illusive mystery the simple realities of nature, until mountains and their bold natural facts are lost behind the cloudy poetry of the writer.

Ruskin helps us to know himself, not the Alps; his mountain chapters, although essentially four thousand years old, are, however, no more an anachronism than the dim primeval spark which smoulders in all of us; their brilliancy *is* that spark fanned into flame.

To follow a chapter of Ruskin's by one of Tyndall's is to bridge forty centuries and realize the full contrast of archaic and modern thought.

This was the drift of my revery as I lay basking on the hot sands of Inyo, realizing fully the geological history and hard, materialistic reality of Mount Whitney, its mineral nature, its chemistry; yet archaic impulse even then held me, and the gaunt, gray old Indian who came slowly toward me must have subtly felt my condition, for he crouched beside me and silently fixed his hawk eye upon the peak.

At last he drew an arrow, sighted along its straight shaft, bringing the obsidian head to bear on Mount Whitney, and in strange fragments of language told me that the peak was an old, old man who watched this valley and cared for the Indians, but who shook the country with earthquakes to punish the whites for injustice toward his tribe.

I looked at his whitened hair and keen, black eye. I watched the spare, bronze face, upon which was written the burden of a hundred dark and gloomy superstitions; and as he trudged away across the sands, I could but feel the liberating power of modern culture which unfetters us from the more than iron bands of self-made myths. My mood vanished with the savage, and I saw the great peak only as it really is, a splendid mass of granite, 14,887 feet high, ice-chiselled and storm-tinted, a great monolith left standing amid the ruins of a bygone geological empire.

13 *

XIV.

THE PEOPLE.

IF mankind were offspring of isothermal lines and topography, we might arrive at a just criticism of Sierra Nevada people by that cheap and rapid method so much in vogue nowadays among physical geographers. Their practice of dragooning the free-agent with wet and dry bulb thermometers would help us to predict the future of Sierra society but little more securely than Madam Sáint John, who also deals in coming events. I fear we have no better than the old way of developing what lies ahead logically from yesterday and to-day, adding large measure of sympathy with human aspiration and faith in divine help.

Why all sorts and conditions of men from every race upon the planet wanted gold, and twenty years ago came here to win it, I shall not concern myself to ask. Nor can I formulate very accurately the proportions of good, bad, and indifferent *dramatis personæ* upon whom the golden curtain of '49 rolled up.

No venerated landmark or sacred restraint held those men in check. There were no precedents for the acting, no play-book, no prompter, no audience. "Anglo-Saxondom's idee" reigned supreme, developing a plot of riotous situation, and inconceivably sudden change. Wit and intellect wrought a condition the most ambitious savages might regard with baffled envy. History would not, if she could, parallel the state of society here from

'49 to '55, nor can we imagine to what height of horror it might have reached had the Sierra drainage held unlimited gold. Those were lively days. The penniless '49er still looks back to them with bleared eyes as the one period of his life. " Dust " was plenty and to be had, if not for digging, at the modest price of a bullet.

To prove the soil's fertility he tells you proudly, how, in those years, wild oats on every hill grew tall enough to be tied across your saddle-bow. This irony of nature has passed away, but the cursed plant ripens its hundredfold in life and manner.

No one familiar with society as it then was feels the least surprise that Mr. Bret Harte should deal so largely in morbid anatomy, or appear to search painfully for a single noble trait to redeem the common bad. Yet not universal bad, for there were not wanting a few strong Christian men who amid all, kept their eyes on the one model, leading lives blameless if obscure.

Broadly, through all kind and condition, shone the virtue of generous, if not self-denying hospitality. A sort of open-handed fraternity banded together the honest miners; they were shoulder to shoulder in common quest of gold, in united effort to make the " camp " lively. The " fraternity " too often emulated that of Cain, or wore a ghastly likeness to the *Commune*. That those desperadoes, who, through the long chain of mining towns outnumbered respectable men, had so generally the fixed habit of killing one another, should rather be written down to their credit; that they never married to hand down lawless traits, seems their crowning virtue.

For a few years the solemn pines looked down on a mad carnival of godless license, a pandemonium in whose picturesque delirium human character crumbled and vanished like dead leaves.

It was stirring and gay, but Melpomene's pathetic face was always under that laughing mask of comedy.

This is the unpromising origin of our Sierra Civilization. It may be instructive to note some early steps of improvement; a protest, first silent, then loud, which went up against disorder and crime; and later, the inauguration of justice, in form if not reality.

There occurs to me an incident illustrating these first essays in civil law; it is vouched for by my friend, an unwilling actor in the affair.

Exactly why horse-stealing should have been so early recognized as a heinous sin it is not easy to discover; however that might be, murderers continued to notch the number of their victims on neatly kept hilts of pistol or knives, in comparative security, long after the horse thief began to meet his hempen fate.

Early in the fifties, on a still, hot summer's afternoon, a certain man, in a camp of the northern mines which shall be nameless, having tracked. his two donkeys and one horse a half-mile, and discovering that a man's track with spur-marks followed them, came back to town and told "the boys," who loitered about a popular saloon, that in his opinion "some Mexican had stole the animals."

Such news as this naturally demanded drinks all round. "Do you know, gentlemen," said one who assumed leadership, "that just naturally to shoot these Greasers ain't the best way. Give 'em a fair jury trial, and rope 'em up with all the majesty of law. That's the cure."

Such words of moderation were well received, and they drank again to "here's'hoping we ketch that Greaser."

As they loafed back to the veranda a Mexican walked over the hill brow, jingling his spurs pleasantly in accord with a whistled waltz.

The advocate for law said in undertone, "That's the cuss."

A rush, a struggle, and the Mexican, bound hand and foot, lay on his back in the bar-room. The camp turned out to a man.

Happily such cries as "String him up!" "Burn the doggoned 'lubricator!'" and other equally pleasant phrases fell unheeded upon his Spanish ear.

A jury, upon which they forced my friend, was quickly gathered in the street, and despite refusals to serve, the crowd hurried them in behind the bar.

A brief statement of the case was made by the *ci devant* advocate, and they shoved the jury into a commodious poker-room, where were seats grouped about neat, green tables. The noise outside in the bar-room by and by died away into complete silence, but from afar down the cañon came confused sounds as of disorderly cheering.

They came nearer, and again the light-hearted noise of human laughter mingled with clinking glasses around the bar.

A low knock at the jury door; the lock burst in, and a dozen smiling fellows asked the verdict.

A foreman promptly answered "*Not guilty.*"

With volleyed oaths, and ominous laying of hands on pistol hilts, the boys slammed the door with, "You'll have to do better than that!"

In half an hour the advocate gently opened the door again.

"Your *opinion*, gentlemen?"

"Guilty!"

"Correct! You can come out. We hung him an hour ago."

The jury took theirs "neat"; and when, after a few minutes, the pleasant village returned to its former tranquillity, it was "allowed" at more than one saloon that "Mexicans 'll know enough to let white men's stock alone after this." One and another exchanged the belief that this sort of thing was more sensible than "'nipping' 'em on sight."

When, before sunset, the bar-keeper concluded to sweep some dust out of his poker-room back-door, he felt a momentary surprise at finding the missing horse dozing under the shadow of an oak, and the two lost donkeys serenely masticating playing-cards, of which many bushels lay in a dusty pile.

He was reminded then that the animals had been there all day.

During three or four years the battle between good and bad became more and more determined, until all positive characters arrayed themselves either for or against public order.

At length, on a sudden, the party for right organized those august mobs, the Vigilance Committees, and quickly began to festoon their more depraved fellow-men from tree to tree. Rogues of sufficient shrewdness got themselves enrolled in the vigilance ranks, and were soon unable to tell themselves from the most virtuous. Those quiet oaks, whose hundreds of sunny years had been spent in lengthening out glorious branches, now found themselves playing the part of public gibbet.

Let it be distinctly understood that I am not passing criticism on the San Francisco organization, which I have never investigated, but on "Committees" in the mountain towns, with whose performance I am familiar.

The Vigilants quickly put out of existence a majority of the worst desperadoes, and, by their swift, merciless action, struck such terror to the rest, that ever after, the right has mainly controlled affairs.

This was, *perhaps*, well. With characteristic promptness they laid down their power, and gave California over

to the constituted authorities. This was magnificent.
They deserve the commendation due success. They
have, however, such a frank, honest way of singing their
praise, such eternal, undisguised and virtuous self-lauda-
tion over the whole matter, that no one else need interrupt
them with fainter notes.

Although this generation has written its indorsement
in full upon the transaction, it may be doubted if history
(how long is it before dispassionate candor speaks?) will
trace an altogether favorable verdict upon her pages.
Possibly, to fulfil the golden round of duty, it is needful
to do right in the right way, and success may not be
proven the eternal test of merit.

That the vigilance committees grasped the moral power
is undeniable; that they used it for the public salvation
is equally true; but the best advocates are far from
showing that with skill and moderation they might not
have thrown their weight into the scale *with* law, and
conquered, by means of legislature, judge, and jury, a
peace wholly free from the stain of lawless blood.

An impartial future may possibly grant the plenary
inspiration of vigilance committees. Perhaps that better
choice was in truth denied them; it may be the hour
demanded a sudden blow of self-defence. Whether better
or best, the act has not left unmixed blessing, although it
now seems as if the lawlessness, which even till these
later years has from time to time manifested itself, is
gradually and surely dying out. Yet to-day, as I write,
State troops are encamped at Amador, to suppress a
spirit which has taken law in its own hand.

With the gradual decline of gold product, something
like social equilibrium asserted itself. By 1860, California had made the vast inspiring stride from barbarism
to vulgarity.

ditions.   Have they forgotten that these are less potent factors in development than the impulse, that what a man *is*, is of far less consequence than what he is *becoming?*

Show these gloomy critics a bare stretch of vulgar Sierra earth, and they will tell you how barren, how valueless it is, ignorant that the art of any Californian can banish every grain of sand into the Pacific's bottom, and gather a residuum of solid gold.   Out of the race of men whom they have in the same shallow way called common, I believe Time shall separate a noble race.

Travelling to-day in foothill Sierras, one may see the old, rude scars of mining; trenches yawn, disordered heaps cumber the ground, yet they are no longer bare. Time, with friendly rain, and wind and flood, slowly, surely, levels all, and a compassionate cover of innocent verdure weaves fresh and cool from mile to mile.   While Nature thus gently heals the humble Earth, God, who is also Nature, moulds and changes Man.

THE END.

Cambridge : Electrotyped and Printed by Welch, Bigelow, & Co.

Printed in the United States
110548LV00002B/204/A